Sustainability and the Political Economy of Welfare

Welfare is commonly conceptualized in socio-economic terms of equity, high-lighting distributive issues within growing economies. While gross domestic product (GDP), income growth and rising material standards of living are normally not questioned as priorities in welfare theories and policymaking, there is growing evidence that Western welfare standards are not generalizable to the rest of the planet if environmental concerns, such as resource depletion or climate change, are considered.

Sustainability and the Political Economy of Welfare raises the issue of what is required to make welfare societies ecologically sustainable. Consisting of three parts, this book regards the current financial, economic and political crisis in welfare state institutions and addresses methodological, theoretical and wider conceptual issues in integrating sustainability. Furthermore, this text is concerned with the main institutional obstacles to the achievement of sustainable welfare and well-being, and how these may feasibly be overcome. How can researchers assist policymakers in promoting synergy between economic, social and environmental policies conducive to globally sustainable welfare systems?

Co-authored by a variety of cross-disciplinary contributors, this book reflects a diversity of research perspectives and methods in a unique mixture of conceptual chapters, historical analyses of different societal sectors and case studies of several EU countries, China and the US. It is well suited for those who are interested in and study welfare, ecological economics and political economy.

Max Koch is a Professor in Social Policy at Lund University, Sweden.

Oksana Mont is a Professor in Sustainable Consumption and Production at Lund University, Sweden.

Routledge Studies in Ecological Economics

For a full list of titles in this series, please visit www.routledge.com.

Sustainability and the Political Economy of Welfare

**Edited by
Max Koch and Oksana Mont**

Routledge

Taylor & Francis Group

LONDON AND NEW YORK

First published 2016
by Routledge
2 Park Square, Milton Park, Abingdon, Oxfordshire OX14 4RN

and by Routledge
711 Third Avenue, New York, NY 10017

First issued in paperback 2017

Routledge is an imprint of the Taylor & Francis Group, an informa business

British Library Cataloguing in Publication Data
A catalogue record for this book is available from the British Library

Library of Congress Cataloging in Publication Data
A catalog record for this book has been requested

ISBN 13: 978-1-138-06588-8 (pbk)
ISBN 13: 978-1-138-92528-1 (hbk)

Typeset in Times New Roman
by Taylor & Francis Books

Contents

Notes on contributors

Eric Brandstedt is a Postdoctoral Researcher at the London School of Economics and Lund University. His PhD thesis is entitled *The Construction of a Sustainable Development in Times of Climate Change* (2013). He has published articles in *Moral Philosophy and Politics* and *Environmental Politics*. Aiming at a formulation of a bottom-up approach to normative theorizing around climate change, his current research concerns the relevance of ethics to climate policy.

Hubert Buch-Hansen is an Associate Professor at the Department of Business and Politics, Copenhagen Business School. His current research focuses on competition, business networks and environmental sustainability. Together with Angela Wigger, he is the author of *The Politics of European Competition Regulation: A Critical Political Economy Perspective*. His articles have been published in journals such as *Ecological Economics, International Sociology, Journal of Common Market Studies, New Political Economy* and *Review of International Political Economy*.

Eric Clark is a Professor of Human Geography and affiliated with the Lund University Centre for Sustainability Studies (LUCSUS). His research interests include political economy, land rent, gentrification, island studies and political ecology. He is currently researching financialization in the EU-FP7 programme Financialisation, Economy, Society and Sustainable Development (FESSUD). Clark edited *Geografiska Annaler Series B: Human Geography* from 1998 to 2008 and currently edits the *Journal of Urban Affairs*. His recent publications include articles in *Annals of the Association of American Geographers, Sustainability Science, Transactions of the Institute of British Geographers, Urban Studies* and *Cultural Geographies*.

Maria Emmelin is a Professor of Global Health, Lund University. Her research interests include public health evaluation and the social determinants of health. She teaches qualitative methodology and has long experience of studying the HIV epidemic in Tanzania and violence against women and children in Ethiopia, Tanzania and Indonesia. She also coordinates a

Swedish-Tanzanian network for methodology development on the role of social capital for health promotion and sustainable welfare.

Roger Hildingsson is a Postdoctoral Researcher at the Department of Political Science, Lund University. His research focuses on environmental politics, climate governance, the environmental state and energy policy. In his PhD thesis, *Governing Decarbonisation*, he examines how the state engages in governing low-carbon transitions. He has also been involved in research on EU climate and energy policy and sustainability governance in Sweden. Currently he is engaged in research on new climate governance initiatives and industrial decarbonization. He has published articles in journals such as *European Political Science, Futures* and *Climatic Change.*

Håkan Johansson is a Professor in Social Work, Lund University. His research interests include civil society, EU studies, social policy and welfare states. He is currently conducting research projects on the 'Europeanization of Swedish civil society organization' and 'Local welfare mixes in Swedish municipalities'. His recent publications include an edited volume on *EU Civil Society: Patterns of Cooperation, Competition and Conflict* (with Sara Kalm).

Erin Kennedy holds Master's degrees in Development Studies from Lund University and in Chinese Society, Public Policy and Law from Fudan University and is currently a PhD student at the School of Social Work, Lund University. In her PhD thesis she explores community engagement strategies that enable stakeholder involvement in planning local climate change action in China. She has co-authored the research reports *Greening the World Economy through Cities* and *The role of Cities in Promoting Green Economy and Global Governance.* She has also co-authored an article in *Energy Policy.*

Jamil Khan is an Associate Professor at the Department of Environmental and Energy Systems Studies, Lund University. His research interests cover urban climate governance, sustainable transport, low carbon transitions and the intersection between welfare and green politics. Recent articles appeared in the *Journal of Cleaner Production* and in the volume *Rethinking the Green State: Environmental Governance Towards Climate and Sustainability Transitions.* He is also co-editor of *Environmental Politics and Deliberative Democracy* (with Karin Bäckstrand, Annica Kronsell and Eva Lövbrand).

Max Koch is a Professor in Social Policy at the School of Social Work, Lund University. An ongoing theme of his research has been the ways in which political and economic restructuring are reflected in social structures, with an emphasis on welfare and employment relations, and also from a comparative perspective. More recently, he has combined these research interests with issues of ecological sustainability, particularly climate change and post-growth societies. His previous books include *Roads to Post-Fordism: Labour Markets and Social Structures in Europe, Capitalism and Climate Change: Theoretical Discussion, Historical Development and Policy Responses* and *Non-Standard Employment in Europe: Paradigms, Prevalence and Policy Responses* (co-edited with Martin Fritz).

Oksana Mont is a Professor in Sustainable Consumption and Production and Deputy Director of the International Institute for Industrial Environmental Economics, Lund University. Her main research area is sustainable consumption and production. She combines research on innovative business models for a circular economy with studies on sustainable lifestyles (collaborative and sharing economy) and sustainable consumption policy and governance (including tools for changing behaviour such as nudging). She has published in the *Journal of Cleaner Production, Journal of Consumer Policy, Journal of Industrial Ecology, Social Responsibility Journal* and others.

Annika Pissin is a Postdoctoral Researcher at the Centre for East and South-East Asian Studies, Lund University. She studied classical and modern Chinese and Anthropology in Heidelberg, Germany, Tainan, China and Leiden, The Netherlands and carries out research on children and childhood in imperial and contemporary China. Her current research focuses on contemporary childhood, particularly marginalized children as well as children using the internet in China.

Kate Soper is Emerita Professor of Philosophy at London Metropolitan University. She has published widely on environmental philosophy, theory of needs, and consumption and cultural theory. Her writings include *What is Nature? Culture, Politics and the Non-Human, Citizenship and Consumption* and *The Politics and Pleasures of Consuming Differently*. She has been a member of the editorial collectives of *Radical Philosophy* and *New Left Review* and a columnist for *Capitalism, Nature, Socialism*. Her study on 'Alternative hedonism and the theory and politics of consumption' was funded in the ESRC/AHRC 'Cultures of Consumption' Programme. She has since participated in a number of research projects on climate change and sustainable consumption.

Foreword

Ian Gough

Welfare and sustainability, despite the efforts of a few pioneers, continue to be discussed and researched in separate silos. It is astonishing to discover that the vast bulk of writings on welfare and contemporary social policy ignore the pressing constraints and closing boundaries of the planetary system. And while global environmental research understands and warns against the growing human impacts of climate change and allied threats to sustainable welfare it does not yet present an integrated social analysis of these risks. So this book is especially welcome.

Drawing on different disciplines – philosophy, economics, political science, geography, social policy, social work and health, environmental sciences and more – it seeks to build bridges between the domains of welfare and sustainability. Yet it is no cobbled-together collection, rather the outcome of extended discussion and collaboration centred around the Pufendorf Institute for Advanced Studies at Lund University, coordinated and led by Max Koch. The result is a bold, trenchant and innovative volume.

Apart from in Chapter 6, 'green growth' is given short shrift. Though more could have been said on this, the tighter focus enables contributors to dive in and tackle the harder questions: what can welfare mean and how can it be advanced in a world of constraint, post-growth and steady-state economics? The first part comes to some clear conclusions here. While the ideas of welfare and well-being embrace irreducibly subjective aspects like 'happiness', to make sense of 'sustainable', inter-generational welfare, an objective, human needs-based ontology is essential (a position endorsed by Pope Francis in his recent encyclical). Further, in Herman Daly's steady-state economy, his 'distributionist' institutions are pivotal but vague; here students of social policy must and can start making a contribution. Again, 'the future is not what it used to be': What does the possibility of a 'broken world' imply for much Western philosophy with its assumptions of optimism and progress? This discussion might skirt close to cultural relativism and pessimism, but Kate Soper in the book's final chapter brings things together by recognizing the centrality of consumption politics in democracies and the overt discontents to which this gives rise, and envisages an 'alternative hedonism' as central to a new social policy.

The second part of the book investigates new eco-social policies to meet climate change-related risks, including redistribution, working-time reduction, personal carbon allowances and voluntary grass-roots action groups. The third part discusses emerging practices at the social-environmental interface, such as social enterprises. The book makes another important contribution here in recognizing that these will emerge in different forms in different parts of the world. It warns against replacing existing one-size-fits-all neoliberal policies with alternatives in the same mould; the future won't be like that.

As the book points out, climate change has been called not just a wicked problem but a super-wicked problem, given its complexities and interrelationships over global space and intergenerational time. One book cannot tackle all this, and this volume concentrates mainly on the advanced 'welfare states' of the West. But this is useful because sustainable welfare is more often discussed within the global South, though the moral obligations are more extreme in the North. This volume mounts a cumulative, consistent and credible case for rethinking the idea of sustainable welfare.

Acknowledgements

This volume is the collaborative effort of many people with different academic backgrounds. Ten researchers from five faculties at Lund University, one researcher from Copenhagen Business School and one from London Metropolitan University brainstormed ideas, conducted joint research, co-authored chapters and provided mutual feedback for over a year. The volume is the outcome of the interdisciplinary research project on 'Sustainable Welfare', coordinated by Max Koch and funded by the Pufendorf Institute for Advanced Studies at Lund University. The research team benefited greatly from the fantastic premises of this institution. We are grateful to its Director Sune Sunesson and for the professional administrative support from his colleagues. We would like to especially thank Eva Persson for her project management and helping us navigate through all the stages of the project – from the funding application to the final Expert Workshop.

The Pufendorf Institute also funded a three-month stay of a guest researcher. It was a privilege to have had Kate Soper, Emerita Professor of Philosophy, London Metropolitan University, as part of our team. She contributed greatly to all stages of the project.

The volume could not have been written without the extremely constructive feedback we received from the participants of our Expert Workshop on Sustainable Welfare that took place on 7–8 May 2015, and which was also funded and hosted by the Pufendorf institute. We would like to thank all the participants who shared their views on the topic of sustainable welfare with us. Special thanks go to the invited speakers from that occasion: Ian Gough (London School of Economics), Inge Røpke (Aalborg University), Jörgen Larsson (Chalmers University of Technology), Petter Næss (Norwegian University of Life Sciences) and Mi Ah Schoyen and Bjørn Hvinden (Oslo and Akershus University College of Applied Science). Nadia Johanisová (Masaryk University, Brno) gave a very interesting additional presentation on 'Eco-Social Enterprise: Satisfying Needs in a Degrowth Future?'

Last but not least we would like to thank Eileen Laurie for her extremely professional and efficient copy-editing of the volume, which has profoundly improved its quality.

Introduction

Research on sustainable welfare: state of the art and outline of the volume

Max Koch and Oksana Mont

Welfare is commonly conceptualized in socio-economic terms of equity, highlighting distributive issues within growing capitalist economies. In times when the unequal distribution of wealth in the 'advanced' capitalist world has reached the levels of the nineteenth century (Piketty, 2014), the question of whether we 'can afford the rich' (Sayer, 2015) is indeed central. However, the traditional answer of welfare researchers – that issues of inequality can be solved by redistributing the primary incomes of capital and labour within economically growing economies – is increasingly controversial. While gross domestic product (GDP), income growth and rising material standards of living are normally not questioned as priorities in welfare theories and policymaking, there is growing evidence that Western production and consumption patterns and the associated welfare standards are not generalizable to the rest of the planet if environmental concerns are to be considered. The existing structures of welfare capitalism are not only challenged by unprecedented levels of inequality but also by the fact that the Earth's carrying capacity is being exceeded in relation to at least three planetary boundaries: climate change, the nitrogen cycle and biodiversity loss (Rockström *et al.*, 2009).[1] The economy, associated production and consumption norms, and welfare standards can no longer be considered as a system operating in a theoretical vacuum. This means taking the environmental limits of economic growth, social welfare, and human needs and wants seriously, as well as understanding that real thresholds and non-linear and irreversible changes exist that have fundamental consequences for humans and other species.

The present volume therefore raises the issue of what would be required to make welfare societies ecologically sustainable. It regards the current financial, economic and political crisis and the corresponding adjustments and recalibrations in welfare state institutions, with which much contemporary welfare literature is concerned, as an impetus to also considering environmental concerns. The volume is furthermore concerned with the main institutional obstacles to the achievement of sustainable welfare and well-being, how these could feasibly be overcome and how researchers can assist policymakers and activists in promoting synergy between economic, social and environmental policies that are conducive to globally sustainable welfare systems.

Research into welfare and sustainability has hitherto been carried out by academics working within the confines of their disciplines with only little contact and cross-fertilization with other fields. Western welfare systems were built on class compromises at national level in post-war circumstances, based around issues of equity and socio-economic (re-)distribution (Koch, 2006). It was assumed that capitalist economies would continue to grow in order to finance welfare services, especially via the taxation of the primary incomes of employers and employees. While much current welfare literature gravitates around the crisis of the national welfare state and the corresponding read-justments, ecological concerns voiced as early as the 1970s have largely been ignored. Yet welfare standards in EU member states and beyond are not only challenged by rescaling and recalibration processes, and migration and demographic changes, but also by global and intergenerational environmental issues. Much recent research points to the fact that Western ideas of 'welfare' and 'prosperity', and especially the associated production and consumption norms, cannot be generalized to the rest of the world (Fritz and Koch, 2016). Tim Jackson (2009: 86), for example, demonstrates that there is as yet 'no credible, socially just, ecologically sustainable scenario of continually growing incomes for a world of nine billion people'. Hence an institutional compromise for a society with sustainable global welfare would need to go beyond the post-war arrangements. A theoretical concept of and interdisciplinary research into what we shall refer to in this volume as 'sustainable welfare' has hitherto not been developed. Such a concept and compromise would be oriented at global level and systematically account for environmental and intergenerational concerns, as well as being the theoretical foundation for policies working towards the establishment of corresponding welfare systems.

By integrating the two previously separate disciplines of welfare and sustainability research and developing corresponding theoretical concepts, as well as outlining and discussing policies and emerging practices of 'sustainable welfare', this volume hence aims to fill a critical gap in research. How does the meaning of welfare change if environmental sustainability is taken seriously? Tentatively, we presuppose that which authors such as Langhelle (1999) and Brandstedt and Emmelin (Chapter 1) call the 'sustainability proviso', which means a widened scope and changed pattern of welfare provision and, parti-cularly, of any distributive principle applied. Considering this proviso means reviewing existing welfare policies accordingly, while welfare theories would need to be made compatible with sustainability approaches. Yet, though progress has been made in a range of disciplines – for example, in the emerging discipline of sustainability science (Clark, 2014) – an integrated theory of 'sustainable welfare' only exists in elementary form at the current time.

Existing research

Various scholars in ecological economics, psychology, social policy and philosophy have started to conceptualize 'welfare', 'prosperity', 'hedonism' and the 'good life' in alternative ways, and also given the lack of evidence for the absolute decoupling of GDP growth from material resource use and CO_2 emissions in the absence of economic growth (Victor, 2008; Soper et al., 2009; Kasser, 2011; Muraca, 2012). While these contributions are fragmented and in need of integration (for an overview, see Koch, 2013), they share the hypothesis that much of what is required for welfare and human flourishing, once a decent material standard of living has been attained, is non-material and that this is achievable at much lower than current levels of matter and energy throughput. First, there is evidence that people in more equal and socially inclusive societies are better off and report greater amounts of well-being than those living in more unequal ones where status competition is particularly pronounced (Wilkinson and Pickett, 2010). Second, consumption researchers argue that in rich countries buying things is not in the first place about the goods themselves but rather about the symbolic message that the act of purchase conveys (Soper et al., 2009). What Hirsch (1976) called the competition for 'positional goods' is mediated through a genuinely social logic that Bourdieu (1984) referred to as 'distinction'. This general societal race to determine legitimate taste is by definition short term, does not contribute anything to human well-being in the long term and contradicts the principal reproductive needs of the earth as an ecological system (Paech, 2012), since such competitive consumption practices are normally bound to matter and energy transformations and necessitate the burning of fossil fuels. Third, well-being and quality of life research demonstrates that humans must have certain psychological needs satisfied in order to flourish and experience personal well-being. These needs include feeling safe and secure as well as feeling competent and efficient. People also require love and intimacy and struggle when living in conditions of loneliness, rejection and exclusion (Kasser, 2011). Yet where 'economic growth is a key goal of a nation' (Kasser, 2011: 195), with its encouragement of self-enhancing, hierarchical, extrinsic and materialistic values, the fundamental needs required for human well-being tend to be undermined.

A great deal of further research takes up relevant aspects of sustainable welfare as outlined above. Hemerijck (2013) and Kazepov (2010), for example, deal with the recalibrations and patterns of rescaling in Western welfare states, but without referring to environmental challenges. Conversely, Kronsell and Bäckstrand (2015) focus on the 'green state' but are much less concerned with its welfare dimension. Rauschmayer *et al.* (2012) share our emphasis on basic human needs and/or capabilities for the establishment of global sustainability as well as our global and intergenerational perspective. However, we focus more on welfare and the necessary changes in associated institutions and systems and also build on the existing degrowth literature. Walker (2012) outlines core principles for environmental justice but does not focus on the relations between the political economy of welfare and sustainability. Stiglitz (2010) puts forward an elaborate analysis of the financial crisis of the advanced capitalist countries yet does not consider the environment. Koch (2012) provides such an analysis of the twofold crisis of finance-driven capitalism, but the focus in that book is on the historical development of climate change, capitalism and the financial crisis as socio-ecological issues and not on the provision of sustainable welfare now and in the future. D'Alisa et al. (2014), Daly (1977), Jackson (2009), Latouche (2010) and Victor (2008) demonstrate the necessity of overcoming the priority of economic growth in policymaking and outline how an economy without growth could function. However, none of these authors is particularly concerned with the provision and institutions of welfare. While our volume builds upon the last-mentioned authors in many ways, it is unique in focusing on the intersection of sustainability and the political economy of welfare.

Sustainable welfare

Until the economic crisis of the 1970s, the boundaries of the national welfare state were generally not challenged. This began to change with the growing awareness that major threats to human welfare transcend both space and time. Climate change is a good example of a transnational and transgenerational phenomenon: greenhouse gases (GHGs) emitted here and now mix with the existing stock of GHGs in the atmosphere, thereby producing global warming and amplifying the risk of negative effects such as droughts and flooding that are dispersed over time and space (that is, including in those geographic zones where the GHGs were not emitted and in the decades to come). Once the transcendent character of contemporary activities is recognized, the question arises as to whose welfare should be represented in the organizational principles of welfare societies (Brandstedt and Emmelin, Chapter 1). We agree with these two authors that the distributive principles underlying existing welfare systems would need to be extended to include those affected in other countries and in the future. Not only the citizens of a given (welfare) state but also non-citizens would need to be taken into account when providing welfare under the sustainability proviso, even if temporally and geographically distant people are not actually governed by a specific nation state (Brandstedt and Emmelin, Chapter 1). Any actual welfare provision would need to consider that the satisfaction of present needs and wants must not undermine the ability of future needs satisfaction. This includes the recognition of critical thresholds and limitations and also that needs, aspirations and wants must be reviewed – and possibly restrained – in order not to violate the sustainability proviso. Hence the very idea of sustainability is a challenge to business as usual.

In addition to universalizability and intertemporality, the satisfaction of human needs is central to the concept of sustainable welfare (Koch and Buch-Hansen, Chapter 2). The central welfare concern is not the unlimited provision with material riches of the 'happy few' in Western societies but rather the satisfaction of basic needs for all humans now and in the future. Needs differ from wants and preferences in that they are non-negotiable and universalizable and that failure to satisfy these produces serious harm (Gough, 2014). Hence needs do not vary over time and across cultures but according to the ways in which a specific culture at a particular point in time attempts to satisfy these. Critical thresholds for the universal provision of human needs (and wants) or for a 'minimally decent life' are to be constantly (re)defined in light of the advances of scientific knowledge. The degree to which more than basic human needs can be provided on a finite planet remains subject to scientific inquiry, and particularly to climate expertise. While we cannot exactly identify the exact kind and amount of need-satisfiers that future peoples will require, all economic systems would need to be assessed according to their ability to produce enough appropriate need-satisfiers.

In summary, our concept of sustainable welfare is oriented towards the satisfaction of human needs within ecological limits, from the intergenerational *and* global perspective. It is only at global level that thresholds for matter and energy throughput as well as for CO_2 emissions can be determined in order to effectively mitigate global environmental challenges such as climate change. At the same time, these biophysical conditions and global thresholds delineate the room for manoeuvre within which national and local economies and societies can evolve[2] and within which welfare beyond basic human needs can be provided. The dimensions and outreach of this concept are reflected in a corresponding 'policy-auditing' (Gough, 2014) approach, according to which existing economic, social and environmental policies as well as material welfare standards would need to be reviewed under the aspect of their generalizability. Beyond basic human needs, material welfare would be regarded as secondary to environmental sustainability. Production and consumption patterns would need to be organized in ways that the global matter and energy throughput and the associated biophysical flows do not exceed levels identified by sustainability science. Accordingly, economic growth as a policy goal would need to be deprioritized relative to the satisfaction of human needs within ecological limits. In relation to climate change, given the fact that absolute decoupling of GDP growth, material resource use and GHG emissions is unlikely for the time being, the reduction of GHG emissions would be given priority over other policy goals including economic growth.

An interdisciplinary approach

With the present volume we intend to contribute to the debate on alternative socio-economic models that has resurfaced in the twofold crisis of the environment and the global financial system and the corresponding pressures on existing welfare systems. Normally, solutions to this twofold crisis are sought within the separate silos of academic disciplines, especially with regard to environmental, economic and welfare discourses. However, the conceptualization and practising of sustainable welfare requires a combination of knowledge, not only from welfare studies and economics, but also from various disciplines that study technological processes, infrastructural developments, policy mechanisms and power structures, and so on. The added value of this volume is therefore the integration of these fields of study into one interdisciplinary approach to sustainable welfare. Reflecting this approach, all but two chapters are the outcomes of cross-disciplinary collaboration and teamwork. This, we hope, creates new windows for creative thinking, unexpected perspectives and forward-looking contributions. The volume is the outcome of the research project 'Sustainable Welfare' at the Pufendorf Institute for Advances Studies at Lund University from, 2014 to 2015. It brings together 12 researchers from five faculties at Lund University, plus one researcher from Copenhagen Business School and one from London Metropolitan University. The represented disciplines employ different toolboxes of methods, the combination of which promises to provide insights that remain hidden whenever methods of individual disciplines are applied in isolation. Reflecting this heterogeneity of research traditions and perspectives, this volume provides a unique mix of conceptual work and empirical and historical studies of different societal sectors and case studies of EU countries, China and the US.

Outline of the volume

The volume has three main parts, each with four chapters that deal with theoretical concepts, policies and emerging practices of sustainable welfare. Part I addresses methodological, theoretical and wider conceptual issues in integrating sustainability and welfare concerns and principles, and brings together philosophical, social science and ecological economics approaches. Chapter 1 by Eric Brandstedt and Maria Emmelin introduces and outlines the main features of a concept of 'sustainable welfare'. The point of departure is the traditional welfare concept against the background of which the issue is raised of 'what it takes to make welfare sustainable' and 'whose welfare should actually be represented'. More specifically and in a global context, the chapter discusses the issue of the appropriate unit for measuring welfare if the ecological boundaries of the Earth are to be taken seriously, outlining the appropriate scope of the welfare state and dealing with potentially acceptable trade-offs between economic development and sustainable welfare goals. The chapter argues that a concept of sustainable welfare per se, as well as a corresponding welfare system, must consider the needs of future human beings and relate to the global level in the same way that environmental challenges relate to human welfare. Subsequent chapters use this chapter as a theoretical point of reference.

Chapter 2 by Max Koch and Hubert Buch-Hansen deals with two theoretical traditions that are directly relevant for the integration of ecological sustainability and the political economy of welfare but which hitherto have not been developed using interaction and cross-fertilization: *steady-state economics* and *degrowth* approaches, on the one hand, and theories of *human need*, on the other. The chapter first explores how the notions of need, welfare and well-being are reflected in growth-critical literature and demonstrates that there are compelling reasons for considering these notions in more depth. It then identifies the differences and commonalities of human need approaches by scholars such as Doyal and Gough, and Max-Neef. Despite their differences, it is argued that these approaches are united in their assumption that some absolute or basic human needs exist that any human being now and in the future has a right to have satisfied. The subsequent section provides an attempt to integrate the two perspectives. Building mainly on Doyle and Gough, health and autonomy are presented as basic human needs, the satisfaction of which should be the focus of any global sustainable welfare system.

Chapter 3 by Kate Soper and Maria Emmelin argues for the importance of mobilizing new cultural forces and rethinking society in order to further support sustainable welfare. This is necessary to counter or qualify the concepts of 'modernization', 'progress' and 'development' associated with the commitment to the growth model of welfare and prosperity, with its economic and social adaptation to the constraints of the global capitalist market. Such an approach means challenging the presumed links between economic expansion and 'higher' standards of living and their current monopoly over definitions of human health and quality of life. The chapter draws on the social complexity and reflexivity of the globalized era to question the presumption that greater equality and social justice, and more enlightened polices on race, gender and human rights, can only be carried on the back of conventional economic growth and its shopping mall culture. While this approach to rethinking ideas of 'welfare', 'prosperity', 'development' and the 'good life' can be aligned with earlier and more traditional romantic antipathies to the 'modern' life, it rejects the puritanical and socially conservative aspects of traditional cultures of resistance to modernity. Instead, it endorses a form of modernization and its representation that seeks to sever the link between progress and economic expansion, while opposing the cultural regression and social conservatism that have hitherto tended to go along with economic backwardness.

Chapter 4 by Eric Brandstedt and Oksana Mont asks how the future is to be envisioned in philosophical and policy debates. Contemporary expectations and scenarios of what future societies are likely to look like are relevant for the feasibility of sustainable welfare as they directly and indirectly impact on mid- and long-term policy strategies that would undermine or facilitate such a transition. A common current expectation is that sustainability challenges constrain our visions of the 'good life' as our ideas about the future would need to fit in with planetary boundaries. This shift from free associations towards future scenarios within limits opens up questions such as whether all people on Earth will lead a universal lifestyle or whether there will be a mushrooming of ideas of the 'good life' at various local levels. The chapter first outlines the philosophical future scenarios and visions of John Rawls and then proceeds to analyse future-oriented policy visions in Sweden. It then contrasts and compares the roles and functions of the assumptions about the future in the theories and policy designs discussed. The chapter concludes with reflections on the practical implications of these assumptions.

Part II is dedicated to the identification and understanding of the structural obstacles and opportunities in establishing sustainable welfare that arise from existing production and consumption patterns at global, national and local levels. The chapters are united in the view that a transition towards sustainable welfare presupposes a redistribution of wealth, work, material resource use and carbon emissions at all these levels. Chapter 5 by Jamil Khan and Eric Clark examines the global political economy from various 'green' and, particularly, 'pro-growth' and 'no-growth' perspectives. It demonstrates that these have overlapping but different understandings of the global political economy and therefore tend to identify different sets of obstacles and opportunities for the anchoring and success of policies oriented towards sustainable welfare. The chapter starts by introducing the variegated landscape of green economic perspectives on global political economy, captured by concepts such as green growth, green economy, steady state and degrowth. It then outlines the policies preferred by these perspectives and the obstacles that are rooted in the global political economy that hinder the implementation of these policies. These include high and increasing levels of inequalities, especially in terms of wealth, institutions of private ownership displacing democratically controlled commons, the growth imperative driving excessive consumption and production, and the rapidly expanding commodification and financialization of ever more spheres of natural and social life. The chapter concludes by identifying the prospects of policies crucial for transitioning towards sustainable welfare that to varying degrees challenge the institutional structures of the global political economy.

Chapter 6 by Håkan Johansson, Jamil Khan and Roger Hildingsson reinterprets the notion of social risk as a key concept in welfare studies. Social risks are generally seen as the result of structural transformation processes causing new problems and risks for various societal groups. Unemployment, sickness, work-related injuries and old age are often portrayed as classic or first-generation social risks that emerged as a result of industrialization and urbanization. A second generation of social risks emerged in relation to individualization and changing demographic structures, giving rise to new social demands and needs. The chapter proposes that a new generation of climate change-related risks is emerging, potentially replacing previous social risks and/or transforming them in unexpected ways. It analyses the ways in which the link between climate change and social risks is portrayed in the reports from the Intergovernmental Panel on Climate Change (IPCC), United Nations Framework Convention on Climate Change (UNFCCC) and other international institutions and outlines types of welfare arrangements that could ameliorate the social risks associated with climate change.

Chapter 7 by Roger Hildingsson and Max Koch discusses the potential of personal carbon emission allowances as eco-social policy instruments. Reflecting the growing significance of climate change as a socio-ecological issue, the chapter begins from an overview of different modes of environmental regulation and associated eco-social policy instruments. Subsequently, it moves to a detailed discussion and comparison of different models of personal carbon emissions allowances schemes and how these could fit into a wider political strategy of socio-ecological transition towards establishing sustainable welfare. The chapter concludes by outlining alternatives to free market or commodification policy strategies in climate change mitigation.

Chapter 8 by Oksana Mont deals with work time reductions as a further important element of a wider eco-social policy strategy. Placing emphasis on sustaining a welfare state in a non-growing economy, it addresses the corresponding readjustments that focus on work time reduction and job creation. It provides an analysis of historical examples of work time reductions in Western Europe, highlighting the issue of why some of these policies were abandoned, while others were sustained. The concluding section suggests alternative ways of operating a welfare system under conditions of generally reduced working hours.

Part III deals with varieties and emerging practices in the establishment of sustainable welfare under different institutional conditions in different parts of the world. It contains a comparative and institutional analysis of nation state trajectories towards sustainable welfare, a sectoral study of social enterprises, a participatory and 'bottom-up' inquiry into low carbon communities and a general reflection on the structural requirements for the establishment of sustainable consumption practices such as 'alternative hedonism'. Chapter 9 by Hubert Buch-Hansen, Annika Pissin and Erin Kennedy takes the existing growth-critical literature, which has largely failed to consider the importance of capitalist diversity for degrowth transitions to steady-state economies, as its point of departure. It seeks to overcome this neglect by bringing into focus diverging institutional and socio-economic settings in three political econo- mies – China, the US and France – and by considering the impacts that these different settings will have for future degrowth transitions. Drawing on various indicators to measure progress in the degrowth transition proposed by O'Neill (2012) – including 'social accounts' such as human well-being and 'biophysical accounts' such as material inputs and CO_2 emissions – the chapter first establishes the status quo of the three countries. Subsequently, it outlines the characteristics of these political economies from the theoretical perspective of capitalist diversity and institutional change, arguing that each represents a distinct form of capitalism. Owing to their diverse political economies, the three countries would face different structural challenges and opportunities when embarking on socially sustainable degrowth trajectories.

Bringing together the emerging field of degrowth research with empirical research on social enterprises and social economy organizations, Chapter 10 by Eric Clark and Håkan Johansson analyses the capacities of social enterprises for facilitating transition to sustainable welfare and degrowth. One consequence of the expansion of market relations is a growing tendency to naturalize market conditions as being necessary, exaggerating the importance of market-based profit-oriented production, while neglecting the importance of social enterprises and forms of non-profit production that have historically contributed, and continue to account for, a considerable share of all production of goods and services in manifold forms. These socio-economic activities are presented in the degrowth literature as alternatives to growth-generating, market-based and profit-oriented economic activities, underlining an understanding of degrowth as conducive to prosperity, conviviality and sustainable welfare. Social enterprises are first examined in relation to broader shifts in politics and political economy. The chapter then considers the notion of 'green social enterprises' from various perspectives, highlighting the role of use value-oriented versus exchange value-oriented investment and decision-making.

Chapter 11 by Erin Kennedy and Annika Pissin deals with imaginaries of low carbon life in China. Within official statements and development plans the term 'low carbon' is frequently used and extends into areas including low carbon economy, low carbon development, low carbon society, low carbon cities and low carbon life. However, this term is commonly used without clarity regarding definition or methods of implementation and measurement. As greenhouse gas emission targets and development plans 'trickle down' from top-level government officials to community-level residents, little knowledge is shared and there is restricted room for ideas about ways of achieving the desired low carbon targets at community level. The purpose of this chapter is to explore the narratives of what is possible and what is imaginable for a low carbon life in China at individual and local levels. It builds on two narrative sources: first, interviews where people from different generations tell their stories of what they want to see in the future and second, through the examination of blogs written by authors in mainland China. The chapter reviews current low carbon policies in China as well as the methods of implementation that are utilized by upper levels of government and implemented at local levels. These top-down approaches are then juxtaposed with the ideas that individuals have concerning low carbon life and how it can be implemented.

Chapter 12 by Kate Soper addresses the interaction of policy and experience in achieving an 'alternative hedonist' lifestyle. The concept of alternative hedonism has sometimes been charged with making too much of individual consumer agency at the cost of taking proper account of the essential role of state and institutional initiatives in promoting sustainable consumption and welfare. However, this concept has never attempted to deny the importance of top-down initiatives but rather emphasizes their reliance upon electoral support and their necessary interaction with the experiences of individuals in modern democracies. The hypothesis is that any avant-garde of consumers who opt to self-police their consumption in the interest of sustainable welfare is likely to remain an ineffective minority unless it is swelled by proactive public policies. In conclusion, it is argued that alternative hedonist frameworks of thinking about the 'good life' can alter conceptions of self-interest among affluent consumers and thus help to set off the relay of political pressures for a fairer global distribution of resources and a more sustainable economic order.

In the Conclusion, Oksana Mont and Max Koch summarize the book's main theoretical and empirical results in relation to the development of the concept of sustainable welfare and outline the structural challenges and opportunities to achieving this in the real world. The two volume editors also identify areas for further research.

Notes

1 Of these boundaries, it is climate change that is the focus of several of the chapters of this book.
2 Degrowth approaches, which are taken up in a range of contributions to this volume, argue that a rescaling of the production and consumption cycle from transnational and national levels towards local levels would be necessary in order to rebalance economy, society and nature (Kallis, 2011).

References

Bourdieu, P. (1984). *Distinction: A Social Critique of the Judgement of Taste*. Cambridge: Harvard University Press.

Clark, E. (2014). *Sustainability Science*. Oxford Bibliographies. Oxford: Oxford University Press.

D'Alisa, G., Demaria, F. and Kallis, G. (eds). (2014). *Degrowth: A Vocabulary for a New Era*. London: Routledge.

Daly, H. (1977). *Steady State Economics*. San Francisco, CA: W. H. Freeman.

Fritz, M. and Koch, M. (2016). Economic development and prosperity patterns around the world: Structural challenges for a global steady-state economy. *Global Environmental Change*, 38, 41–48.

Gough, I. (2014). *Climate Change and Sustainable Welfare: An Argument for the Centrality of Human Needs*. Centre for Analysis of Social Exclusion. Working Paper No. 182. London: London School of Economics.

Hemerijck, A. (2013). *Changing Welfare States*. Oxford: Oxford University Press.

Hirsch, F. (1976). *The Social Limits to Growth*. Cambridge, MA: Harvard University Press.

Jackson, T. (2009). *Prosperity without Growth? The Transition to a Sustainable Economy*. London: Sustainable Development Commission.

Kallis, G. (2011). In defence of degrowth. *Ecological Economics*, 70, 873–880.

Kasser, T. (2011). Cultural values and the well-being of future generations: A cross-national study. *Journal of Cross-Cultural Psychology*, 42, 206–215.

Kazepov, Y. (ed.). (2010). *Rescaling Social Policies towards Multilevel Governance in Europe*. Aldershot: Ashgate.

Koch, M. (2006). *Roads to Post-Fordism. Labour Markets and Social Structures in Europe*. Aldershot: Ashgate.

Koch, M. (2012). *Capitalism and Climate Change: Theoretical Analysis, Historical Development and Policy Responses*. Basingstoke: Palgrave Macmillan.

Koch, M. (2013). Welfare after growth: Theoretical discussion and policy implications. *International Journal of Social Quality*, 3(1), 4–20.

Kronsell, A. and Bäckstrand, K. (eds). (2015). *Rethinking the Green State: Environmental Governance towards Climate and Sustainability Transitions*. London: Routledge.

Langhelle, O. (1999). Sustainable development: Exploring the ethics of our common future. *International Political Science Review*, 20(2), 129–149.

Latouche, S. (2010). *Farewell to Growth*. Cambridge: Polity.

Muraca, B. (2012). Towards a fair degrowth society: Justice and the right to a 'good life' beyond growth. *Futures*, 44, 535–545.

O'Neill, D. W. (2012). Measuring progress in the degrowth transition to a steady-state economy. *Ecological Economics*, 84, 221–231.

Paech, N. (2012). *Liberation from Excess: The Road to Post-Growth Economy*. Munich: Oekom.

Piketty, T. (2014). *Capital in the 21st Century*. Cambridge, MA: Harvard University Press.

Rauschmayer, F., Omann, I. and Frühmann, J. (eds). (2012). *Sustainable Development: Capabilities, Needs and Well-Being*. London: Routledge.

Rockström, J., Steffen, W., Noone, K., Persson, Å., Chapin, F. S., Lambin, E., Lenton, T. M., Scheffer, M., Folke, C., Schellnhuber, H., Nykvist, B., De Wit, C. A., Hughes, T., van der Leeuw, S., Rodhe, H., Sörlin, S., Snyder, P. K., Costanza, R., Svedin, U., Falkenmark, M., Karlberg, L., Corell, L. V., Fabry, J., Hansen, J., Walker, B., Liverman, D., Richardson, K., Crutzen, P. and Foley, J. (2009). Planetary boundaries: Exploring the safe operating space for humanity. *Ecology and Society*, 14(2), 32.

Sayer, A. (2015). *Why We Can't Afford the Rich*. Bristol: Policy Press.

Soper, K., Ryle, M. H. and Thomas, L. (2009). *The Politics and Pleasures of Consuming Differently*. Basingstoke: Palgrave Macmillan.

Stiglitz, J. (2010). *Freefall. Free Markets and the Sinking of the Global Economy*. London: Penguin.

Victor, P. (2008). *Managing without Growth: Slower by Design, Not Disaster*. Cheltenham: Edward Elgar.

Walker, G. (2012). *Environmental Justice: Concepts, Evidence and Politics*. London: Routledge.

Wilkinson, R. and Pickett, K. (2010). *The Spirit Level. Why Equality is Better for Everyone*. London: Penguin.

Part I

Perspectives on sustainable welfare

1   The concept of sustainable welfare

Eric Brandstedt and Maria Emmelin

Introduction

A common idea nowadays is that traditional welfare states, development and economic growth are environmentally destructive. A related problem with economic growth is the so-called 'hedonic treadmill': although gross domestic product (GDP) increases over time, the reported subjective well-being of people in the developed world seems to remain the same (Easterlin, 1974). When these are put together, the following hypothesis can be formed: making the welfare state sustainable should also increase individual welfare, and there are no trade-offs, sacrifices or conflicts between the objectives of sustainability and welfare. In this chapter, we will scrutinize and criticize this conjecture. We will do so by taking a step back in order to consider this basic issue: the concept of welfare and the contention that it must be made sustainable.

A conceptually clear approach to sustainable welfare should meet two requirements. It should in a descriptively adequate way account for the concept of welfare and provide an account of what it means to make welfare sustainable. In the current debate, however, it is rare that both or even one of these conditions are met. First, there are theories about welfare, well-being or the good life that all neglect the crucial question of what it means to make welfare sustainable. These fail to respond to a most pressing concern for contemporary politics and theory, that is, meeting a sustainability proviso. Second, there are normative approaches to sustainability that, although they do heed the sustainability proviso, still fail because they pay too little attention to the descriptive adequacy of the underlying conception of welfare. The latter failure is no less damaging than the first. It risks giving the false impression that, when making welfare sustainable, one does not have to account for the conceptual clarity of the concept of welfare. This could mean that normative approaches fail to account for some of the most troubling features of the sustainability issue. If they rely on a truncated, but descriptively inadequate, ideal of the good life, then they are insufficient guides for the kind of policies needed for reaching sustainability.

These two *distinct* objectives of the idea of sustainable welfare are scrutinized in the following way. First, we relate to some traditional discussion points in the welfare debate in order to delineate the concept of welfare. Second, we evaluate traditional conceptions of welfare in terms of how well these manage to respond to the sustainability proviso. Basically, we ask whether we find the sustainability proviso internal to an acceptable conception of welfare. Or, in other words, is the sustainable life coextensive with the good life? We argue that it is *not* because the requirements of sustainability (that is, reconsidering the currency of welfare and recalibrating the patterns of distribution of welfare) cannot fully be motivated in terms of improvements in individual welfare. For such reasons, we cannot justify heeding a sustainability proviso by merely appealing to the constraints internal to the concept of welfare. Instead we suggest, by way of conclusion, that working towards sustainable welfare necessitates policies not directly grounded in individual welfare. If sustainability is accepted as a compelling normative ideal, one should instead focus on the conditions under which such an individually demanding social goal could be attained. These conditions could, for instance, be illuminated by the concept of 'social capital'. The question of sustainable welfare that is relevant to policy would then be: How can social capital, over and above individual welfare, be mobilized for the collective good of sustainability?

The concept of welfare

Welfare, welfare economics and welfare politics

We shall begin with some preliminary remarks on the terminology and background of the welfare debate (see Griffin, 1986; Sumner, 1996). Welfare can be defined as the *subjective* condition of faring or doing well; in other words, what is 'good for' a person. In this sense, welfare is approximately equivalent to 'individual well-being', 'individual interest', and 'individual good' (Sumner, 1996). 'Welfarism' is the view that well-being is the only value that matters ethically. The traditional welfarist position is utilitarianism and the following developments of '(new) welfare economics'. Traditionally, welfare has been understood in terms of felt pleasure satisfaction; however, due to the increasing dominance of new welfare economics, it has become commonplace to equate welfare with (revealed) preference satisfaction. Here it is important to emphasize that welfare is not the same as provision of material goods and services, since this is a common and unfortunate confusion. Welfarist theorists are generally sceptical of making material goods – for example, GDP or per capita income (PCI) – *constitutive* of welfare, because these are viewed as lacking any intrinsic value and are only valuable insofar as they increase welfare. Although nobody denies that access to, for instance, economic resources is an important means of attaining welfare, one should resist the temptation to equate this *with* welfare. The point could be expressed as a more general formality requirement for theories of welfare: the nature of welfare should be distinguished from the sources or determinants of welfare (e.g. knowledge, friendship, money, health). Welfare theorists are generally interested in analysing the former (i.e. in meeting the formality requirement) although they occasionally, and erroneously, merely provide a list of the latter.

The analysis of welfare focuses on so-called 'prudential values', that is, what is 'good for' a person, which should be distinguished from other kinds of values, such as aesthetic, ethical and – arguably – perfectionist values. In the analysis of the concept of welfare, one must thus avoid mixing and confusing these different kinds of values. For instance, one should avoid moralizing the concept, that is, allowing for the conceptual possibility that what is good for a subject (i.e. her welfare) is different from what she ought to care about morally (i.e. what is ethically good) and from what is good for her *qua*, her status as a human being (i.e. the perfectionist good). It should, however, be noted that distinguishing between prudential values and perfectionist ones is not without controversy: there are some theories purportedly about the nature of welfare, such as the capability approach, that understand welfare in perfectionist terms.

To distinguish prudential value from moral value is, however, less controversial. We should nonetheless clarify how the analysis of welfare differs from a more general discussion of social justice. In such a debate, welfare is generally scrutinized on the basis of a normative adequacy requirement. The classic example, which also sets the tone for the subsequent debate, is from Amartya Sen (1980), who posed the question, 'Equality of what?' G. A. Cohen (1989) similarly poses the question, 'What is the currency of egalitarian justice?' On the basis of the normative presupposition of egalitarianism, Sen, Cohen and others examine different proposals for the appropriate units being distributed equally. However, that is not an analysis of the concept of welfare as such, and is not how we will analyse it.

Instead of normative adequacy, we will adopt descriptive adequacy as the basic requirement for the analysis. We want the analysis of welfare to be as general as possible and not just applicable under specific normative conditions. Additionally, the analysis should ensure fidelity to pre-theoretical intuitions (i.e. judgements that we make about whether our lives are going well or badly) and be free of distorting biases (see Sumner, 1996, for a longer discussion of the requirements of descriptive adequacy for welfare).

The rudiments of a descriptively adequate concept of welfare

In presenting some of the most popular conceptions of welfare in this section, we point to some general problems that each of these face. The situation is, however, generally worse for some than for others, as can be seen when distinguishing between objective and subjective accounts of welfare. Sumner (1996: 38) defines their difference in the following way: '[s]ubjective theories make our well-being logically dependent on our attitudes of favour and disfavour. Objective theories deny this dependency'. Given this definition, we can see how subjective accounts have a certain edge due to the subject-relative nature of welfare (Sumner, 1996: 42–44). In reference to the conditions for descriptive adequacy introduced above, the search for a theory of welfare should focus on prudential values. This means not only that it must be a theory about what it means for an individual's life to go well, but further, to be going well from his or her point of view. This subject-relativity of the concept of welfare speaks in favour of subjectivist accounts, since these make welfare dependent on the subject's own concerns.

Beginning with the subjective theories of welfare, a distinction can be drawn between 'state of mind' theories (e.g. pleasure, pain) and 'state of the world' theories (e.g. preferences) (Griffin, 1986: 7). Hedonism, which is the classical state of mind theory, is the set of views that understand welfare as an introspectively discriminable experience (either as a positive feeling, that is, the sensation model, or by the fact that some external object is being liked or disliked, that is, the attitude model). In the words of Sumner (1996: 92):

> The resulting theory tells us that our lives are going well when we are having pleasurable feelings and badly when we are having painful ones, that you are better off than me if you are having more of the former or fewer of the latter, that something benefits me when it causes the former and harms me when it causes the latter, and so on.

The thing that hedonism seems to get right is that welfare is, at least partly, constituted by pleasurable experiences; if a thing is fully disconnected from the subject's mind, it is hard to see in what sense it can benefit the subject seen from the subject's point of view. However, the problem with hedonism is that it makes too much of this 'experience requirement' (cf. Griffin, 1986: 13). Even if it is a necessary requirement for welfare, it is certainly not a sufficient one. To illustrate this point, one could relate briefly to the classic example from Robert Nozick of the 'experience machine' (1974). In this famous thought experiment, Nozick asks whether we would plug in to an experience machine that would simulate any kind of pleasurable experience we want while floating in a tank with electrodes attached to our brain. Nozick's intuition, shared by most commentators, is that we would not want to plug in, although plugging in would reliably lead to the maximizing of felt pleasure satisfaction. The exact reason for not doing so is disputed, but relates to the inauthenticity of machine-induced pleasurable satisfaction. This seems to point to a general problem for a subjective, state of mind, theory of welfare.

One may thus wonder whether a move to a state of the world theory, such as the desire account, is more promising. According to its simplest version (and the one commonly assumed by welfare economists), welfare is understood as the satisfaction of actual desires. Welfare just consists in getting what one wants, where these wants can be understood, for instance, in terms of revealed preferences in the market place. However, we have all experienced that getting what we want is no guarantee for being better off – an afternoon spent in a shopping frenzy may result in only fatigue and emptiness, although this activity was exactly what we wanted to do. A more sophisticated desire account presents itself: perhaps it is not the actual desire satisfaction that makes us better off, but rather the satisfaction of desires informed by the true nature of the desired object. Perhaps if we were knowledgeable about the true nature of spending the better half of a day in a crowded shopping centre, we would not have chosen to do this instead of spending the time sitting in an armchair. One of the problems with the desire account – and any other state of the world theory – is that it ignores the experience requirement, and this seems in many, though not all, cases to be counterintuitive.

Perhaps the most promising conception of welfare is found in a hybrid between the two hitherto considered accounts: welfare as 'authentic happiness' or, synonymously, 'authentic life satisfaction' (Sumner, 1996: 172). This conception of welfare agrees with the hedonist one about the experience requirement, but adds the requirement of authenticity that is somewhat similar to that of the sophisticated desire account. The resulting account of welfare thus states that something is good for a subject if and only if she authentically endorses it or experiences it as satisfying as an informed and autonomous subject. Now, this account is not without objections, but we contend that it is the most promising account for meeting the requirements of descriptive adequacy introduced above.

Let us turn to objective accounts, which here can be exemplified with a basic needs account. It is worth pointing out again that we believe that an analysis of welfare ought to make descriptive adequacy its first priority, and only after this has been accounted for should we turn to normative adequacy. This is, however, not how basic needs accounts are normally conceived; these are instead usually justified by normative or moral reasons (see, for example, O'Neill, 2011; Gough, 2014). James Griffin describes the strategy that usually underlies needs accounts as follows: 'instead of starting with a notion [of welfare] that we might later fit into morality, we start with morality and ask which notion fits it' (Griffin, 1986: 40). This is a strategy that, however morally justifiable and laudable, risks leading to lacunas in the descriptive adequacy of welfare.

The basic idea behind a needs account of welfare is that, for an individual to lead a good life, she must – at least – have her basic needs satisfied. The importance of needs is explained by drawing attention to the fact that, if the basic needs of an individual are not met, she necessarily suffers serious harm (see Feinberg, 1973). To make the account distinct from the desire account it is important to qualify needs as being 'basic' (or 'fundamental', 'absolute', 'non-volitional'), as distinguished from non-basic (or 'instrumental', 'volitional') (see Thomson, 1987; Wiggins, 1998; Frankfurt, 1984). The difference between desires and basic needs might then be explained by pointing out that 'desire' is an intensional transitive verb, unlike 'need', and thus does not allow for substitutions as in the following sentences: if 'P wants a glass of water', it is not necessarily true that 'P wants a glass of H_2O'; however, if 'P needs a glass of water', then 'P needs a glass of H_2O'. Furthermore, one may argue that, for true statements of basic needs, such as 'P needs water in order to survive', it is not meaningful to even ask 'but does P really need water?' All needs, whether instrumental or basic, are needed to obtain some aim or end. This is true in the case of an instrumental need, such as the need to add something sweet to coffee to improve its taste, as well as in the case of a basic need, such as the need for water, which is needed for survival. But, arguably, there is a difference related to the end states, which in cases of basic needs are said to be of such great importance that we could not do without them. Some basic needs are needed for survival (e.g. water, health); others are needed in order to avoid falling below some minimal threshold of a decent life (e.g. autonomy, recognition). Such needs just seem to be the fundamental and constitute an absolute basis for a good life, no matter whose life it is, or what one otherwise wants or decides to do.

What should then be said of the analysis of welfare in terms of basic needs? A general worry is that this will turn out to be too restrictive and not cover all that matters for an individual's welfare. Although no one would deny that the provision of basic needs is a component of a good life, it is much less obvious that nothing else matters for subjective welfare. In the words of Sumner (1996: 54)

> [i]t is certainly true that we are standardly benefited by the satisfaction of basic needs for nourishment, sanitation, security, companionship, and the like. But it is equally true that we can profit by satisfying mere likes or preferences or even whims.

Now, a defender of a needs account may add that the threshold that is supposed to separate prudentially and morally important basic needs from instrumental needs is not set at mere survival, but includes provision for what is needed for the optimal development of critical interests (cf. Gough, 2014: 15). Alternatively, it might be developed in terms of capabilities and functionings (e.g. Sen, 1992). However, the deeper problem here is that widening or deepening the range of the end states that are supposed to mark basic needs could have unwanted consequences. It could, on the one hand, drain the normative urgency of the claims considered (it is less normatively compelling to provide for everyone's highest attainable standard of health than to provide for what is needed to maintain a minimally decent life) and, on the other hand, it risks collapsing the account of welfare into a desire theory. The specification is faced with the following dilemma: in order to make the needs account descriptively adequate as an analysis of welfare, it is not enough to ground needs upon bare survival or the basics for a minimally decent life – there is much more that matters to us prudentially – but in order to make the account both distinct and normatively compelling, the threshold must be set relatively low. We conclude from this that analysing welfare in terms of basic needs is less promising than the subjective accounts considered. When we now move on to consider which conception of welfare is best equipped to account for the sustainability proviso, then the evaluation of the respective analyses is turned on its head.

The sustainability proviso

The idea of 'sustainability' dates back to the 1970s, but in its current form it is rooted in the Brundtland Report (WCED, 1987). Here the overarching argument is that development must be made sustainable, which is defined as: 'development that meets the needs of the present without compromising the ability of future generations to meet their own needs' (WCED, 1987: 43). The less-often quoted qualification of the definition goes as follows:

> It [sustainable development] contains within it two key concepts:
>
> - the concept of 'needs', in particular the essential needs of the world's poor, to which overriding priority should be given, and
> - the idea of limitations imposed by the state of technology and social organization on the environment's ability to meet present and future needs.
>
> (WCED, 1987: 43)

Following Oluf Langhelle's analysis of the concept of sustainable development, one might distinguish between 'the goal of development', that is, 'the satisfaction of human needs and aspirations' (WCED, 1987: 43), and the 'proviso of sustainability', that is, 'that each generation is permitted to pursue its interests only in ways that do not undermine the ability of future generations to meet their own needs' (Langhelle, 1999: 133). Although this understanding of 'sustainability' is not beyond dispute, one can safely say that it captures two essential features of the received understanding of sustainability (cf. Brandstedt 2013). To make development sustainable means *widening the scope* of consideration to include global and intergenerational impacts *and* the consequent need to *reconsider the units and patterns* of distribution assumed in relevant practices. Let us elaborate somewhat on these two features of the sustainability proviso.

Before the environmental awakening of the 1970s and prior to the full advance of globalization, the boundaries of the nation state were generally not challenged. In discussions of the welfare state, it was uncontroversial to assign to the state exclusive responsibility for maintaining the welfare of its citizens. Similarly, in political philosophy, it was commonplace to assume the closed confines of a nation state as both the site and scope of theories of justice, such as in (Rawls, 1971: 457). However, due to the growing awareness of the fact that causal relations transcend space and time, such narrow scope for the principles of welfare distribution, or more generally the principles of justice, is no longer a tenable default position. Globalization and ecological interdependence constitute the background to any contemporary discussion of politics. Climate change is the clearest example of an essentially transnational and transgenerational phenomenon: greenhouse gases from activities carried out here and now are mixing with the existing stock of heat-trapping gases in the atmosphere, which is producing increased global warming and exacerbating the negative effects that are dispersed over space and time. If the transboundary character of contemporary activities is properly recognized, the following question arises: whose welfare should be represented in justifications of principles for organizing a society today? A reasonable answer is that the scope of distributive principles must be widened to include all those affected (see Näsström, 2011 for a discussion of the so-called 'all-affected principle'), even if the nation state can still be maintained as the site of justice (Abizadeh, 2007). In other words, even if it may be possible to maintain that those governed by principles of justice are necessarily citizens of a nation state, the minimal requirement states that these principles should also take into account the claims of some non-citizens. We can thus conclude that the traditional, restrictive, view of the scope of principles of distribution of welfare is unsatisfactory in our world today. Any principle for the distribution of welfare must adopt a broadened scope and consider the impact that the provision of welfare has on the interests of geographically and temporally distant people – even if the underlying distributive principle is still only meant to govern the citizens of a specific nation state.

Once the scope of justice is widened beyond the traditional national realm, the following normative question arises: How does this widened scope affect the normative foundation of traditional distributive principles? Due to this global and intergenerational expansion, many more interests are relevant in the justificatory process; does this mean that we must rethink the understanding of the relevant interests and their respective weighting? In order to keep this exposition brief, we could here distinguish between distributive units (or currency) and distributive patterns. The main proposals of distributive units in the debate are: 'primary goods' (Rawls, 1971), 'resources' (Dworkin, 1981) and 'access to advantage' (Cohen, 1989), 'capabilities' (Sen, 1992). The main proposals of different patterns for distributive principles are: maximizing (defended by various utilitarians), maximin (Rawls, 1971), equality (e.g. Cohen, 1989) and sufficiency (Frankfurt, 1987). Together, these two dimensions of justice make up a rich array of combinations – much too many to consider here. The only claim that we can assert at this stage is that the sustainability proviso, with the broadened scope introduced above, calls into question *any* proposed unit and pattern for distribution in a society. The recognition that led the Brundtland report – as well as the more general debate, for instance, Meadows *et al.* (1972) – towards the affirmation of a sustainability proviso was that there is something amiss in the traditional ways of understanding development and economic growth. In the definition of sustainable development presented above, this recognition was manifested in the contention that the satisfaction of present-day needs and aspirations must not compromise the ability of future needs satisfaction (and, more generally, in the idea of 'limitations'). This means that some needs and aspirations must be held in check and restrained in order to avoid violating the sustainability proviso. The exact specification of the kind of trade-offs involved here is still up for debate. We can only conclude that any proposed distributive principle must reconsider the currency and patterning in light of the extended scope of the sustainability proviso. To put it differently, the very idea of sustainability is a challenge to business as usual.

To make things more concrete, let us specify the limits imposed by the sustainability proviso, focusing on climate change. The maximum disturbance of the climate system is commonly set at the temperature target of two degrees Celsius above that of pre-industrial temperature levels. This target is generally justified as a marking a 'safe operating space' of a relatively stable climate condition, one that humans and other species are adapted to (Rockström *et al.*, 2009). This goal was recognized by leading politicians of most member states of the United Nations Framework Convention on Climate Change (UNFCCC) in 2009, in the so-called 'Copenhagen Accord', as being the threshold for 'dangerous climate change'.

More concretely still, one could argue that the world at large thus has a 'carbon budget', specifying how much oil, coal and gas can be burned in order to have a reasonable chance of meeting the temperature target (Allen *et al.*, 2009). On the basis of the best available computer models, Allen *et al.* have calculated the carbon budget as being in the ballpark region of 1 trillion metric tonnes of carbon. The current stock of carbon in the atmosphere is 586 billion metric tonnes (GtC), which means that we have already emitted more than half of this target and, as emission trends are increasing, we are likely to exceed the trillionth tonne in less than 24 years. In a widely read opinion piece from 2012, Bill McKibben draws attention to a report from the Carbon Tracker Initiative, which alerted people to the full scale of the climate crisis by listing the amount of carbon contained in the proven coal, oil and gas reserves of the fossil fuel industry, which is 2,795 GtC. He writes: 'We have five times as much oil and coal and gas on the books as climate scientists think is safe to burn. We'd have to keep 80 percent of those reserves locked away underground to avoid that fate' (McKibben, 2012).

Now, given the expected market value of those reserves – estimated to be around $27 trillion – and the fact that the fossil fuel industry sustains large parts of the global economy, heeding the sustainability proviso will obviously require some sacrifices. At any rate, it will mean forfeiting carbon-based consumption as a way to mitigate climate change and benefit future generations. The question, however, is whether this necessarily amounts to sacrifices in individual welfare. To answer this, we analyse the main conceptions of welfare through the lens of sustainability in the following section.

Making welfare sustainable

A common idea in accounts of welfare is that some (internal) limits designate the nature of welfare (cf. O'Neill, 2011; Gough, 2014): pleasure is thought to be good only to the extent that it is moderate and balanced; there are limits to basic needs set by the dependencies of the human predicament; functionings are defined in terms of limited human abilities, etc. This suggests an answer to the test of normative adequacy that sustainability presents. Perhaps we can achieve sustainability just by ensuring that internal limits to welfare are heeded, making sure that individuals lead happy lives. In this section, we will argue that this idea, even if suggestive, is misconceived.

More specifically, the argument is that objective accounts now appear to be more promising than the subjective accounts considered. The basic explanation of this is that it is subjective wants, desires and preferences that to a large extent drive the problems of sustainability. Even so, neither do objective accounts give the right answer to sustainability – at least not as they are commonly presented. Even if it is probably correct that individual welfare will need to be formed more in alignment with that which objective accounts suggest, the reason for this is not primarily because we will then lead a better life as seen from the agent's own point of view, but rather because it is normatively required on the basis of the sustainability proviso. The alternative explanation that we will put forward is that the necessary limits are instead external to the nature of welfare, which amounts to saying that we must choose to lead less good lives (seen from the subject's point of view) for some external reason. In other words, we must be prepared for sacrifices in individual welfare.

One commonly finds arguments to the effect that solving the sustainability issue will at the same stroke bring about happiness. These 'win-win' arguments are commonplace within such disparate groups as environmentalists and neoclassical economists. The first group often claims that a consumerist culture drives climate change as well as making us subjectively unhappy. Thus, if we put a stop to consumerism, we will mitigate climate change and, as a positive side effect, create conditions for happier lives. Among the more pro-market proponents of the second group, the win-win potential comes from the purported relation between mitigating climate change and making investments for long-term market returns. The appeal of win-win arguments is that they seem promising in light of the radically non-ideal condition that we are presently in, with the lack of collective willingness to reorient the economy at a global level (e.g. Soper, 2008; see also Chapter 12). If the fate of future generations, small island states, the poorest people of the world and nature are not enough to motivate sufficient abatement action, one may thus hope that climate change can be solved for the seemingly unrelated reasons that people will lead happier lives, or that market returns are secured over time.

The underlying rationale is the same as that which has motivated attempts to equate prudential values with moral values in the general discussion of welfare. It could take form in ways that correspond to the different conceptions of welfare that we have considered. Based on the subjective accounts, hedonism and desire theories, one could argue that to be genuinely happy today one must give up certain unsustainable desires, either because this increases experienced happiness or because it clears away a distraction to that which we genuinely desire. Based on the objective accounts, premised on needs or capabilities, one could argue that to be genuinely happy today certain unsustainable desires must be given up, either because these are non-basic wants whose priority should be demoted to basic needs, or because some basic functionings are threatened by such unsustainable desires. This shows that we do not need to introduce a new conception of welfare to account for the sustainability pressures, but existing accounts can be revised to handle the new threat (we should note that they are not accounts of the sources of welfare and so are not committed to the carbon economy as a source of welfare). However, the question is not whether normative adjustments are possible to any conception of welfare, but whether these rearrangements are required for internal reasons of welfare maximization or for some external normative reason. Our answer, in short, is that the case is better argued on the basis of an objective account: if indeed welfare consists in the satisfaction of basic needs or functionings, then the conflict between the good life and the sustainable life is not as clear as it is in subjective accounts.

Subjective accounts seem to fare less well. Consider hedonism. Is the hedonistically happy life the sustainable life? The way the argument for this answer must be framed is by arguing that unsustainable lifestyles are inherently flawed because they cause the subjects' lives to contain less hedonic happiness than they otherwise could have. We appear to find examples of such arguments in the happiness literature, as briefly referred to above, for instance, with the 'hedonic treadmill'. However, what such studies illustrate is not that environmentally less destructive practices necessarily maximize hedonic happiness; they only point to the fact that hedonic experiences are satiable. Even if it is true that further economic growth and the consumerist culture do not lead to reports of increasing subjective happiness, this does not mean that degrowth – or say, a more frugal lifestyle – will either. The hedonic treadmill is likely to turn whether it is powered by fossil fuel or renewable energy.

That is not to say that there are no prudential reasons to give up carbon activities in a hedonist conception of welfare. If a consumerist lifestyle only causes stress, fatigue or weariness, it is unlikely to be the best source of hedonistic happiness – something to which Kate Soper's 'alternative hedonism' is an important reminder (cf. Soper 2008; Chapter 12). Yet there is another reason why this will not give us the full answer to sustainability. Regardless of how prudent 'alternative hedonism' is, there is no guarantee that the pursuit of the good life envisioned will not conflict with the sustainability proviso. Even if it is true that people find low carbon activities deeply rewarding and opt for these for hedonistic reasons to some extent, this only points to the fact that high carbon activities are not a necessary condition for hedonistic happiness. This still leaves open the possibility that long-haul flights and Sunday afternoon drives with petrol-guzzling sport-utility vehicles are possible, even if not necessary, sources of hedonistic happiness. If we take experienced hedonic happiness as our standard for correctness in designing policies for sustainability, it is not enough to point to the fact that some people today find amusement in more frugal lifestyle choices because it is also true that people still enjoy high carbon activities – and that is exactly the problem.[1]

In what sense, then, does an objective account of welfare fare better? Basically, the strengths of objective accounts – and perhaps of needs accounts in particular – are the mirror image of the weaknesses of subjective accounts when applied to a normative ethical agenda. An objective account has the resources to handle the problem of 'adaptive preferences' (Elster, 1982), it does not rely on the narrow and deceptive model of *Homo economicus*, it can account for distinctions between more or less serious claims and, perhaps most importantly, in relation to sustainability, it clearly recognizes the existence of limits (for a good summary of these strengths, see Gough 2014: 3–4; see also Chapter 2). There are indeed benefits to this account if it is to be used as a standard of sustainable welfare. However, the point is that *these strengths stem from the moralizing of welfare that the basic needs account proposes.* Consider, for instance, the way in which Gough argues that human needs, unlike desires, can account for differences in moral seriousness: 'human needs explicitly introduce moral criteria into the conception and appraisal of human well-being' (2014: 4).

The introduction of a criterion of normative adequacy is not at all misplaced in the discussion of the welfare state. The basic structure of the welfare state must be justified by evaluating its distributive profile and general organization, for instance, in terms of the sustainability proviso. Several of the subsequent chapters of this anthology take on this task in greater detail (in particular Chapter 2, which provides a needs-based evaluation of the political economy of sustainable welfare; see also Chapter 5, which considers some of the obstacles to a transition to a sustainable welfare state and Chapter 6, which considers recalibrations of the welfare state prompted by the new risks of climate change).

The critique against the win-win strategy considered above may seem to make the task of reorganizing society towards a sustainable welfare state even more daunting. It is therefore important to end with the following proposal: there are other ways of accommodating change than in finding support in terms of individual welfare. Even if one agrees – and we do – with what is argued in Chapter 12, namely that it is imperative that the sustainability proviso is perceived to be in the interests of electorates, this does not mean that sustainability will stand and fall by the close link to individual welfare criticized above. Citizens may be motivated not only to act on what is good for them, but also by what is good for the community. The key to unlocking the necessary conditions for collective action in a sustainable welfare state could, for instance, be found in the idea of social capital (see, for example, Putnam, 1993). In a society with high social capital, trusting individuals are capable of transcending more confined norms of collective action. In such settings, altruism is not confined to caring for relatives based on reciprocal interaction; it is additionally possible for individuals to act on norms of non-reciprocal altruism, that is, to make sacrifices for the common good, although that may come at a rather high cost to the individual herself (see Haidt, 2012). We also see social capital as being an entry point for moving into a complex endeavour to influence norms and attitudes. Here the awareness of the differences between participation in *bonding, bridging* and *linking* social networks is needed as well as an understanding of the potential negative effects of mobilizing social capital. Perhaps this should be the focus of future work (cf. Chapters 10–12), rather than trying to make the seemingly disparate notions of welfare and sustainability fully coincide.

Conclusion

In conclusion, meeting the sustainability proviso in contemporary welfare states requires reconsidering the units and patterning of welfare. The necessary rearrangements are better explained by objective rather than subjective accounts of welfare. However, the objective accounts of welfare are, at the same time, disassociated from the descriptive adequacy of the concept of welfare. Focusing the welfare state, for instance, on basic needs rather than on subjective preferences seems conducive to meeting the sustainability proviso, but less obviously conducive to individual welfare. If we look from the opposite direction, focusing on some subjective understanding of welfare is good advice if the only objective is to maximize welfare, but less promising if the aim is that of a sustainable welfare state. This tension should be confronted in any discussion of sustainable welfare. Even if more study is needed to fully clarify these frictions, we hope that enough has been said above to motivate a shift of focus in the debate. If we think that it is important to meet the sustainability proviso, the normative debate should not focus primarily on prudential arguments, but rather on how social capital can be mobilized for the collective good of sustainability.

Note

1 Something similar is true of the desire-based account. We must be open to the possibility that what we desire – even under ideal conditions – is simply incompatible with what sustainability requires. There is, for instance, nothing inherently undesirable with overseas holidays (even knowing that the flight produces a great deal of carbon dioxide emissions). Solving climate change will not be fully in line with satisfying individual desires as long we do not have a basic desire for the well-being of not just our own children, but for that of unknown and unrelated future generations. For a more developed critique against desire and preference-based accounts of sustainable welfare, see Gough (2014).

References

Abizadeh, A. (2007). Cooperation, pervasive impact, and coercion: On the scope (not site) of distributive justice. *Philosophy & Public Affairs*, 35(4), 318–358.

Allen, M. R., Frame, D. J., Huntingford, C., Jones, C. D., Lowe, J. A., Meinshausen, M. and Meinshausen, N. (2009). Warming caused by cumulative carbon emissions towards the trillionth tonne. *Nature*, 458, 1163–1166.

Brandstedt, E. (2013). *The Construction of a Sustainable Development in Times of Climate Change*. Lund: MediaTryck.

Cohen, G. A. (1989). On the currency of egalitarian justice. *Ethics*, 99, 906–944.

Dworkin, R. (1981). What is equality? Part 2: Equality of resources. *Philosophy & Public Affairs*, 10, 283–345.

Easterlin, R. A. (1974). Does Economic Growth Improve the Human Lot? Some Empirical Evidence. In P. A. David and M. W. Reder (eds), *Nations and Households in Economic Growth* (89–125). New York: Academic Press.

Elster, J. (1982). Sour Grapes: Utilitarianism and the Genesis of Wants. In A. Sen and B. Williams (eds), *Utilitarianism and Beyond*. Cambridge: Cambridge University Press.

Feinberg, J. (1973). *Social Philosophy*. New Jersey: Prentice Hall.

Frankfurt, H. (1984). Necessity and desire. *Philosophy and Phenomenological Research*, 45, 1–13.

Frankfurt, H. (1987). Equality as a moral ideal. *Ethics*, 98, 21–43.

Gough, I. (2014). Climate change and sustainable welfare: An argument for the centrality of human needs, CASE papers, CASE/182. London: Centre for Analysis of Social Exclusion, London School of Economics and Political Science.

Griffin, J. (1986). *Well-Being: Its Meaning, Measurement, and Moral Importance*. Oxford: Oxford University Press.

Haidt, J. (2012). *The Righteous Mind: Why Good People are Divided by Politics and Religion*. New York: Pantheon.

Langhelle, O. (1999). Sustainable development: Exploring the ethics of our common future. *International Political Science Review*, 20(2), 129–149.

McKibben, B. (2012). Global warming's terrifying new math. *Rolling Stone*, 1162. 19 July. www.rollingstone.com/politics/news/global-warmings-terrifying-new-math-20120719?page=5 (accessed 7. 1. 15).

Meadows, D. H., Meadows, D. L., Randers, J., and Behrens I, W. (1972). *The Limits to Growth: A Report for the Club of Rome's Project on the Predicament of Mankind*. New York: Universe Books.

Näsström, S. (2011). The challenge of the all-affected principle. *Political Studies*, 59, 116–134.

Nozick, R. (1974). *Anarchy, State and Utopia*. Oxford: Blackwell.

O'Neill, J. (2011). The Overshadowing of Needs. In F. Rauschmayer, I. Omann and J. Frühmann (eds), *Sustainable Development* (25–43). London: Routledge.

Putnam, R. D. (1993) *Making Democracy Work: Civic Traditions in Modern Italy*. Princeton, NJ: Princeton University Press.

Rawls, J. (1971). *A Theory of Justice*. Cambridge, MA: Harvard University Press.

Rockström, J., Steffen, W., Noone, K., Persson, Å., Chapin I, F. S., Lambin, E., Lenton, T. M., Scheffer, M., Folke, C., Schellnhuber, H. J., Nykvist, B., de Wit, C. A., Hughes, T., van der Leeuw, S., Rodhe, H., Sörlin, S., Snyder, P. K., Costanza, R., Svedin, U., Falkenmark, M., Karlberg, L., Corell, R. W., Fabry, V. J., Hansen, J., Walker, B., Liverman, D., Richardson, K., Crutzen, P. and Foley, J. (2009). Planetary boundaries: Exploring the safe operating space for humanity. *Ecology and Society*, 14(2), 1–32.

Sen, A. (1980). Equality of What? In *The Tanner Lecture on Human Values* 1. Cambridge: Cambridge University Press.

Sen, A. (1992). *Inequality Reexamined*. Oxford: Clarendon Press.

Soper, K. (2008). Alternative hedonism, cultural theory and the role of aesthetic revisioning. *Cultural Studies*, 22(5), 567–587.

Sumner, L.W. (1996). *Welfare, Happiness, and Ethics*. Oxford: Clarendon Press.

Thomson, G. (1987). *Needs*. London: Routledge & Kegan Paul.

WCED (World Commission on Environment and Development) (1987). *Our Common Future. The Report of the World Commission on Environment and Development*. New York: Oxford University Press.

Wiggins, D. (1998). *Needs, Values, Truth*. New York: Oxford University Press.

2 Human needs, steady-state economics and sustainable welfare

Max Koch and Hubert Buch-Hansen

Introduction

The standard avenue in economics is to downplay if not deny the legitimacy of any distinction between needs and wants or preferences. A consequence of this view is the assumption of rational consumer sovereignty, insatiability and the indefiniteness of wants as well as a corresponding disinterest in the notion of human need. Yet the idea that individuals are best placed to judge the adequateness of their wants/needs is severely compromised if there are limits to people's knowledge and to their rationality in choosing the optimal means to their chosen ends. Regarding environmental limits, Hodgson (2013: 197) emphasizes that many people 'neither understand nor accept the conclusions of the science of climate change' and are therefore unlikely to make the 'right choices'. Moreover, if preferences adapt to circumstances, it is questionable 'how choice in markets (can) provide a means of comparing the wellbeing of people in different circumstances, especially over global space and inter-generational time' (Gough, 2014a: 3). Indeed, preference satisfaction theory appears to be especially unsuited for the consideration of the well-being of future generations, since their preferences cannot be revealed through their choice of behaviour (O'Neill, 2011). In this chapter we aim to contribute towards a systematic consideration of basic human needs in the political economy of sustainable welfare. More particularly, while Chapter 1 dealt with wider conceptual issues of sustainable welfare, we delineate the general characteristics of a welfare system of a non-growing economy by integrating the concept of basic human needs with growth-critical approaches. We do this by incorporating into Herman Daly's steady-state economy perspective the notion of sustainable welfare institutions that facilitate the satisfaction of human needs. Paradoxically, despite the fact that growth-critical scholars frequently refer to human needs, they have, as yet, not considered the issue in any detail, let alone gone very far in relating their approaches to existing concepts of human need (see, however, Muraca, 2013). As a corollary, the two theoretical traditions have largely evolved without interaction or cross-fertilization. Attempting to overcome this split in research into sustainable welfare, the chapter is divided into three sections. The first section demonstrates how the notions of wants and needs are reflected in the growth-critical literature using the example of the steady-state economy. The second section identifies the differences and commonalities of the human needs approaches proposed by scholars such as Doyal and Gough (1991) and Max-Neef (1991). The third section outlines the potential for an integration of the two perspectives in the context of a global sustainable welfare system.

Steady-state economics and human needs

The steady-state economy is the currently most developed vision of a non-growing economic system that functions within ecological boundaries. This makes it a logical entry point for reflections on human needs and sustainable welfare. The steady-state economy perspective was first presented by Herman E. Daly in a string of publications from the 1970s onwards (e.g. Daly, 1973, 1991, 1996), but over the years a number of other scholars have also contributed to the development of the perspective (e.g. Dietz and O'Neill, 2013). The steady-state economy is an economic system that does not grow in the sense that it keeps two factors at a constant level: the population of artefacts (stocks of physical wealth) and the number of people. The goal is to keep the level of *throughput* as low as possible, with throughput denoting 'flows of matter and energy from the first stage of production (depletion of low-entropy materials from the environment) to the last stage of consumption (pollution of the environment with high-entropy wastes and exotic materials)' (Daly, 1991: 17).

Daly (1991: 50–76) proposes that three institutions are crucial for maintaining a steady-state economy. The first is a system of government-auctioned physical depletion permits that keeps the stock of physical artefacts constant and matter–energy throughput at sustainable levels. Such a system could include a government authority that, on the basis of the best available scientific knowledge, annually determines an overall quota for the use of a specific natural resource, after which it auctions off permits to private actors on the market. These actors can then either use or trade the permits that they have bought (Dietz and O'Neill, 2013: 64–65). The second is a population stabilization institution which serves to keep the 'stock of people' within ecological limits. This could involve the more or less controversial ideas of 'transferable birth licences', economic incentives in the form of tax breaks to families with few children as well as immigration reforms (see Dietz and O'Neill, 2013: 81–83). The third is a distributist institution aiming to reduce inequality. Indeed, the legitimacy and long-term maintenance of all social orders requires that structural inequalities are held within certain acceptable limits. In capitalist societies, the state, particularly in its welfare dimension, is the institution that attempts to ensure this to be the case (Koch and Fritz, 2015). In the case of a steady-state economy, Daly (1991: 53–56) explicitly proposes an arrangement of setting maximum limits on income and wealth and minimum limits on income.

In combination, these institutions – which we in the following refer to as the three institutional pillars of steady-state economies – serve to make the economic system operate in an environmentally and socially sustainable manner. Daly is not in favour of abandoning growth in all sectors of the economy but of viewing it as a 'process to be consciously and politically monitored and regulated' (Barry, 2012: 133). Hence, while two basic physical magnitudes, population and artefacts, are to be held relatively constant in a steady-state economy, mainly qualitative parameters such as 'culture, genetic inheritance, knowledge, goodness, ethical codes ... the embodied technology, the design, and the product mix of the aggregate total stock of artifacts' (Daly, 1991: 16–17) are free and welcome to evolve. This is also reflected in Daly's distinction between 'growth' and 'development', whereby the former refers to a quantitative increase of gross domestic product (GDP) and the latter to qualitative change.

The steady-state economy is defined in terms of biophysical limits and material flows, rather than in terms of GDP or social goals (O'Neill 2012: 222) and, as a result, Daly's main focus is not the issue of human needs (albeit see Daly and Farley, 2011: 277–280). The question is hence how to relate human needs to a steady-state economy? Answering this question would seem to require a material analysis of use values and of their relations to energy and physical flows as well as of the parallels between the two. Money and capital are qualitatively homogenous, quantitatively unlimited, divisible, mobile and reversible according to their exchange-value moment, while their energy and matter, or use-value aspect, is qualitatively heterogeneous, quantitatively limited, indivisible, locationally unique and irreversible (Koch 2012: 26–35). However, though not explicitly dealing with the notion of needs in a steady-state economy, Daly does present a powerful critique of the doctrines of the 'relativity of scarcity' and 'insatiability of wants' upon which neoclassical economics and the growth paradigm are based. Apart from pointing out that, in fact, scarcity is absolute inasmuch as we live on a finite planet, Daly notes that it is highly problematic not to differentiate between different forms of wants; that is, for neoclassical economists, no wants can be considered more important than others, meaning that 'even wants created by advertising are granted absolute status' and that even such wants are considered insatiable (Daly, 1991: 41). Against this notion, and drawing on John M. Keynes, Daly introduces the distinction between absolute and relative wants: *absolute wants* are felt by human beings regardless of the condition of other human beings, whereas the satisfaction of *relative wants* make human beings feel superior to others (Daly, 1991: 40) The statement attributed to John Stuart Mill that 'men do not desire to be rich, but richer than other men' neatly captures the essence of relative wants.

While absolute wants are satiable, relative wants are not. Daly questions the capability of economic growth in improving societal welfare in relative terms on the grounds that either the additional wealth produced is distributed equally, in which case no one is made better off – or those who already are well off are favoured disproportionally, as a result of which inequality increases.

Moreover, a range of wants cannot be satisfied through economic growth, and indeed the pursuit of growth may run counter to the satisfaction of human wants such as leisure time and planetary well-being (Daly, 1991: 41). However, these reflections on wants are not properly integrated into the notion of the steady-state economy. Neither in early works on steady-state economics (Daly, 1991), nor in a more recent introduction to ecological economics – in which Max-Neef's matrix of human needs is presented (Daly and Farley, 2011: 279–280) – is there an explanation of how human needs could and should be satisfied within the framework of a non-growing economy. In this respect, contributions to the steady-state economy are similar to a related branch of growth-critical scholarship, namely, degrowth research (Koch, 2015). Degrowth literature frequently highlights the importance of satisfying human needs. For instance, at the first conference on degrowth, held in Paris in 2008, a declaration was issued which stated that 'the objectives of degrowth are to meet basic human needs and ensure a high quality of life, while reducing the ecological impact of the global economy to a sustainable level, equitably distributed between nations' (Research and Degrowth, 2010: 524). Yet, paradoxically, neither here nor in other degrowth publications that highlight the importance of satisfying human needs (see, for example, Demaria *et al.*, 2013; Klitgaard and Krall, 2012) is it specified what is understood by human needs. The following section therefore reviews the most influential theories of human need.

Theories of human need

All need theories are faced with issues such as what needs actually are, how these relate to competing concepts such as wants, motivations or capabilities, and whether some kind of taxonomy of needs can be constructed and operationalized for empirical research. However, all theorists of human needs agree on the notion that human needs differ from wants and preferences in that they are non-negotiable (Gasper, 1996: 6) and can be applied universally to all humans now and in the future. Any failure to satisfy them always has a detrimental effect on the overall health of an individual (Doyal and Gough, 1991). While needs theories can be traced back to Aristotle, the two most influential needs approaches within welfare research have been tabled by Max-Neef (1991) and Doyal and Gough (1991). Max-Neef (1991: 17) understands human needs as a system, that is, as interrelated and interactive and in a non-hierarchical way. Simultaneities, complementarities and trade-offs are characteristics of the process of needs satisfaction. He proposed a two-dimensional typology, distinguishing between nine 'axiological needs' (subsistence, protection, affection, understanding, participation, identity, idleness, creation and freedom) and four 'existential' categories: being, doing, having and interacting. Max-Neef (1991: 17) also introduced the crucial distinction between needs and satisfiers. While 'needs' are conceived dualistically as 'deprivation' and 'potential', 'satisfiers' represent 'different forms of being, having, doing and interacting, which contribute to the "actualisation" of these deprivations or potentials' (Jackson *et al.*,

2004: 11). While the satisfaction of need yields positive feelings, their dissatisfaction yields negative ones. If a need is not satisfied, the corresponding negative feeling or deprivation will produce a drive to satisfy this need. For example, the need of subsistence may be undermined due to a lack of food. The corresponding negative feeling is hunger, arousing the drive to eat. Hence, food itself is not considered a need but rather a satisfier of the need for subsistence. As a corollary, there is a variety of alternatives, that is, different kinds of food, for the satisfaction of this need. Similarly, housing may be seen as a satisfier of the need for protection, democracy of the need of participation. Certain satisfiers such as sport may be related to different needs such as leisure, participation, identity and creation. In contrast to preferences, needs cannot normally be substituted: 'The person who suffers from malnutrition requires immediate objects of nutrition – not better housing or a more satisfying leisure' (O'Neill, 2011: 33).

Whereas needs are finite, few and classifiable, satisfiers tend to be 'culturally determined, and numerous in variety' (Max-Neef, 1991: 18). In other words, needs do not vary over time and across cultures, but the ways in which a particular culture at a particular time attempts to satisfy those needs do. Cultural change in this context is the transition from one particular satisfier or set of satisfiers in favour of another. Unsatisfied needs are regarded as 'poverties', thereby broadening the concept of poverty beyond income and monetary measures. 'Development' then means the alleviation of multiple poverties and becomes the equivalent of individual self-realization or flourishing. The distinction between basic needs and economic goods questions the commonly assumed positive relationship between increased material consumption and increased satisfaction of needs, particularly non-material needs, and the primacy and unidimensional role of economic growth in the creation and improvement of human well-being. Hence, theories of human need 'allow to tease apart what is consumed in the consumer society from what contributes to human well-being' (Jackson *et al.*, 2004: 18). This distinction was also at the heart of Erich Fromm's *To Have or to Be?* and can be found in many of the writings of philosophers of well-being: between desires that are 'subjectively felt and whose satisfaction leads to momentary pleasure' and 'objectively valid needs' that are 'rooted in human nature and whose realisation is conducive to human growth' (Fromm, 1976: 4).

Doyal and Gough developed their approach independently and in parallel with that of Max-Neef. Contrary to the latter, the former is hierarchical, moving from universal goods, through basic needs to intermediate needs. It departs from Immanuel Kant's argument that individuals must have both the physical and mental capacity to act and be responsible. The universality of need is due to the assumption that, if needs are not satisfied then 'serious harm' of some objective kind will result. Doyal and Gough (1991: 50) understand 'serious harm' to be the 'fundamental disablement in the pursuit of one's vision of the good, whatever that vision is'. Basic needs are then 'universalisable preconditions for non-impaired participation in any form of life' (Gough, 2014a: 8).

The key question is what physical and mental capacities a person must possess to pursue goals, whatever these goals are. Health and personal autonomy were identified as the most basic human needs. While physical and mental health is an absolute precondition for completing a range of practical tasks in any society, autonomy is defined as 'the ability to make informed choices about what should be done and how to go about doing it' (Doyal and Gough, 1991: 53). Irrespective of the further particulars of societal contexts, the three key variables for individual autonomy are cognitive and emotional capacity, cultural understanding (e.g. acquisition of language and other social skills) and autonomy of agency (a range of opportunities to actually undertake socially significant activities). Like in Max-Neef's approach, need satisfiers are subsequently distinguished from needs. However, in Doyal and Gough's approach, 'universal satisfier characteristics' conceptually bridge the two. These characteristics of satisfiers are intended to apply to all cultures at all times and are grouped in 11 categories, whereby the first six contribute to physical and mental health and the last five to autonomy: adequate nutritional food and water, protective housing, non-hazardous work environment, non-hazardous physical environment, appropriate healthcare, security in childhood, significant primary relationships, physical security, economic security, safe birth control and child-bearing, and basic and adequate education.

Thresholds are key to any needs approach in that there are lower and lowest levels at which a 'minimally decent life' can be achieved.

> Where an agent suffers a loss in one dimension of need that takes her below a certain minimal threshold, there will not be a gain in some other dimension of need that will compensate for that loss. If a person is suffering from severe malnutrition then that immediate need must be satisfied.
>
> (O'Neill, 2011: 32)

Doyal and Gough argue for a 'minimum optimorum' or 'minopt' concept to define critical thresholds of intermediate needs:

> This is the minimum quantity of any given intermediate need satisfaction required to produce the optimum level of basic need satisfaction. The underlying assumption here is that the relationship is asymptotic: additional increments of a satisfier characteristic generating decreasing increments of basic need satisfaction until at the minopt point no additional benefit is derived.
>
> (Gough, 2014b: 378)

In practice, Doyal and Gough endorsed the needs levels achieved by the country with the highest overall standards of basic need satisfaction. In the early 1990s, this country was Sweden. Soper (1993) criticized this argument on the grounds that the extravagance of the Swedish energy use, and thus Sweden's socio-economic and welfare model, is in fact not generalizable to all other peoples of the world. Gough accepted the critique and reformulated his approach in the following way: 'If, due to past industrialism, population growth, environmental degradation and climate change, we can achieve less than optimal generalizable satisfaction of basic needs, then so be it. We will be forever living in a world of constraint' (Gough, 2014b: 378). The concept of human need has thus to be constantly updated and is

> historically open to the continual improvements in understanding that have characterised human progress. But at any one time, there is a body of best knowledge to which international appeal can be made. Put starkly, our theory is relative in time but absolute in space.
>
> (Gough, 2014b: 378)

It follows for a theory of sustainable welfare that it is, in principle, possible to provide satisfaction of basic human needs on a global scale. However, the extent to which more than basic needs (and wants) can be provided on a finite planet remains subject to scientific inquiry.

In relation to the needs of future generations and long-term sustainability, Gough argues that their basic needs are the same as those of the present. Likewise, the broad categories of universal satisfier characteristics are assumed to apply: 'Future people will have needs for affiliation, cognitive and emotional expression, understanding and critical thought' (Gough, 2014a: 15). Indeed, compared to the indeterminacy of future generations' preferences, a 'theory of needs provides some firm foundations on which to build sustainability targets for public policy' (Gough 2014a: 16). Similarly, O'Neill (2011: 33) writes that 'each generation needs to pass down the conditions for livelihood and good health, for social affiliation, for the development of capacities for practical reasoning, for engaging with the wider natural world and so on'. While the present generation remains largely ignorant about the 'detailed nature and quantum need satisfiers that future peoples in future contexts will require' (Gough, 2014a: 16), Doyal and Gough (1991: 230–236) nevertheless clarify that all economic systems would need to be assessed according to their ability to produce enough appropriate need satisfiers. Applying the protection-from-harm-of-future-generations principle to climate change, Gough (2014a: 22) argues that climate policy should be an urgent priority, since 'significant climate mitigation can be accomplished without compromising the needs of present persons'. The fact that many social groups can be seriously harmed by climate change entails obligations to strangers provided by the welfare state:

> public rights or entitlements to the means to human welfare in general and to minimum standards of well-being in particular, independent of rights based on property or income. Only the state can guarantee strong entitlements to people of this sort, though this does not require that it directly provides the satisfiers.
>
> (Gough, 2014b: 361)

A move from prioritizing the provision of capital accumulation in an abstract monetary sense towards the promotion of particular use values that satisfy human needs would echo basic characteristics of a steady-state economy. Indeed, Gough postulates that 'similar auditing' would be 'necessary of institutions providing for biological reproduction and care of children, the transmission and renewal of cultural understandings, and the exercise of political authority' (Gough, 2014a: 17).

Sustainable welfare and needs satisfaction

Human needs differ from wants and preferences in that they are non-negotiable and universalizable, and that failure to satisfy them produces serious harm. In contrast to Max-Neef, who emphasizes the interrelatedness of 11 human needs, Doyal and Gough propose a hierarchical model with two basic needs. Though in many cases Doyal and Gough would regard needs as 'intermediary' that are seen as 'basic' in Max-Neef, there is significant overlap in relation to what is regarded a 'need' in general.[1] In addition, both models have the distinction between basic needs and satisfiers in common. Hence, needs do not vary over time and across cultures but according to the ways in which a specific culture at a particular point in time attempts to satisfy them. In his more recent work, Gough has addressed issues of sustainability, intergenerational concerns and universality more directly than other needs or capability theorists. For example, he explicitly mentions the necessity of tackling climate change without compromising the needs of future generations and suggests principles of 'policy auditing' from a human needs perspective. Critical thresholds for the universal provision of human needs (and wants) or for a 'minimally decent life' are to be constantly (re-)defined in light of the advancement of scientific knowledge. For this auditing process, climate expertise, sustainability science but also steady-state economy and degrowth approaches could play important parts. They would however need to be integrated.

Using Daly's three institutional pillars necessary for the functioning of a steady-state economy (i.e. a physical depletion quota institution, a population stabilization institution and a distributist institution) as our point of departure, we can now integrate the notion of needs into the vision of a post-growth socio-economic order. The former two institutional pillars would ensure that economy and society are reproduced within ecological boundaries. At the same time, these would determine the bio-physical parameters within which the satisfaction of human needs in a specific time and place is provided. The third pillar, the distributist institution, aims to ensure a certain level of equality. We would certainly agree with Daly that the redistribution of economic resources is a crucial necessity, if a steady-state economy is to constitute a viable way of organizing economic life. Yet we also suspect that the third institutional pillar of any steady-state economy would have to do more than 'merely' distribute resources. It would also need to facilitate the satisfaction of basic human needs, which is not reducible to matters of (re)distribution. In other words, distributist institutions are necessary but insufficient, inasmuch as it is doubtful whether a steady-state economy that fails to facilitate the satisfaction of the two basic human needs identified by Doyal and Gough would enjoy the necessary popular support. Our tentative suggestion would be that, in place of an exclusively distributist institution, the third steady-state economy pillar should be complemented by a set of institutions oriented at the provision of sustainable welfare, which we, in turn, understand to be the facilitation of the satisfaction of basic human needs. We deliberately write *facilitate* because no welfare system can directly satisfy human needs. For instance, the institutions of a steady-state economy neither can nor should prevent an individual from leading a lifestyle that destroys his or her own physical health.[2] But any steady-state economy should aim to provide an institutional framework within which it is *possible* for humans and communities to satisfy their own basic needs. In particular, it should ensure that citizens have access to nutritional food, clean water, healthcare and education.

When theorizing sustainable welfare and the satisfaction of human needs as a dimension of the steady-state economy, the existence of two levels of abstraction should be distinguished: at a relatively high level of abstraction, the principles underlying the steady-state economy and human needs are addressed in general terms, that is, in terms of the lowest possible matter and energy throughput, constant artefacts and population, as well as the provision of the two basic human needs of autonomy and physical and mental health; at a lower and more concrete level of abstraction, both the institutions that provide Daly's core steady-state economy and those that ensure the satisfaction of the basic human needs are addressed in relation to specific locations at given points in time. This distinction corresponds to the one made in the historical materialist tradition between capitalism as a 'mode of production' and as a 'social formation', that is, as it actually manifests itself in time and space (Althusser and Balibar, 1998; Poulantzas, 1975; Koch, 2012). Just as contemporary capitalist societies are diverse, so would steady-state economies take many different forms in different places, as would the sustainable welfare institutions by means of which the satisfaction of the aforementioned human needs would be facilitated (see Chapter 9). There are two main reasons for this. The first is that such institutions would be shaped by open-ended political struggles. The other is that, owing to existing ideational and material structures, institutional change almost never involves a clean break with the past. On the contrary it generally involves 'the rearrangement or recombination of institutional principles and practices in new and creative ways' as well as 'the blending of new elements into already existing institutional arrangements' (Campbell, 2010: 98–99).[3] In the event that the introduction of a steady-state economy was politically decided in any 'overdeveloped' country, it is thus very likely that various institutional principles and practices underpinning existing welfare arrangements would be preserved in some form and recalibrated in a plurality of creative ways, as they are synthesized with degrowth/steady-state economy and sustainable welfare principles.[4] In other words, the institutions of local steady-state economies and their corresponding sustainable welfare systems would vary across space and to some degree resemble currently existing economic and welfare institutions.

Recapitulating the purposes and structures of Western European welfare institutions from the post-war period, these have often been understood in terms of the provision of citizens with access to healthcare, education, housing and social security. To the extent that these institutions actually did or do so, they are relevant in relation to the satisfaction of the 11 'universal characteristics of needs satisfiers' mentioned by Doyal and Gough, most directly perhaps to 'appropriate health care', 'appropriate education', 'protective housing', and 'economic security'. However, existing welfare regimes have always differed considerably with respect to how and to what extent they offer their citizens social protection (Esping-Andersen, 1990). Moreover, the 'Keynesian' welfare state of the decades following the Second World War has been transformed everywhere into what Cerny (2010) labelled the 'competition state'. Forms of state 'supply management', where welfare goals such as social equity are subordinated to a location's competitive situation, have substituted previous Keynesian ideas of equity-oriented 'demand management', while the state authority itself has been rescaled from the national to transnational (European) and local levels (Brenner, 2004; Koch, 2008; Kazepov, 2010). Whereas the post-war welfare state aimed to shield its citizens from market forces by providing universal social protection, the competition state promotes marketization and 'activation' for the sake of a location's improved competitive position (Buch-Hansen and Wigger, 2011). In these circumstances, the extent to which an individual's human needs are satisfied becomes a matter of an individual's market performance relative to other human beings – and a matter of a (nation) state's competitiveness relative to other states.

Though the Keynesian welfare state in many ways performed better than the modern Schumpeterian competition state in facilitating the satisfaction of human needs for the majority of its citizens, we nevertheless point to three issues that together suggest that much wider transitions than a simple return to the post-war national welfare compromise would be necessary to provide sustainable welfare in the sense of a satisfaction of basic human needs on a global scale as well as for present and future generations. First, the Keynesian welfare state emerged largely due to working-class pressure for better wages and social security and because political and economic elites saw it as a way of minimizing working-class support for communism (Lipietz, 1992: 5–8). The welfare state was not primarily embraced by these elites because it satisfied the human needs of workers, but because it proved remarkably capable of facilitating economic growth. Indeed, by providing a reasonably educated and healthy labour force and by ensuring a high level of aggregate demand by means of social transfers, the state helped to ensure the expanded reproduction of capitalism in its Fordist period (Koch, 2006). Needs satisfaction was far from being the policy priority in this welfare arrangement.

Second, in the post-war circumstances, welfare was commonly conceptualized in terms of socio-economic equity, highlighting distributive issues, while social policy was mostly conceived as the 'public management of social risks' (Esping-Andersen, 1990). Growing capitalist economies were presupposed in most development models in order to finance welfare services via the taxation of the primary incomes of employers and employees. While much current welfare literature circles around the crisis of the various national post-war welfare arrangements and their readjustments following the 2008 financial and economic crisis, ecological concerns, which had been issued as early as in the 1970s (Meadows *et al.*, 1972), are still largely being ignored. The direct and indirect climate change-related risks mentioned in Gough *et al.* (2008: 325) are normally not regarded as 'social risks' and therefore not as an issue that is worthwhile taking up in social policy research circles (see Chapter 6 in this volume). Yet there is much recent research pointing to the fact that Western production, consumption and welfare standards cannot be generalized to the rest of the world (Jackson, 2009: 488; see Introduction and Chapter 1 in this volume). Many authors have alluded to the finiteness of natural resources, due to which we would need between four and five Earths to fuel global production and consumption patterns on the scale of current Western countries. Meanwhile, hopes that social-democratic welfare regimes would also perform best in ecological terms and gradually turn into eco-social states (Gough et al., 2008) could not be verified in comparative empirical research (Koch and Fritz, 2014). It is hence highly unlikely that a sustainable welfare system within a future steady-state economy could facilitate the satisfaction of human needs by simply emulating Western welfare policies of the post-war period.

Third, we conclude that a different sort of compromise than the Fordist class compromise and a different sort of rescaling than the current European one would be necessary preconditions for any sustainable welfare system within the context of a global steady-state economy. Any institutional compromise for a sustainable welfare society would need to go beyond the national scale and encompass the entire globe as well as other social groupings than classes. It is only at the global level that thresholds for matter and energy throughput and population quota can be determined in order to effectively mitigate global environmental challenges such as climate change. At the same time, these bio-physical terms achieved at global level would delineate the room for manoeuvre within which national and local economies and societies could evolve. In relation to the Atlantic space, it is especially through a transition of regulatory power from traditional national welfare institutions to local levels that human needs satisfaction within the third steady-state economy pillar could be facilitated and made compatible with globally identified ecological limits. Indeed, without arguing that everything should or could be produced locally, several contributions to degrowth, the steady-state economy, social enterprises and cooperatives have argued for the need to replace today's global capitalist system with economies based on cooperative principles and oriented towards local production and consumption cycles (Dietz and

O'Neill, 2013; Latouche, 2009; Lewis and Conaty, 2012). However, it is not only from academic research but also from emerging practices of new and different ways of living such as ecovillages, transition towns and social enterprises that local sustainable welfare systems can draw inspiration in their attempts to provide basic human needs (see Chapter 10 in this volume).

Conclusion

Sustainable welfare and the satisfaction of basic human needs for all, now and in the future, are unlikely to be achieved under the imperative of economic growth. Conversely, degrowth and steady-state economy approaches that are oriented at long-term sustainability have as yet not sufficiently focused on needs and social welfare. This chapter set out to complement existing growth-critical approaches, namely Daly's steady-state economy, with theories of human need. We outlined the basic features of a welfare system of a global steady-state economy, which, while differing from one location to the next, would every-where respect ecological limits and aim to facilitate the satisfaction of basic human needs for all inhabitants of the planet. While due to planetary limits, existing Western welfare systems cannot be generalized to the rest of the world, the issue of whether a global sustainable welfare system is capable of providing more than basic human needs is an empirical one, or, in Ian Gough's words, a matter of 'policy auditing', during which critical thresholds for the universal provision of human needs (and wants) would constantly need to be (re-)defined in the light of the best available scientific knowledge.

Reaching an agreement on a steady-state economy that includes a sustain-able welfare component as one of its institutional pillars (the content and form of which would vary from one location to the next) will be far from easy. The apparently unsurmountable structural obstacles for such a transition include the hegemony of the growth discourse and the ensuing lack of political will, the widespread and deeply ingrained consumer culture in the rich countries (but see Chapter 12 in this volume) and a massive concentration of economic resources and power in the hands of organizations and individuals who profit from a continuation of the current growth model. Any transition to sustainable welfare (see also Chapter 1 of this volume) will hence run into strong opposition in that 'there will undoubtedly be strenuous pushback from powerful elements of society who perceive that they have more to lose than to gain from general sustainability' (Rees, 2014: 97). Yet it is also true that sustainable welfare would serve the interest of the large majority of this planet's people – not to mention the unborn generations – and this may provide some hope that sustainability transitions could ultimately gain the required momentum.

Notes

1   There is also considerable overlap between what Nussbaum regards as central cap-abilities (see Chapter 1) and Max-Neef's and Doyal and Gough's human needs.

However, as Gasper (2014) has demonstrated, when Nussbaum argues for the universalizability of capabilities and identifies them in cross-cultural ways, she appears to be heavily relying on a needs approach: 'Human need is a relatively stable matter, and thus there is some hope that we can give an account of basic human needs that will remain reasonably constant over time' (Nussbaum, 2006: 278).

2 This is not to say that the state should not attempt regulating behaviour, for instance through the taxation of unhealthy and ecologically harmful products and 'naming and blaming' strategies similar to state anti-smoking campaigns.

3 See Mahoney and Thelen (2010) for an overview of theories of gradual institutional change, and Angelin *et al.* (2014) for an application of this approach to contemporary welfare institutions in Sweden and Germany.

4 See Buch-Hansen (2014) for a theoretical overview over the contents and degrees of institutional change in different varieties of capitalism en route to a steady-state economy and Fritz and Koch (2014) for a comparative empirical analysis of the potentials and structural challenges of 38 countries in such a transition.

References

Althusser, E. and Balibar, E. (1998). *Reading Capital*. London: Verso.

Angelin, A., Johannson, H. and Koch, M. (2014). Patterns of institutional change in minimum income protection in Sweden and Germany. *Journal of International and Comparative Social Policy*, 30(2), 165–199.

Barry, J. (2012). Towards a Political Economy of Sustainability. In M. Pelling, D. Manuel-Navarrete and M. Redcliffe (eds), *Climate Change and the Crisis of Capitalism* (129–141). London: Routledge.

Brenner, N. (2004). Urban governance and production of new state spaces in Western Europe, 1960–2000. *Review of International Political Economy*, 11(3), 447–488.

Buch-Hansen, H. (2014). Capitalist diversity and de-growth trajectories to steady-state economies. *Ecological Economics*, 106, 173–179.

Buch-Hansen, H. and Wigger, A. (2011). *The Politics of European Competition Regulation*. London: Routledge.

Campbell, J. L. (2010). Institutional Reproduction and Change. In G. Morgan, J. L. Campbell, C. Crouch, O. K. Pedersen and R. Whitley (eds), *The Oxford Handbook of Comparative Institutional Analysis* (87–116). Oxford: Oxford University Press.

Cerny, P. G. (2010). The competition state today: From raison d'État to raison du Monde. *Policy Studies*, 31(1), 5–21.

Daly, H. E. (ed.). (1973). *Toward a Steady-State Economy*. San Francisco, CA: W. H. Freeman and Company.

Daly, H. E. (1991). *Steady-State Economics*, 2. Washington, DC: Island Press.

Daly, H. E. (1996). *Beyond Growth*. Boston, MA: Beacon Press.

Daly, H. E. and Farley, J. (2011). *Ecological Economics*. Washington, DC: Island Press.

Demaria, F., Schneider, F., Sekulova, F. and Martinez-Alier, J. (2013). What is degrowth? From an activist slogan to a social movement. *Environmental Values*, 22 (2), 191–215.

Dietz, R. and O'Neill, D. (2013). *Enough is Enough. Building a Sustainable Economy in a World of Finite Resources*. San Francisco, CA: Berrett-Koehler Publishers.

Doyal, L. and Gough, I. (1991) *A Theory of Human Need*. Basingstoke: Macmillan.

Esping-Andersen, G. (1990). *The Three Worlds of Welfare Capitalism*. Cambridge: Polity Press.

42   *Max Koch and Hubert Buch-Hansen*

Fritz, M. and Koch, M. (2014). Potentials for prosperity without growth: Ecological sustainability, social inclusion and the quality of life in 38 countries. *Ecological Economics*, 108, 191–199.

Fromm, E. (1976) *To Have or to Be?* London: Jonathan Cape.

Gasper, D. (1996). *Needs and Basic Needs. A Clarification of Meanings, Levels and Different Streams of Work.* Working Paper Series No. 210. The Hague: Institute of Social Studies.

Gasper, D. (2014). Logos, Pathos and Ethos in Martha C. Nussbaum's Capability Approach to Hum Dev. In F. Comin, and M. C. Nussbaum (eds), *Capabilities, Gender, Equality. Towards Fundamental Entitlements* (96–130). Cambridge: Cambridge University Press.

Gough, I. (2014a). *Climate Change and Sustainable Welfare: An Argument for the Centrality of Human Needs.* Centre for Analysis of Social Exclusion, Working Paper No. 182. London: London School of Economics.

Gough, I. (2014b). Lists and Thresholds: Comparing the Doyal-Gough Theory of Human Need with Nussbaum's Capabilities Approach. In F. Comin and M. C. Nussbaum (eds), *Capabilities, Gender, Equality. Towards Fundamental Entitlements* (357–381). Cambridge: Cambridge University Press.

Gough, I., Meadowcroft, J., Dryzek, J., Gerhards, J., Lengfield, H., Markandya, A. and Ortiz, R. (2008). JESP symposium: Climate change and social policy. *Journal of European Social Policy*, 18, 25–44.

Hodgson, G. M. (2013). *From Pleasure Machines to Moral Communities: An Evolutionary Economics without Homo Economicus.* Chicago, IL: University of Chicago Press.

Jackson, T. (2009). *Prosperity without Growth? The Transition to a Sustainable Economy.* London: Sustainable Development Commission.

Jackson, T., Jager, W. and Stagl, S. (2004). Beyond insatiability: Needs theory, consumption and sustainability. Sustainable Technologies Programme, Working Paper 2004/2, Centre for Environmental Strategy: University of Surrey.

Kazepov, Y. (2010). *Rescaling Social Policies: Towards Multilevel Governance in Europe.* Aldershot: Ashgate.

Klitgaard, K. A. and Krall, L. (2012). Ecological economics, degrowth, and institutional change. *Ecological Economics*, 84, 247–253.

Koch, M. (2006). *Roads to Post-Fordism: Labour Markets and Social Structures in Europe.* Aldershot: Ashgate.

Koch, M. (2008). The state in European employment regulation. *Journal of European Integration*, 30(2), 255–272.

Koch, M. (2012). *Capitalism and Climate Change: Theoretical Discussion, Historical Development and Policy Responses.* Basingstoke: Palgrave Macmillan.

Koch, M. (2015). Climate change, capitalism and degrowth trajectories to a global steady-state economy. *International Critical Thought*, 5(4), 439–452.

Koch, M. and Fritz, M. (2014). Building the eco-social state: Do welfare regimes matter? *Journal of Social Policy*, 43(4), 679–703.

Koch, M. and Fritz. M. (2015). Green States in Europe: A Comparative View. In K. Backstrand and A. Kronsell (eds), *Rethinking the Green State. Environmental Governance towards Climate and Sustainability Transitions.* London: Routledge.

Latouche, S. (2009). *Farewell to Growth.* Cambridge: Polity Press.

Lewis, M., and Conaty, P. (2012). *The Resilience Imperative. Cooperative Transitions to a Steady-State Economy.* Gabriola Island: New Society Publishers.

Lipietz, A. (1992). *Towards a New Economic Order. Postfordism, Ecology and Democracy.* Cambridge: Polity Press.

Mahoney, J. and Thelen, K. (eds) (2010). *Explaining Institutional Change. Ambiguity, Agency and Power.* Cambridge: Cambridge University Press.

Max-Neef, M. (1991) *Human Scale Development. Conception, Application and Further Reflections.* New York and London: The Apex Press.

Meadows, D. H., Meadows, D. L., Randers, J. and Behrens, W. (1972). *The Limits to Growth.* New York: Universe Books.

Muraca, B. (2013). Decroissance: A project for a radical transformation of society. *Environmental Values,* 22(2), 147–169.

Nussbaum, M. (2006). *Frontiers of Justice: Disability, Nationality, Species Membership.* Harvard, CT: The Belknap Press.

O'Neill, D. W. (2012). Measuring progress in the degrowth transition to a steady state economy. *Ecological Economics,* 84, 221–231.

O'Neill, J. (2011). The Overshadowing of Needs. In F. Rauschmayer, I. Omann and J. Frühmann (eds), *Sustainable Development* (25–43). London: Routledge.

Poulantzas, N. (1975). *Political Power and Social Classes.* London: Verso.

Rees, W. E. (2014). Are Prosperity and Sustainability Compatible? In S. Novkovic and T. Webb (eds), *Co-operatives in a Post-Growth Era* (83–100). London: Zed Books.

Research and Degrowth (2010). Degrowth declaration of the Paris 2008 conference. *Journal of Cleaner Production,* 18(6), 523–524.

Soper, K. (1993). A theory of human need. *New Left Review,* 197, 113–128.

3 Reconceptualizing prosperity
Some reflections on the impact of globalization on health and welfare

Kate Soper and Maria Emmelin

Introduction

This chapter takes its cue from Tim Jackson's pioneering arguments on the macro-economic and social preconditions of a sustainable global order, and echoes the call for a redefined 'prosperity without growth' in meeting them (Jackson, 2004, 2009). Its particular focus is on the changing perceptions that are essential to furthering policies of sustainable welfare, a theme that it pursues within two related frames of thinking. First, at a more abstract and exclusively conceptual level, it explores (with special reference to Western affluence) the revised ideas of 'progress', 'prosperity' and 'development' that would be involved in a transition to a degrowth economic and political order. And it presents this new 'politics of prosperity' as intrinsic to the cultural revolution needed to inspire public support for that transition – and for the changed understandings of welfare discussed in this volume. At a less abstract and speculative level, the next section expands on this theme by illustrating some of the negative impacts of globalized modernization on health in developing economies, focusing on the issues of violence against women, non-communicable disease, and the role that mobilizing or creating social capital may have in mitigating the breakdown of traditional community support systems. While this approach to rethinking ideas of 'welfare', 'prosperity', 'development' and the 'good life' can be aligned with earlier romantic antipathies to the 'modern' (we refer briefly to some aspects of Irish history in exemplification), it rejects the puritanism and social conservatisms of traditional cultures of resistance to modernity. The subsequent section argues instead for an approach to modernization and its representation that would sever the link between progress and economic expansion while resisting cultural regression. In making a case for this, it looks at some of the more recent critical responses to Euro-American-driven ideas of welfare and 'development', reviews some of the tensions between objective assessments of needs and capabilities and the more directly personal assessments of individuals themselves, and relates findings in these areas of welfare study to the larger conceptual shifts explored at the beginning of the chapter at a more abstract level.

Revising perceptions of 'progress' and 'prosperity'

Concepts of 'progress', 'modernization' and 'development' have almost always hitherto, and especially during the last 150 years, been associated with economic expansion and industrialization (cf. Victor, 2008: 8–26). These have also proved to be the predisposing vehicles of enlightened social and sexual policies, secularization, and progressive cultural movements. What counts as modern is progressive, and economic growth has been its condition. In the light, however, of the now very pressing environmental and social reasons for moving to a post-growth economy, we can no longer so automatically link 'progress' and its kindred ideas with advancements in a prosperity conceived primarily in terms of increased economic wealth, whether social or individual. Ideas of 'progress' need instead to be associated with the critique of growth and its unsustainable reliance on an ever expanding consumer culture. Since they have so dramatically exceeded the carrying capacity of the planet, nations with the least sustainable environmental footprint should no longer be thought of as developmental models for the so-called 'developing' nations. Conversely, the less Westernized and industrialized nations and communities might now be viewed as potentially offering more sustainable (and therefore one can argue, more progressive) norms of welfare and modes of providing for it.

Admittedly, at least in the case of the concept of 'development', there is an established field of ethical critique and a number of moves in welfare theory that have challenged, or sought to qualify, that set of associations (Crocker, 1991; Sachs, 1992; Gasper, 2008; Gasper and St Clair, 2010). Sen and his followers have notably claimed that the objective of development is the expansion of human capabilities rather than economic growth (Sen, 1999: 35–53). Expounding on this aspect of Sen's argument, David Clark has made the point that:

> while growth may be necessary for development, it is not always sufficient. In broad terms it is possible to distinguish between growth mediated and support led development. The former operates through rapid and broad based economic growth, which facilitates the expansion of basic capabilities through higher employment, improved prosperity and better social services. The latter works primarily through proficient welfare programmes that support health, education and social security.
> (Clark, 2006)

But the capabilities approach has, on the whole, had rather little to say about sustainability, and has generally presented growth as an essential ongoing condition of development, while conceiving development itself in terms of the Western model of self-enhancement and the embrace of its political, economic and legal institutions. Nussbaum's equivocal position here is illustrative. While claiming that 'we do not have to win the respect of others by being productive ... society is held together by a wide range of attachments and concerns, only some of which concern productivity' (Nussbaum, 2006: 160), she also wants to promote education for profit and economic growth and talks of skills 'needed for a flourishing economy' (Nussbaum, 2010: 10). Robert Lane, too, while acknowledging that economic growth does not guarantee any enhancement in *individual* well-being once a certain level of income has been reached, claims that happiness is improved by economic growth because of the collective goods that it brings such as health and education (Lane, 2000: 63). But that position of course presumes equality of access to such goods within the nation, and quite abstracts from global exploitations of those less fortunate in the accumulation of national wealth in the first place.

On the whole, then, it is only those welfare theorists and economists advocating degrowth or steady-state economics as essential to sustainable living who to date have seriously challenged the link between economic expansion and development.[1] Since then, Latouche has arguably pressed the case for rethinking the concept of 'development' with most rhetorical zeal in his denunciations of the 'ethnocentrism of development' and imperialistic colonization that have sacrificed the Global South to the Global North and destroyed its self-sufficiency (Latouche, 2009: 20–30, 61; cf. Belpomme, 2007). We might also note here Hornborg's argument that 'mainstream modern perceptions of "development" can be viewed as a cultural illusion confusing a privileged position in social space with an advanced position in historical time' (Hornborg, 2009: 239) and the overall critique of development economics associated with world system analysis and ecological unequal exchange studies (Wallerstein, 2004; Hornborg, 2011).

To offer general support for these calls for conceptual revision of the idea of 'development' is not to deny the urgency of correcting for fundamental forms of oppression and affliction in the more impoverished communities, nor the importance of meeting basic needs of survival and well-being (Doyal and Gough, 1991; Gough, 2014; Koch and Fritz, 2014; Chapter 2 in this volume). But it is to highlight the continuing failure of existing development policies and programmes to deliver even on that fairly minimal agenda and thus to recognize the extent to which economic growth has failed to correlate with either alleviation of poverty or a fairer distribution of wealth (UNDP, 2013). It is also to challenge the current monopoly of growth-oriented ways of thinking over ideas about social welfare and individual fulfilment.

Further light can be shed on this project of revaluation by looking at some of the ways in which traditional and less modernized (and often colonized) societies have in the past been represented relative to the metropolitan and imperial centres of power. We might here cite in illustration the case of Ireland, where by reason of its subordination to the exemplary modern state, Gaelic culture came to be seen as archaic or premodern relative to the anglicizing influence and, as such, to be either transcended or preserved depending on the particular political sentiment and cultural loyalties of the observer (Cleary, 2005: 3). So while some celebrated a premodern Ireland of 'saints and scholars' as a place distinguished by its spirituality rather than its economic advances or progressive social policy;[2] others saw Irish backwardness as mired in an obsolete religious and patriarchal culture, and as part of the problem of Anglo–Irish relations, not the transcendence of it. It was an insult to be defied and sublated rather than reworked and revalued; Ireland's aberrant relationship to capitalism was regarded as indicative of something anomalous and in need of correction, and there were also many who, without necessarily being great friends of capitalism, and broadly supportive of the nationalist cause, found the endorsement of a premodern Ireland associated with that cause hugely problematic, not least by virtue of its social conservatism and offensive gender politics. The preservationist impulse towards Gaelic Ireland was also condemned as reinforcing English hegemony by colluding in the imperialist's sentimental patronage (Kiberd, 2009: 45–48).

Romantic visions of Ireland as a bulwark against modernity were largely discredited with independence, further undermined by the post-1960s' economic developments (including EU membership in 1973) and wholly swept away during the so-called Celtic Tiger years, when Ireland became a model of neo-liberal entrepreneurialism. But those years themselves, of course, then proved very short-lived and pretty disastrous, and when the boom gave way to recession, the follies and corruption of the 'Celtic Tiger' mode of modernizing capitalism were more fully exposed (Allen, 2007a, 2007b; O'Toole, 2009). Among its effects was the creation of a huge abyss between the wealthy elite and the rest of the population of a kind that had already taken place else-where, and in its essentials there was no departure from the usual course of boom and bust capitalism with its material legacy of new, but never occupied building and half-completed construction work – of a capitalism that, as David Harvey put it, 'builds a physical landscape appropriate to its own condition at a particular moment in time, only to have to destroy it, usually in the course of a crisis, at a subsequent point in time' (Harvey, 1989: 93).

The Irish case, then, instantiates an economic and cultural evolution of some interest to the reconceptualization of progress and modernity with which we are here concerned. With respect to the transition to a post-growth economic and political order, one might, for example, here defend the relevance of resuscitating something of the 'spirituality'[3] and sober consumption that the defendants of a premodernized conception of the colonized nation sought to pit against the materialism and commercializing values of the colonizer. And nations that currently figure as relatively 'backward' might reconstitute themselves in a period of historical transition informed by such conceptual reconstruction as in the vanguard by comparison with the 'overdevelopment' characteristic of the imperial powers or metropolitan centres that have rendered them marginal and premodern by comparison (Cleary, 2005: 6).[4]

But any attempt in our own times to invoke that vision would, of course, have to be reworked in ways that severed the link between 'progress' and economic expansion while opposing the social conservatism that has so often gone together with economic backwardness. In place of a stadial and evolu-tionist conception of history, a degrowth understanding committed to social justice and a fairer distribution of environmental resources would need to offer a more complex narrative on the old–new divide, a transcendence of the current binary opposition between 'progress' and elegiac 'nostalgia'. Against the grain of those who denounce sustainable policies for taking us 'back to the stone age', a cultural outlook of this kind would recast certain forms of ret-rospection as potentially avant-garde. But it would do so in ways that dis-sociated that nostalgia from any endorsement of the patrician and patriarchal relations of premodern societies. It would claim, that is, a politically progressive role for keeping faith with past ways of doing and making, provided that goes together with a critique of the social and sexual exploitations of the labour processes of earlier communities (cf. Williams, 1977: 184, 36–7; Ryle, 2009).

A renewal of more craft-based ways of working might provide one example of how older patterns of living could be restored and reconfigured in the con-text of an economic order committed to sustainable welfare. By reason of its emphasis on skill, attention to detail and personal involvement, craft production obviously runs counter to prevailing views on the mental–manual division of labour (cf. Sennett, 2008) and is incompatible with the timeline imperatives of the 'work and spend' economy. But in a slower-paced society, many more might be able to benefit from the particular forms of concentration in work and self-fulfilment that craft can provide. And, as Juliet Schor has pointed out, defending her view of 'plenitude' as an alternative to 'business as usual' approaches to well-being, craft production can now take advantage of a wide array of eco-friendly smart technologies:

> We are circling back and plenitude is a synthesis of the pre- and post-modern. From the former it borrows the vision of skilled artisans producing for their own use as well as for the market .... From the postmodern period comes advanced technology and smart, ecologically parsimonious design. It's the perfect synthesis. Technology obviates the arduous and back-breaking labour of the preindustrial. Artisan labour avoids the alienation of the modern factory and office.
>
> (Schor, 2010: 127)

Those working in these new ways would also, of course, enjoy more disposable time – time, as André Gorz has argued, that would not so much exempt people from doing anything at all, but open up possibilities for everyone to engage in a host of private or public activities – activities which would no longer need to be profitable in order to flourish (Gorz, 1989). In this process, idleness and free time would cease to be seen as threats to commerce but rather as the forms in which a more genuine prosperity, and the trust and participation in social networks associated with enhanced social capital, can be realized (Putnam, 1993, 2000; cf. Chapters 1, 8 and 12 in this volume). Education, instead of being promoted as a forcing house for the economy, would be defended as the place to prepare individuals to enjoy the free time made available in a post-consumerist era. And aesthetic resources and satisfactions, instead of being downgraded and marginalized, would become more central and universally available. In all these ways, the acceptance of a more frugal and materially *reproductive* provision for needs of the kind essential to promoting a universally accessible and sustainable level of welfare would be compensated for by an expansion of less resource-hungry but arguably more sophisticated and gratifying cultural occupations.

Health, development and overdevelopment

In certain areas of welfare, however, notably health, it might well be thought perverse to favour traditional modes of provision, or to question the benefits of economic growth. Yet even here the picture is complex. For, while increased GDP generally correlates with improved life expectancy, this is not always the case. In certain regions, improvements have come not through economic expansion but as a result of local changes in health policies and the prioritization of education. Even where economic growth has brought benefits, these have seldom been extended to everyone, with the poorest remaining the most deprived, especially in countries characterized by great economic inequities. What also emerges from studies in sub-Saharan Africa, is the overriding importance attached to social norms, social networks and community-based activities in the understanding of what it means to be healthy and how best to promote this (Frumence *et al.*, 2011; Berhane *et al.*, 2001). Yet it is these same networks and forms of social capital that tend to be undermined by an increasing emphasis on individual economic advance and commodification. On the other hand, research has shown that, where public health interventions have mobilized traditional community networks, it has proved possible to influence social norms in beneficial ways in order to promote health. In the case of the HIV/AIDS epidemic in the Kagera region of Tanzania, utilizing the existing structural and cognitive social capital emanating from participation in social networks, it was possible to positively influence norms of HIV-related risk behaviour and then to counter rather than encourage the spread of the HIV epidemic (Frumence, 2011).

It is in relation to health, moreover, that we encounter one of the more striking instances of the way in which first-world affluence is now proving counterproductive even for its own populations and is generating quite serious problems of its own (lifestyle-related stress, lack of exercise, growing problems of mental health and obesity). In this case, we have a twofold ground on which to question the appropriateness of the consumerist model of the 'good life'. Not only may extension of this model to developing countries prove less sustainable and successful than more traditional methods of provision, it can also be said to foster ways of living that are intrinsically unhealthy. The adoption, for example, of Westernized conceptions of prosperity has led to a massive increase in car use instead of cycling in places such as China and India – with the added irony that this comes at a point at which attempts are being made to reverse that trend in Western societies because of its adverse impact on public health! A related example of what are now sometimes described by the Chinese as 'wealth deficits' (meaning the downsides of becoming richer in monetary terms) is provided by the huge rise in obesity in China since the 1980s, where the Ministry of Health estimated in 2012 that 300 million were obese in a population of 1.2 billion, making it second only to the USA in the numbers of the overweight. Diabetes is also on the rise, with a tripling of the number of children under 14 suffering from diabetes over the last 25 years (French, 2015). The ill effects of modernization are also evident in the spread of non-communicable diseases in many countries in sub-Saharan Africa. This comes on top of an existing burden of communicable diseases such as HIV/AIDS, and is now threatening to offset the benefits of lower rates of respiratory infections, diarrhoeal diseases and tuberculosis (Dalal *et al.*, 2011; Lozano *et al.*, 2012). In 2010 the Global Burden of Disease study presented heart diseases and diabetes as the top ten leading causes of death in southern sub-Saharan Africa (Lozano *et al.* 2012). Smoking is yet another health threat connected to modernization. An increased awareness of its severe health consequences has led to restrictions in its use in most countries of the Global North, making the tobacco industry intensify their efforts to promote smoking, especially in low- and middle-income countries of the Global South (Sebrié and Glantz, 2006).

These illustrations are merely indicative of certain tendencies that run counter to mainstream perceptions and claims about the necessary links between economic development and improved health, and are not offered as in any sense comprehensive of what is clearly a complex field of study. But what they do suggest is that there are a number of differing grounds on which to challenge the view that health benefits automatically follow upon economic modernization. Without disputing the role played by Western medical science in improving many aspects of health on a global scale, impositions of its biomedical model that are insensitive to the norms and practices in other cultures can prove damaging to pre-existing community-based forms of welfare provision, or counterproductive in other respects. As we have noted, too, economic modernization also brings its own health hazards, and the lifestyle promoted by consumer culture and its model of 'development' is by no means an uncomplicated blessing in respect of physical and mental well-being.

Uncoupling gender and sexual emancipation from economic growth

We have already implied that rendering welfare expectations and provision consistent with the observation of environmental limits will depend in part on invoking a discursive space in which ideas of social and cultural progress (on gender, ethnicity, sexual orientation, etc.) are no longer presented as so closely tied to the economic growth and modernization that have hitherto almost always been the vehicle of emancipated social and cultural agendas. Here, then, in this third part, we elaborate on these issues a little further.

There is no denying that traditional cultures, whose patterns of work and consumption we might in certain respects want to retain or resuscitate in the interests of sustainability, have usually been regressive in other respects, notably on gender relations and sexuality. Our example of Ireland is an obvious case of this, and the general pattern is manifest still in many parts of the world today: hence the commonly held presumption of those aspiring to social/sexual emancipation that the expanding market and its secular consumer society can alone provide for it. Yet there are reasons to challenge, or, at the very least, to want to qualify this presumption. Oppressed, marginal and subaltern groups have in recent times discovered that they have not always had their emancipatory interests best served by the forms of 'development' associated with the expansion of the market and its modernizing trends. In acknowledging this, feminist scholars in development studies have pointed to the danger of 'exporting' gender policies from the Global North to the Global South and the obvious risk that it carries of a continuation of colonial relations and dependencies (Baell, 1998; Connelly *et al.*, 2000; Kilby and Olivieri, 2008; Moser, 2005; Schech, 1998). Research on gender and violence has been said to be particularly prone to the risk of decontextualization because of its tendency to overlook differences in public discourses, legal systems and gendered norms. Some have also argued that, since development policy has been infiltrated by a paradigm that is so heavily influenced by notions of Western modernity, there is an obvious risk that it has not benefited the poor and marginalized, or women exposed to violence (Connelly *et al.*, 2000). The policy focus, for example, in the case of intimate personal violence against women, on female-only projects actually marginalized women from broader (and male) power structures and therefore failed to empower women. Feminists from the Global South have criticized the general view of 'women of the Global South' in development policies from the Global North for being racist and ethnocentric, and for viewing women as a homogenous and victimized group with limited agency. These critiques have prompted calls for renewed approaches to gender and development with more emphasis on cooperation and partnership (Schech, 1998; Baell, 1998), and greater scepticism about the extent to which women's rights can be advanced within a neoliberal framework (Kilby and Olivieri, 2008). The importance of including local feminist groups and activists from the Global South in the dialogue is being recognized, and in many countries of the Global South, which are now targets for development collaboration, there is a body of feminist activists involved in policymaking. In cooperation with development agencies of the Global North, they can provide a more sensitive and contextualized channel for women to express themselves on issues of intimate personal violence and thus enhance their political agency.

All this indicates a need at a more theoretical level to provide accounts that are sensitive to the respective strengths and weaknesses of both the 'thinner' (and more objective, essentialist, Enlightenment–humanistic ...) and the 'thicker' (subjective, relativistic, culturally pluralist, 'postmodernist'...) approaches to welfare needs (Gasper, 2008; cf. Doyal and Gough, 1991; Chapter 2 in this volume). 'Thin' approaches have the virtue of recalling us to the needs for health provision, political representation and protection from abuse of those who are least empowered to understand their own deprivation or to claim their own rights to satisfaction. And in response to those who would argue that any attempt to represent the needs of others is guilty of a patronizing and undemocratic imputation or imposition of needs (cf. McInnes, 1977; Fitzgerald, 1977; Heller, 1980), the 'thin' theorist can always point to the potential inequalities in the distribution of goods that are licensed by allowing individual claimants to be the sole arbiters of their needed status. 'Thick' theorists, on the other hand, would claim to be more alert to the ways in which the welfare governance of 'experts' can be promoted at the expense of realizing the more situated and subjectively informed needs of claimants themselves. They are, we might say, more reluctant to endorse an older-style paternalism rather than a more locally relevant, or choice-oriented conception of welfare provision.

In recent times, emancipatory social movements have reflected the tensions between these opposing theoretical perspectives in their struggle for democratic credentials. It is clear in the case of the feminist movement that this was in large part constituted through resistance to the idea that men could continue to represent the needs of women or be the sole arbiters on welfare provision in matters relating to them. At the same time, many Western feminists working within the framework of Enlightenment conceptions of selfhood and well-being, have proceeded to expose the role of patriarchy and religious fundamentalism in non-Western societies in denying the most oppressed groups of women any proper knowledge of their 'true' needs and potential as emancipated persons. They have also endorsed Western biomedical norms and criteria of health in defending women in other cultures from the abuse of such practices as female genital mutilation and shielding them from ignorant and ill-judged forms of medical practice. In this sense, even as these feminists have conducted an immanent critique of the inherent masculinity of a supposedly universal Enlightenment humanism, they themselves have also invoked a transcultural and universalistic understanding of female needs and medical norms in their criticisms of the repressions and bigotry of other cultures. Yet this Enlightenment feminism has also, in turn, been criticized from a postmodernist feminist perspective for its collusion in the cultural 'imperialism' of the West and the imposition of its rationalist and individualistic approach to self-realization.[5]

Similar tensions resurface in any attempt to defend the global relevance and universal applicability of a relativist or 'thick' theory concept of welfare 'needs' as encompassing everything essential to functioning as a citizen within a given social milieu. For formulations of this kind, which presume the co-existence between 'social functioning' and the exercise of citizenship, obviously invoke specific – Western and Enlightenment – conceptions of what it is to be a member of a community and must necessarily raise questions about the propriety or applicability to other cultures of its associated models of governance, social cohesion and participation. In very impoverished communities, or those without, or with only very partial, political rights, participation as a citizen will not be a normal aspect of one's 'embedded' social being, and any needs essential to such participation will therefore not figure in the package of needed provision. In this sense, to endorse a 'thick' or culturally relative position that defines needs in terms of what is essential to the social functioning of situated individuals is also implicitly to condone the failure of provision for democratic and human rights in many social contexts. It suggests that needs are being met even where basic human rights are not enjoyed. In a fundamentalist Islamic regime such as that under the Taliban in Afghanistan, for example, women in this account might be said to have their needs met as culturally embedded and socially functioning individuals precisely in virtue of the *absence* of provision for their fuller political participation as citizens. 'Thick' theorists tend to promote their position as a critique of what they see as the undemocratically ethnocentric optic of 'thin' perspectives on human well-being. But in defending democracy they themselves, of course, remain implicitly committed to precisely that liberal–Enlightenment framework of thinking about rights, autonomy, citizenship and social participation that is lacking in many of the cultural contexts whose divergence from Western norms and values they are also calling on us to respect and defend (cf. Alkire, 2005: 242–249). Nor is it possible see how emancipation from violence, abuse and humiliation can be defended without recourse to that Enlightenment framework of thinking.

Yet even as we acknowledge the importance of Western influence in this respect, we should also note its more negative economic impacts on gender emancipation – not least in its recent moves to co-opt women into the work world and its shopping mall culture, rather than promote other aspects of self-realization. Although it has certainly advanced their interests in many respects, the successes of the feminist movement have been essentially cultural, and female emancipation in affluent societies has not unsettled the presiding structures and institutions of economic power, nor led to greener and fairer ways of thinking about human prosperity. On the contrary, movements for sexual emancipation have been co-opted by Western markets, with 'Third Wave' feminism and 'girl power' providing the springboard for all sorts of consumer-oriented media interventions, brand development and advertising spin. Cultural critics, moreover, have tended to celebrate the licence given to self-making, gender performance and the reconstruction of identity by consumer culture rather than to criticize its forms of hedonism (de Grazie and Furlough, 1996; Nava, 1992; Radner, 1995; for more critical perspectives see Littler, 2009: 171–187, 2008; Schor, 2008). The emphasis on empowerment through consumption has also meant that problematic developments in consumer culture have been undercriticized, most notably its continuing environmental and social exploitations, and its pressures on women to see themselves as 'liberated' only insofar as they show themselves ready to conform to the careerism and intensive pressures of the contemporary work world.

Nor has the impact of consumer culture on sexuality been confined to Western societies, even if the forms it takes elsewhere are always mediated by specific regional conditions and social traditions. Today, for example, we can see its effects on youth culture in some African countries, where recent studies have shown how a consumerist approach to wealth can influence new, and by no means obviously liberating, forms of sexual behaviour. A study among university students in Uganda indicates that young women (and also boys) involve themselves in transactional sex in order to live up to the increasingly materialistic demands of consumption, thereby also increasing their vulnerability to sexually transmitted infections. In cases of this kind, so far from enabling a more authentic emancipation, the aspirations engendered by a globalized consumer culture have led to an increased commodification of the self (Choudry, 2015).

Conclusion

We have here argued for the importance of mobilizing new cultural forces centred around revised understandings of 'modernization', 'progress', 'prosperity' and 'development' as a condition of furthering support for sustainable welfare and the post-growth economic order on which it must surely ultimately depend. At the conceptual level, we have presented a new 'politics of prosperity' as needing to counter the presumed links between economic expansion and 'higher' standards of living and their current monopoly over definitions of human well-being and quality of life. We have also sought to indicate ways in which a less growth-led approach to thinking about 'progress' and 'development' could result in new forms of representation of the relationship between past and present, tradition and modernity, and influence fairer and more sustainable methods of living and working in the future. At a more empirical level, we have drawn on critical strands in development studies and global health research to argue for a more considered view of the presumption that economic growth is always the essential condition of improved health. While we do not dispute the crucial role of Western medicine in improving many aspects of health on a global scale, we have suggested that it can be counterproductive if deployed without proper regard for indigenous norms and practices. We have also drawn attention to the health hazards associated with Western affluence itself and the negative impact in that respect of the modernized conception of the 'good life'.

Likewise in the area of gender relations and sexuality, we have acknowledged the key role of modernization as a vehicle of more 'enlightened' attitudes while also seeking to qualify the view that these can today only be carried on the back of economic development and its shopping mall culture. We have here defended an approach that seeks to sever the link between progress and economic expansion while nonetheless opposing the cultural regression and social conservatism that have hitherto tended to go together with economic backwardness. Overall, then, we are suggesting in this context that, if we are to be sensitive to the ways in which market liberalism can be said both to have advanced the self-realization of previously oppressed constituencies but also in other ways to have skewed or foreclosed their opportunities, then we require a discourse on welfare that defends certain Western-led assessments of health and well-being while rejecting the more market-driven and consumerist conceptions of the modernizing discourse on personal 'development'. The general implication here is that we need concepts of 'development', 'progress' and the like that continue to endorse humanist–Enlightenment conceptions of well-being and personal emancipation in certain key respects, while also exposing the ways in which a neoliberal and highly market-driven programme for delivering on that Enlightenment agenda may now be actively subverting it.

Notes

1 Most influentially, perhaps, among the economists themselves, Goodland and Daly, in the distinction they drew some while back between market-driven growth in output and 'development' in the sense of qualitative enhancement (Goodland and Daly, 1996).
2 As Eamonn De Valera famously put it on the fiftieth anniversary of the founding of the Gaelic League in his St Patrick's Day speech of 1943:'The ideal Ireland that we would have, the Ireland that we dreamed of, would be the home of a people who valued material wealth only as a basis for right living, of a people who, satisfied with frugal comfort, devoted their leisure to the things of the spirit ... – The home, in short, of a people living the life that God desires that men should live'. According to Yeats, too, although he couched the idea in more aristocratic–aesthetic terms, Ireland was to be valued as a place that had escaped the general corruption of a secular modernity – that was spiritually opposed to the unholy trinity of British materialism, middle-class mass culture and orthodox Christianity (cf. Nolan, 2005: 158).
3 We use the term in quotation marks for lack of a more precise vocabulary. We do not intend to imply that a less acquisitive consumption would necessarily be coloured by religious belief or ascetic practice, only that it would be less driven by the quest for material possessions, more socially and environmentally aware and more committed to aesthetic and relational forms of gratification.
4 Cf. James Joyce's speculation on Ireland: 'had we been allowed to develop our own civilisation instead of this mock English one imposed on us, and which has never suited us, think of what an original, interesting civilisation we might have produced' (cited in Kiberd, 2009: 33).
5 For further discussion and reflection on these tensions, see Benhabib, 1992; Fraser, 1989; Nicholson, 1995; Nussbaum, 1992; Soper, 2001.

References

Alkire, S. (2005). Needs and Capabilities. In S. Reader (ed.), *The Philosophy of Need* (220–251). Cambridge: Cambridge University Press.
Allen, K. (2007a). *The Corporate Takeover of Ireland*. Dublin: Irish Academic Press.
Allen, K. (2007b). *Ireland's Economic Crash: A Radical Agenda for Change*. Dublin: The Liffey Press.
Baell, J. (1998). Trickle-down or rising tide? Lessons on mainstreaming gender policy from Colombia and South Africa. *Social Policy and Administration*, 32(5), 513–534.
Belpomme, D. (2007). *Avant qu'il ne soit trop tard*. Paris: Fayard.
Benhabib, S. (1992). *Situating the Self: Gender, Community, and Postmodernism in Contemporary Ethics*. Cambridge: Polity Press.
Berhane, Y., Gossaye, Y., Emmelin, M. and Högberg, U. (2001). Women's health in a rural setting in societal transition in Ethiopia. *Social Science & Medicine*, 53(11), 1525–1539.

Choudry, V. (2015). Trading in sexual currency – Transactional sex, sexual coercion and sexual behaviour among young people in Uganda. Doctoral thesis. Lund: Lund University.

Clark, D. A. (ed.) (2006). Capability Approach. In *The Elgar Companion to Development Studies.* Cheltenham: Edward Elgar.

Cleary, J. (2005). Ireland and Modernity. In J. Cleary and C. Connolly (eds), *Cambridge Companion to Modern Irish Culture* (1–24). Cambridge: Cambridge University Press.

Connelly, M. P., Murray, L., MacDonald, M. and Parpart, J. L. (eds) (2000). Feminism and development: theoretical perspectives. *Theoretical Perspectives on Gender and Development* (51–159). Ottawa: International Development Research Centre.

Crocker, D. A. (1991). Towards development ethics. *World Development,* (19)5, 457–483.

Dalal, S., Beunza, J. J., Volmink, J., Adebamowo, C., Bajunirwe, F. and Njelekela, M. (2011). Non-communicable diseases in sub-Saharan Africa: What we know now. *International Journal of Epidemiology,* 40(4), 885–901.

Doyal, L., and Gough, I. (1991). *A Theory of Human Need.* London: Macmillan.

Fitzgerald, R. (1977). The Ambiguity and Rhetoric of Need. In R. Fitzgerald (ed.), *Human Needs and Politics* (195–212). Rushcutters Bay: Pergamon.

French, P. (2015). Fat China: How are policymakers tackling rising obesity? *The Guardian,* 12 February.

Fraser, N. (1989). *Unruly Practices: Power, Discourse and Gender in Contemporary Social Theory.* Cambridge: Polity.

Frumence, G. (2011). The role of social capital in HIV prevention: Experiences from the Kagera region of Tanzania. Doctoral thesis Umeå: Department of Public Health and Clinical Medicine, Umeå University.

Frumence, G., Eriksson, M., Killewo, J., Lennarth, N. and Emmelin, M. (2011). Exploring the role of cognitive and structural social capital in the declining trends of HIV/AIDS in the Kagera region of Tanzania – A grounded theory study. *African Journal of Aids Research,* 10, 1–13.

Gasper, D. (2008). Culture and development ethics: Needs, women's rights and Western theories. *Development and Change,* 27(4), 627–661.

Gasper, D. and St Clair, A. L. (eds) (2010). *Development Ethics.* London: Ashgate.

Goodland, R. and Daly, H. (1996). Environmental sustainability: Universal and non-negotiable, *Ecological Applications,* 6(4), 1002–1017.

Gorz, A. (1989). *Critique of Economic Reason,* trans. C. Turner. London: Verso.

Gough, I. (2014). *Climate Change and Sustainable Welfare: An Argument for the Centrality of Human Needs.* Centre for Analysis of Social Exclusion, Working Paper No. 182. London: London School of Economics.

de Grazie, V. and Furlough, E. (eds) (1996). *The Sex of Things: Gender and Consumption in Historical Perspective.* Berkeley: University of California Press.

Harvey, D. (1989). The Urban Process under Capitalism: A Framework for Analysis. In D. Harvey, *The Urban Experience* (50–89). Oxford: Blackwell.

Heller, A. (1980). Can 'True' and 'False' Needs be Posited? In K. Lederer (ed.), *Human Needs* (213–227). Cambridge, MA: Oelgeschlager, Gunn and Hain.

Hornborg, A. (2009). Zero-sum world: Challenges in conceptualizing environmental load displacement and ecologically unequal exchange in the world system. *International Journal of Comparative Sociology,* 50(3–4), 237–262.

Hornborg, A. (2011). *Global Ecology and Unequal Exchange: Fetishism in a Zero-Sum World.* New York: Routledge.

Jackson, T. (2004). *Chasing Progress: Beyond Measuring Economic Growth*. London: New Economics Foundation.

Jackson, T. (2009). *Prosperity without Growth*. London: Sustainable Development Commission.

Kiberd, D. (2009). *Ulysses and Us: The Art of Everyday Living*. London: Faber and Faber.

Kilby, P. and Olivieri, K. (2008). Gender and Australian aid policy: Can women's rights be advanced within a neo-liberal framework? *Australian Journal of International Affairs*, 63(3), 319–331.

Koch, M. and Fritz, M. (2014). Building the eco-social state: Do welfare regimes matter? *Journal of Social Policy*, 43(4), 679–703.

Lane, R. (2000). *The Loss of Happiness in Market Democracies*. New Haven, CT and London: Yale University Press.

Latouche, S. (2009). *Farewell to Growth*, trans. D. Macey. Cambridge: Polity.

Littler, J. (2008). *Radical Consumption? Shopping for Change in Contemporary Culture*. Milton Keynes: Open University Press.

Littler, J. (2009). Gendering Anti-Consumerism: Alternative Genealogies, Consumer Whores and the Role of Ressentiment. In K. Soper, M. Ryle and L. Thomas (eds), *The Politics and Pleasures of Consuming Differently*. London: Routledge.

Lozano, R., Naghavi, M., Foreman, K., Lim, S., Shibuya, K. and Lipshultz, S. (2012). Global and regional mortality from 235 causes of death for 20 age groups in 1990 and 2010: A systematic analysis for the Global Burden of Disease Study 2010. *Lancet*, 380(9859), 2095–2128.

McInnes, N. (1977). The Politics of Need and who Needs Politics. In R. Fitzgerald (ed.), *Human Needs and Politics* (228–245). Rushcutters Bay, NSW: Pergamon.

Moser, C. (2005). Has gender mainstreaming failed? – A comment on international development agency experiences in the South. *International Feminist Journal of Politics*, 7(4), 576–590.

Nava, M. (1992). *Changing Cultures: Feminism, Youth and Consumerism*. London: Sage.

Nicholson, L. (ed.) (1995). *Feminist Contentions*. New York: Routledge.

Nolan, E. (2005). Modernisation and the Irish Revival. In J. Cleary and C. Connolly (eds) *Cambridge Companion to Modern Irish Culture* (157–172). Cambridge: Cambridge University Press.

Nussbaum, M. (1992). Human functioning and social justice. *Public Theory*, 2(2), 202–246.

Nussbaum, M. (2006). *Frontiers of Justice*. Cambridge, MA: Harvard University Press.

Nussbaum, M. (2010). *Not For Profit*. Prinecton, NJ: Princeton University Press.

O'Toole, F. (2009). *Ship of Fools: How Stupidity and Corruption Sank the Celtic Tiger*. London: Faber and Faber.

Putnam, R. D. (1993). *Making Democracy Work: Civic Traditions in Modern Italy*. Princeton, NJ: Princeton University Press.

Putnam, R. D. (2000). *Bowling Alone: The Collapse and Revival of American Community*. New York: Simon & Schuster.

Radner, H. (1995). *Shopping Around: Feminine Culture and the Pursuit of Pleasures*. New York: Routledge.

Ryle, M. (2009). The Past, the Future and the Golden Age: Some Contemporary Versions of Pastoral. In K. Soper, M. Ryle and L. Thomas (eds), *The Politics and Pleasures of Consuming Differently* (43–58). London: Palgrave Macmillan.

Sachs, W. (ed.) (1992). *The Development Dictionary.* London: Zed Books.

Schech, S. (1998). Between tradition and post-coloniality: The location of gender in Australian development policy. *Australian Geographer,* 29(3), 389–404.

Schor, J. (2008). Juliet Schor, an interview by Jo Littler. Tackling turbo consumption. *Cultural Studies,* 22(5), 588–598.

Schor, J. (2010). *Plenitude.* London: Penguin.

Sebrié, E. and Glantz, S. A. (2006). The tobacco industry in developing countries. *British Medical Journal,* 332(7537), 313–314.

Sen, A. (1999). *Development as Freedom.* Oxford: Oxford University Press.

Sennett, R. (2008). *The Craftsman.* London: Penguin.

Soper, K. (2001). Feminism, Liberalism, Enlightenment. In M. Evans (ed.), *The Edinburgh Companion to Contemporary Liberalism* (197–207). Edinburgh: Edinburgh University Press.

Victor, P. (2008). *Managing Growth: Slower by Design, not Disaster.* Cheltenham: Edward Elgar.

UNDP (2013). *Humanity Divided: Confronting Inequality in Developing Countries.* New York: United Nations Development Programme.

Wallerstein, I. (2004). *World System Analysis: An Introduction.* London: Duke University.

Williams, R. (1977). *Marxism and Literature.* Oxford: Oxford University Press.

4 The future is not what it used to be

On the role and function of assumptions in visions of the future

Eric Brandstedt and Oksana Mont

Introduction

'Our future is what we can predict', wrote John Herman Randall (1939) and continued 'but what will be in its actuality cannot be foreseen – at least by men. Just as the past was not what it has become, so the future is not what it will become'. This provokes the question: how is the future envisioned in present-day theorizing? A plethora of visions of the future are circulating in mass media, research papers and political speeches. Nowadays a common expectation is that sustainability challenges ought to constrain visions of the 'good life', as our dreams have to be contained within the planetary boundaries. The shift from envisioning freely to dreaming within limits challenges the things taken for granted in existing visions of the future.

One can be blind to the assumptions that affect, condition or constrain visions of the future. For instance, one can be very optimistic about the future but, at the same time, pessimistic about some aspects of the future world, like the misanthrope who believes in the power of technological progress, or the harsh market-sceptic who is optimistic about the resilience of nature. What if we have brighter prospects with regard to the world now than we shall have in the future? What if the future is a 'broken world', whereas the present is still thought to be well-functioning and reliable? This comparison of perspectives and underlying assumptions is the topic of this chapter. We aim to explore underlying explicit and implicit assumptions about the future by analysing future visions developed in future-oriented theorizing in political philosophy and in policy visions developed by various societal actors.

The chapter is structured as follows. The next section scrutinizes different ways of relating to the future from the standpoint of political philosophy. In section three, we analyse policy visions. In the fourth section, we introduce a thought experiment of a bleak future where the world has been broken as a consequence of climate change, radical resource scarcity and economic melt-down. From this perspective, we try to unveil some of the changing conditions in that future compared to our present, with a particular focus on the role and function of the assumptions relevant to goals, principles and content of visions of the future. We believe that the change of perspective will have an impact on the justification of the goals, principles and content of the theories and political visions about the future. Today can look very different, depending on the conception of the future that has shaped the retrospection.

Favourable and optimistic assumptions in philosophy

John Rawls's *A Theory of Justice* (1971) is generally considered one of the most important and influential works in political philosophy of the twentieth century. As a result, it may be used here as a paradigmatic example of how the future is envisioned in contemporary political philosophy.

With the risk of stating something that is common knowledge, we shall provide some background to Rawls's theory of justice. It is a contractualist theory, where justice is the agreed-upon solution after a process of reflective deliberation by rational people situated in an idealized choice situation. This 'original position' is a situation in which parties gather, under the 'veil of ignorance', with the goal of arriving at just principles to regulate the 'basic structure' of their society. The veil of ignorance masks morally irrelevant features of the parties, such as their class, social status, abilities, which generation they belong to, etc., but one thing that they do know is that 'their society is subject to the circumstances of justice' (Rawls, 1971: 137). These circumstances are described as: moderate scarcity of resources, relative equality of powers and mutual disinterest. They are, in Rawls's words, 'the normal conditions under which human cooperation is both possible and necessary' (Rawls, 1971: 126). In this situation, justice functions as a solution as to how such people can relate to one another and how surplus resources can be distributed fairly.

The conception of justice that Rawls argues would be chosen in the original position is that of 'justice as fairness'. It consists of the following two principles (Rawls, 1971: 302):

> (1) each person is to have an equal right to the most extensive total system of equal basic liberties compatible with a similar system of liberty for all

(the liberty principle), which is lexically prior to the following twofold principle,

> (2) social and economic inequalities are to be arranged so that they are both: (a) to the greatest benefit of the least advantaged [the difference principle], consistent with the just savings principle, and (b) attached to offices and positions open to all under conditions of fair equality of opportunity

(the equal opportunity principle). The focus of this section is on what Rawls calls the 'savings problem' – the question of justice between generations. In the presented statement of justice as fairness, Rawls's solution to this problem, the 'just savings principle' is presented as a constraint to the difference principle.

In the following, we will present the reasoning that leads to this end, concentrating on the assumptions made.

To begin with, one can note that Rawls asserts that a theory of justice would be incomplete without considering this problem, but also notes that the challenge that it presents 'subjects any ethical theory to severe if not impossible tests' (Rawls, 1971: 284). The savings problem is problematic because the intergenerational setting differs in notable ways from the intragenerational setting (cf. Gardiner, 2011). One such difference is pointed out in the following: 'It is a natural fact that generations are spread out in time and actual exchanges between them take place only in one direction. We can do something for posterity but it can do nothing for us' (Rawls, 1971: 291). In other words, there is no direct reciprocity between non-overlapping generations; the present generation may either benefit or harm future generations, while the latter are unable to affect the former. Thus, for instance, the present generation could harm future generations by consuming non-renewable resources or passing on the costs of climate change, and there is nothing posterity can do to prevent this. Since justice is often thought to arise in contexts of reciprocal relations, it may seem inapplicable to the non-reciprocal relation between different non-contemporary generations (cf. Heyd, 2009).

Another difference is highlighted in Rawls's critique against utilitarianism applied intergenerationally. He writes (1971: 287, emphasis added):

> Thus it seems evident, for example, that the classical principle of utility leads in the wrong direction for questions of justice between generations. For if one takes the size of the population as variable, and postulates a high marginal productivity of capital and a very distant time horizon, maximizing total utility may lead to an excessive rate of accumulation (at least in the near future). Since from a moral point of view there are no grounds for discounting future well-being on the basis of pure time preference, the conclusion is all the more likely that the greater advantages of future generations will be sufficiently large to compensate for present sacrifices. This may prove true if only because with more capital and better technology it will be possible to support a sufficiently large population. *Thus the utilitarian doctrine may direct us to demand heavy sacrifices of the poorer generations for the sake of greater advantages for later ones that are far better off.*

The worry that Rawls grapples with in this quote is the potential unfairness of intergenerational savings. If we approach the savings problem from a traditional utilitarian perspective, with the aim of maximizing total net utility, then earlier generations will generally be required to invest (i.e. forfeit consumption) to the benefit of more populous, and better-off, later generations. Such intergenerational savings may seem unfair: why should relatively poorer generations give up a benefit to relatively wealthier generations? Although the savings rate will be somewhat lowered by taking into account the law of diminishing marginal utility, it will at any rate still be positive for earlier generations (cf. Gosseries, 2001: 313). One can note two interesting assumptions that Rawls makes here. The first is that he, at least principally (see Rawls, 1971: 295 for some reservations), assumes that discounting on the basis of pure time preferences is unacceptable, meaning that there is no justified way in which future benefits or costs can be counted for less simply because they are in the future. The second assumption is that he contends that the worst off generation is the first gen- eration and that each subsequent generation will be, relatively speaking, better off than its predecessor.

The latter assumption leads to the 'problem of the first generation', which in turn explains Rawls's resistance to a strategy of merely extending his intragenerational theory of justice to the intergenerational setting. Take the difference principle as an example: one could argue that social and economic inequalities between generations are to be arranged so that they are to the benefit of the least advantaged generation. But this does not make sense, he argues, since 'there is no way for later generations to improve the situation of the least fortunate first generation. The principle is inapplicable and it would seem to imply, if anything, that there be no saving at all' (Rawls, 1971: 291). There are two reasons why intergenerational savings cannot be motivated by the thought that they maximize the prospects of the worst off generation. The first is that, since the worst off generation is the first in line, they cannot benefit from any scheme of intergenerational cooperation. By the time any intergenerational cooperation has borne fruit, the first generation is long gone. The second reason is a simple feature of intergenerational savings, namely, that they require sacrifices to get off the ground: in order for there to be any such scheme, the first generation and all other generations of the 'accumulation phase' (further described below) will need to leave more to the next generation than they inherit from the previous one. The first reason explains why Rawls rejects the extension of the difference principle. As for the second reason, while it seemingly makes intergenerational savings unjust, Rawls argues that such feelings are misplaced: 'The savings principle repre- sents an interpretation, arrived at in the original position, of the previously accepted *natural duty to uphold and to further just institutions*' (Rawls, 1971: 289, emphasis added).

However, even if we accept the natural duty to uphold and advance just institutions as being normatively desirable, we still need, given Rawls's methodo- logical approach, to vindicate this principle by showing that it can be rationally adopted in the original position. This is not as straightforward as one would perhaps imagine. The veil of ignorance, as explained above, masks morally irrelevant features, including the generation that the parties belong to. This forces the parties to choose principles, 'the consequences of which they are prepared to live with whatever generation they turn out to belong to' (Rawls, 1971: 137). There are, however, two ways in which this can be modelled with the original position. First, by assuming that the parties are composed of a general assembly of everyone who will live at some point in time – making it a truly intergenerational contract. The problem with this interpretation, according to Rawls, is that it would 'stretch fantasy too far' (Rawls, 1971: 139; cf. Heyd, 2009: 172f). That is why he instead proposes a second understanding of the original position: the 'present time of entry' interpretation. According to this, the parties do not know which generation they belong to, but do know that they all belong to the one and same generation. Now the savings problem can be reformulated to highlight the difficulty alluded to. Whereas the veil of ignorance generally functions in order to prevent partial preferences from influencing the basic structure of society, this does not seem to hold in the case of savings. Since the parties know that they are contemporaries, they can rationally advance their generation-specific interests by refusing to adopt any intergenerational savings. Earlier generations have either saved or not saved resources, but either way the parties of the original position do best by not saving (Rawls, 1971: 140).

Rawls elaborates two different solutions to this problem. The first is to make a different motivational assumption about the parties of the original position. In the description of the circumstances of justice introduced above, the parties are assumed to be mutually disinterested. If the parties instead are assumed to be like heads of families, caring about the well-being of their line of descendants (Rawls, 1971: 292), then the problem of the first generation can be overcome and a just savings principle can be justified. Although this solves the problem, it is a solution ridden with many problems, as Jane English (1977) convincingly argued and Rawls later accepted. One issue with this solution is that tinkering with the motivation of the parties, in effect, builds in the just savings principle into the premises of the argument rather than independently justifying it (English, 1977: 93). After the critique from English and others, Rawls retracted the motivational assumption, arguing instead for a simpler solution. The solution can be found in that which he had already presented as the formal constraints – generality, universality, etc. – on the concept of right already assumed in the original position (Rawls, 1971: 130ff). In particular, he argued, 'the parties are to agree to a savings principle subject to the condition that they must want all previous generations to have followed it' (Rawls, 2001: 160).

Rawls's savings problem and the general theoretical problems that he struggled with have now been presented. Let us end this section by providing some more specific details about his just savings principle. We saw above that the just savings principle is presented as a constraint to the difference principle. What this means is that 'the appropriate expectation in applying the difference principle is that of the long-term prospects of the least favoured extending over future generations' (Rawls, 1971: 285). A consequence of this is that intergenerational savings are juxtaposed to intragenerational equality, or, in other words, future savings are financed at the expense of the presently worse off (viz. by lowering the social minimum). The general reason for why inter-generational savings are not financed by the presently better off is a consequence of the assumptions that Rawls makes and, in particular, of the idea of the difference principle. Once the difference principle has been applied, any existing intragenerational inequality is maximally beneficial for the least advantaged in society. If the better off are also required to make intergenerational savings, which would further reduce intragenerational inequality, then this would, in consequence, come at a price for the least advantaged group. Thus, there is no way of making the presently better off single-handedly finance just savings without this, in effect, being at the expense of the presently worse off.

Another characteristic of Rawls's just savings principle is that it is a two-stage principle: first there is an accumulation phase and thereafter a steady-state phase. In Rawls's words (1971: 287): 'Eventually once just institutions are firmly established, the net accumulation required falls to zero. At this point a society meets its duty of justice by maintaining just institutions and preserving their material base'. Most importantly, the aim of the intergenerational savings is not an abundance of wealth; rather it is just institutions (Rawls, 1971: 290). The point of this is to handle and mitigate the problem of the excessive rates of accumulation that the utilitarian doctrine seems to be forced to accept. The just savings principle, unlike the utility principle, is satiable: after just institutions have been established, there is no longer any need for real capital accumulation.[1] 'In fact', Rawls argues, 'beyond some point it is more likely to be a positive hindrance, a meaningless distraction at best if not a temptation to indulgence and emptiness' (Rawls, 1971: 290).

Favourable and optimistic assumptions in policy

Let us now explore these issues in visions of the future presented in policy visions by Swedish actors. The purpose of these policy visions is not to develop utopias but to provide a quite realistic picture of a future that could take place; thus they are less visionary in this regard. They typically present a somewhat improved situation from that of the current one, but seldom do they picture a future reality that turns everything on its head, like, for example, imagining a society with low or no economic growth. Let us now examine several policy visions and try to discern what assumptions about human nature and what governing principles of our society these visions are based on, which of these are explicitly mentioned in the visions and which are not. Which of these implicit assumptions are brought in from the present day into the future? We are interested in learning about what kinds of basic principles, for example, justice and freedom, the visions are based on and whether any contradictions between these principles are acknowledged and articulated in these documents. How are these contradictions dealt with, if at all? Do the visions foresee a steady-state situation of some sort after a period of accumulation, as suggested by Rawls?

We analyse two visions developed by Swedish authorities: Boverket – the Swedish National Board of Housing, Building and Planning, which is responsible for satisfying the basic need for shelter, and Tillväxtverket – the Swedish Agency for Economic and Regional Growth, which is responsible for economic growth. These actors have developed their own vision of life in

Sweden in 2025 or how their organization will drive forward societal development over the next 10 to 15 years. In addition we explore future challenges identified by Framtidskommissionen (Commission on the Future of Sweden).

The Swedish National Board of Housing, Building and Planning's *Vision for Sweden 2025* provides inspiration for measures that promote sustainable social development at all levels of society – from the national to the local (Boverket, 2012). The idea behind developing this vision is that it can be used as a conceptual foundation for preparing strategies for sustainable development at different levels. The vision presents a picture of an urbanized society, in which people live in the three largest urban regions with polycentric city structures: 'big becomes even bigger'. This suggests that the accumulation phase described by Rawls will still be ongoing in 2025.

The vision is *optimistic* in its language and in terms of the better future world that it presents; foreseeable hardships will be minimized thanks to technical solutions. The vision is explicitly optimistic when it comes to satisfying the needs of all: 'everyone now has a selection available to them in type of housing and place of residence, corresponding to their needs' (Boverket, 2012: 11). Thus, the goal of intragenerational justice seems to be satisfied in this vision, at least in terms of access to housing. There is, however, almost no mention of intergenerational justice – towards future generations – as it is implicitly assumed that the future generations will be better off than the current ones and are supposedly living happily in the three largest cities.

Economic growth is viewed as the prerequisite for societal development and this is reflected in visions of growing cities, digitization and increased trade with China and India. Growing tourism and the hospitality industry in Sweden are seen as important contributors to economic growth: 'A general rise in living standards worldwide has provided more opportunities for travel and more recreation. People from near and far visit all corners of Sweden' (Boverket, 2012: 31). However, there is no discussion about the negative environmental impacts associated with increased travelling, nor is there any mention of the dangers of natural habitats being destroyed by excessive tourism, which could undermine the very basis of the tourism industry itself.

Nevertheless, these visions acknowledge that *greenhouse gas emissions* will greatly affect the world in 2025, but note that there are also abundant solutions that reduce any negative impacts on the climate, for example, monetary charges and infrastructural projects that encourage people to use public transport and bicycles more often and thus reduce the use of private cars. Here again, the contradiction between individual interest and the *freedom* to use a private car, and public interest and the 'responsibility' to use public transport is not discussed. Frictions that may arise when measures are introduced to reduce private car use are discerned neither from the point of view of individuals (infringement of one's freedom) nor from the perspective of car manufacturers (infringement of vested interests). Increasing urbanization and the construction of buildings in an energy-efficient way is seen as contributing to public health and biological diversity and also implicitly as an investment in future generations – the accumulative phase. Yet the potential adverse effects of urbanization and the deurbanization movements emerging in other countries that are a result of economic instability, unemployment and the escalating cost of housing are not reflected upon.

The issue of resource availability is critical for the discussion of both inter- and intragenerational justice. However, this is not explicitly discussed in the vision: neither the equal distribution of available resources between people populating the Earth now, nor the access to resources of future generations. What is recognized in the vision is that available resources have different natures. Those that are renewable, such as hydropower, can be extracted on a continuous basis; those that are renewed at a slow rate, for example, forests, can be extracted at intervals 'and only until such time as the raw material is exhausted or is no longer economical to extract, such as mining' (Boverket, 2012: 29). It is implied that the recycling of resources and the reuse of materials will compensate and substitute for resource scarcity and that technological advances will make further extraction of resources economically viable or will lead to the discovery of substitutes that may not necessarily rely on renewables.

Consumption is an important activity in 2025 that takes place both in shopping centres and in small shops, more of which are being opened all the time (Boverket, 2012). Shopping is made easy as people can inspect and view goods at display premises and then have them delivered to their homes. This is justified by the reduced use of cars for making shopping trips, but consumption, per se, as an activity linked to environmental impacts, is not scrutinized. Rawls's idea about the need for early generations to save is not directly compatible with the picture presented in the vision. On the other hand, it is envisioned that economic and technical development creates possibilities for resource-saving lifestyles, where people prefer to reuse items instead of buying new ones. However, it remains unclear how the shift from buying new to buying second-hand goods is going to take place in the minds of individuals and manufacturers and to what extent this can contribute to saving virgin resources.

The vision developed by the Swedish Agency for Economic and Regional Growth is for use by the agency itself. Their slogan is 'We are Tillväxtverket – we get Sweden to grow' (Tillväxtverket, 2013). The primary goal of the agency is to strengthen regional development and facilitate business and entrepreneurship in Sweden. The role of the vision is to create consensus and a common steering platform that helps the agency to fulfil its mandate. Its primary purpose is the communication of the main values of the agency to stakeholders and employees. Unlike the *Vision for Sweden 2025* presented above, this vision does not set a specific time frame and acknowledges that 'nobody knows exactly how much time it will take to reach the set goals'. The vision is seen as showing a clear, inspiring and united direction for common goals towards Sweden being a model for entrepreneurship with sustainable growth.

The Swedish Agency for Economic and Regional Growth sees a successful Sweden where investments for growth are made with the understanding that this contributes to potential growth for future generations. However, the vision fails to recognize the potential conflict between increasing growth of contemporary businesses and economy and the option of growth for future generations. This indicates the belief in abundance of natural resources; trust in the power of entrepreneurship and technological solutions and the conviction that economic activity, especially production and consumption, can increase without any limits – that there is room for both current and future generations to grow. Natural limits are left out of the equation.

The explicit goals for the Swedish Agency for Economic and Regional Growth are seen in facilitating the establishment and growth of more businesses and in strengthening regional development. It is stated that the organization is working proactively for *sustainable growth* in Sweden by enabling entre-preneurship and especially innovative entrepreneurship. Unsurprisingly, the vision of the Swedish Agency for Economic and Regional Growth takes for granted that growth is a desirable goal for society. No discussion is offered on how exactly entrepreneurship and the growth of businesses contribute to increased quality of life or in what way these may affect the state of the envir-onment and the availability of resources for current and future generations. The vision is silent about the possibility that economic growth may undermine the very basis that future generations depend upon to develop businesses and ensure quality of life. The two aforementioned visions share the belief in untamed economic growth and technical optimism as prerequisites and safeguards of inter- and intragenerational justice.

In addition to the two visions presented above, we also assessed the outcome of the future-oriented work of Framtidskommissionen (Commission on the Future of Sweden) in order to identify the challenges facing Sweden in the longer term, between 2020 and 2050. The final report, *Future Challenges for Sweden*, proposed answers to questions like: What will life in Sweden look like and what challenges lie ahead for Swedish society? The commission worked for one-and-a-half years in a collaborative manner via 40 seminars, meetings and social media engagement with all societal actors in Sweden, from school pupils to municipalities, business leaders and government officials.

The main focus of the final report is the challenges associated with sustainable growth, labour market integration, democracy, demographic development, gender equality and social cohesion (Framtidskommissionen, 2013). However, the main task of the commission was not to develop proposals as to how future challenges could be met, but rather to describe the future challenges projecting from present-day challenges.

One such challenge is the need to maintain economic growth as the major prerequisite for societal development. This challenge is in line with the con-cerns about stagnating economic growth presented by the Swedish Agency for Economic and Regional Growth. The report stipulates that lack of economic growth cannot save the environment since environmental conservation and pollution prevention require significant economic resources. Not surprisingly the report stresses that development presupposes a market economy, but also comments on human rights and democracy (Hojem, 2013). Although the wording of relations between markets and human rights and democracy as opposites is telling in itself, the authors fail to acknowledge the role that free markets play in facilitating or simply allowing economic inequality, injustice and the violation of human rights in many production chains. They chose to ignore the increasingly insistent discourse about the need to put the idea of economic growth under scrutiny and instead have the goal of sustainable growth and the development of a green economy – an economy that can continue to generate resources that enhance economic welfare and human well-being, while reducing the environmental impacts and the consumption of finite natural resources (Hojem, 2013).

Interestingly the report highlights the ambition of handing over a society to the next generation in which major environmental problems have been solved without creating additional environmental problems outside Swedish borders, as is stipulated in the generational goal (Naturvårdsverket, 2012). However, the report is silent about potential conflicts between the goal of stimulating economic growth and the need to preserve the environment in Sweden or even to reduce environmental emissions associated with production and consumption.

Other challenges identified by the commission are mostly the present-day challenges that need to be resolved within the next five to ten years. However, these are hard to translate into long-term visions of Swedish lifestyles in 2050 as neither the future-oriented vocabulary nor visionary and long-term thinking were discussed in this work.

Looking back on today and forward to tomorrow

A way of understanding and synthesizing the disparate visions introduced above is by thinking of these in retrospect. The problem, however, is that we may not be able to access such a perspective with any certainty: the future may not be what we expect it to be today. What can be done, however, is to introduce a thought experiment, without any definitive claim to accuracy, either in the description of the past or in the predictions for the future, as in Tim Mulgan's 2011 book, *Ethics for a Broken World*. Mulgan challenges readers to envision a philosophy class taught in a future 'broken world', seriously impacted by climate change and with insufficient resources to meet everyone's basic needs. The students are assigned the task of trying to make sense of the 'affluent philosophers' – those who lived in the much brighter 'affluent world'. These students must try to understand their present world through the 'smug and insular' perspective of their affluent ancestor. How could the 'evil practices' that ruined the world have been so dominant and gone unchallenged to such a large extent?

The differences between the broken world and the past affluent world could be described in terms of changes in background assumptions (Mulgan, 2011: 1–8, 2014). Summarizing and generalizing from Mulgan's presentation, these changes concern: (1) *Natural abundance*, the assumption of favourable conditions, as in natural or ecological abundance such that all basic needs could be met without any compromise to basic liberties, both presently and in the future; (2) *optimism*, the assumption that one's descendants will inherit a better world than the one they inherited from one's ancestors; (3) *acceptance of inequality*, the assumption that the inequalities between people and nations are the price of affluence; (4) *the consumer society*, the assumption that the seemingly inefficient and wasteful wear-and-tear organization of the economy is the natural organization of an affluent society; (5) *economic growth*, the assumption that economic growth is both possible and desirable and that production volumes can increase without limit; (6) *technological optimism*, the assumption that any natural obstacle can always be overcome by technological innovation and that any shortage in one resource be compensated by a natural or man-made substitute; (7) *stability*, the assumption of the natural world as stable, permanent, abundant and largely unaffected by human activity. This list is just a selection of conditions that could be pointed to as characterizing differences between the present affluent world and a future broken world.

Although the exercise that Mulgan undertakes is naturally highly speculative, it functions here as a way of organizing the assumptions introduced in the sections above. It helps unveil assumptions made in contemporary theorizing and policymaking, which otherwise might have been hard to discern as they are deeply entrenched in contemporary cultures, traditions and habits. The broken world perspective functions as a useful device for detecting blind spots and undetected assumptions. It does so by reversing the traditional perspective of looking forward from the present, to that of looking backward to the present.

We can now turn to an analysis of some of the assumptions introduced above in the presentation of Rawls's just savings principle and detected in the visions developed by societal actors. It is, of course, not possible to discuss all of these, let alone in great detail. Our intention is to briefly relate to some of the most salient and interesting assumptions, as seen from the broken world perspective. Beginning with Rawls, two questions can serve to organize the analysis: (1) What (potentially problematic) assumptions are made in the problem formulation of the savings problem? And (2) What (potentially problematic) assumptions are made in the proposed solution to the savings problem?

The problem of justice between generations is, according to Rawls, primarily one of fairly distributing the burdens of creating and maintaining just institutions. More specifically the problem is motivating a just savings principle to govern all generations, from the very first one in the accumulation phase to later ones in the steady-state phase. The problem appears intractable because generations are assumed to stand in non-reciprocal relationships and because it requests that purportedly poorer generations save for better-off generations. This problem formulation is far from being beyond dispute; in fact, it can be challenged from multiple directions.

One may, for instance, challenge the problem formulation by questioning the underlying, and implicit, assumption of optimism. Although Rawls is characteristically vague about at what stage he assumed his contemporaries to be, it is nonetheless clear that his general view is cautiously optimistic (cf. Mulgan, 2011: 174). He seems to assume, if not continued economic growth, at least that each subsequent generation will be better off than its predecessor. What would challenging such assumptions mean for Rawls's theory? It would perhaps not throw it overboard. The risk of a broken future introduces a new threat to the institutional order. Whether we are in the accumulation or steady-state phase, this would likely mean that many more, but different, savings are required to create or maintain an institutional order. Given the discussion above about the place for the just savings principle in Rawls's theoretical framework, more savings are tantamount to a lowered social minimum intragenerationally. In other words, the threat of a broken world means giving up some policies that could benefit the presently worst off in order to ensure further intergenerational savings. Perhaps the social minimum can no longer be guided by people's reasonable expectations, but by a basic needs principle (cf. Chapters 1 and 2 in this volume). The dire prospect of a broken future would also challenge the nature, or composition, of savings, by making some kinds of savings mandatory, such as climate change mitigation and adaptation. Differently expressed, the broken world perspective might introduce new constraints to capital accumulation and maintenance: it may no longer be accumulated or maintained in ways that exacerbate the immanent risks of a broken world.

Moving on to analysing Rawls's solution to the savings problem, some other assumptions can be examined. Rawls's considered solution was to appeal to the constraints of the concept of right assumed in the original position, in particular that which is gathered under the idea of 'ideal theory' (cf. Simmons, 2010). The prospect of a broken future seems to challenge the assumptions of ideal theory in different ways: for instance, the assumptions of favourable conditions as a part of the circumstances of justice. In his ideal theory, Rawls works under the assumption that basic liberties never compete with basic needs (cf. Mulgan, 2011: 168). Although Rawls explicitly added that basic needs are prioritized over basic liberties if we are not in the circumstances of justice (Rawls, 2005 [1993]: 7), he might be criticized for not making this point more central (cf. Brandstedt, 2015). Perhaps the most pressing intergenerational concern is precisely this tension. Perhaps present freedoms and liberties, such as reproductive freedom, transport and mobility needs, or even free speech (e.g. banning climate change denials) should be compromised, and legitimately so, to the benefit of future basic needs (cf. Mulgan 2011: 183). This is work for a so-called non-ideal theory, which Rawls did not pursue in any detail.

Turning to the visions from the Swedish National Board of Housing, Building and Planning, the Swedish Agency for Economic and Regional Growth and the Commission on the Future of Sweden, it can be noted that these are built on ideas of enthusiasm, economic growth, technological optimism and the prevalence of the consumer society. All three visions recognize that the world is not stable and that there are some limitations to natural resources and pollution sinks, at least implicitly, even though these conditions do not play a prominent role in the pictures of the future that the visions present. Although the visions do mention the importance of addressing inequality, they fail to present a coherent picture of what an equal world might look like. No vision explicitly talked about future generations and justice towards them. The Commission on the Future of Sweden mentions the generational goal as an important guide when devising visions of the future, but has not provided any specifics as to how this goal might be achieved. Since the visions do not specifically address the issue of intergenerational justice, consequently they do not discuss the differences between intra- and intergenerational justice and the unidirectionality of relations in intergenerational settings. All of the visions explicitly have economic growth as a goal or a main prerequisite for societal development, but none of the visions picture a steady-state phase that could follow the accumulation phase, as proposed by Rawls. The visions explicitly present a future where there are no contradictions; however, there are in fact a great number of conflicts that have not been discussed or resolved, for example between private and societal interests or between social and environmental impacts.

Most of the visions fail to indicate how the identified current problems, for example inequality, unemployment and injustice, are going to affect the future, especially under the condition previously mentioned of having no conflict between needs and liberties. We are already aware that win–win situations tend to work in the short run or have critical limitations in terms of their effectiveness or cause rebound effects elsewhere. This means that it might be hard to avoid more drastic measures that will have to cost in the short run, but which will bear fruit in the long run, so that the broken world remains a mere thought experiment.

Conclusion

By way of conclusion it can be noted that many silent assumptions are embedded in the process of envisioning the future. From the perspective of the broken world, optimism appears to unite the otherwise disparate visions analysed here. They all assume that our descendants will be better off than we are, that natural resources will be readily available and continuously substituted by alternatives that will be available due to the development of new technologies and that all basic needs can be satisfied without compromising any individual freedoms. In the visions, markets are trusted, everyone's individual freedoms are respected and all people are given an equal voice.

Present-day assumptions could be seen as inconsistent, in conflict with or false from the perspective of the future. Present-day institutions, values and norms are shaped by the prevailing economic paradigm and coloured by contemporary discourse on sustainability. We found that many examples of the blindness and narrow-mindedness of modern society with regard to the econ-omy, environment and social issues transcend time and how this perspective is mirrored in assumptions about the future made in forecasts, as well as the ways in which visionaries are influenced by prevalent institutions and thus develop scenarios that continue with problematic values and norms well into the future. Optimism about the future may, for example, legitimize delayed or half-hearted climate change abatement actions. Asking the question of what if we are the last generation that was better off than our descendants may help us take the necessary steps in shifting the course from 'business as usual' economic growth and short-term utility maximization towards strategies that are critical for both inter- and intragenerational justice and for the long-term survival of the human species.

Note

1 This feature of Rawls's just savings principle is reminiscent of the kind of steady state envisioned by many earlier philosophers and economists, such as Adam Smith (1904 [1776]), John Stuart Mill (1985 [1848]) and John Maynard Keynes (1936). It is also affiliated to Herman Daly's work on steady-state economics (e.g. 1974; see also Chapter 2 in this volume).

References

Boverket (2012). *Vision för Sverige 2025*. Stockholm: Boverket.

Brandstedt, E. (2015). The Circumstances of Intergenerational Justice. *Moral Philosophy and Politics*, 2(1), 33–56.

Daly, H. (1974). Steady-state economics versus growthmania: A critique of the orthodox conceptions of growth, wants, scarcity, and efficiency. *Policy Sciences*, 5, 149–167.

English, J. (1977). Justice between generations. *Philosophical Studies*, 31, 91–104.

Framtidskommissionen (2013). *Future Challenges for Sweden. Final Report of the Commission on the Future of Sweden*. Stockholm: The Commission on the Future of Sweden.

Gardiner, S. (2011). Rawls and climate change: Does Rawlsian political philosophy pass the global test? *Critical Review of International Social and Political Philosophy*, 14(2), 125–151.

Gosseries, A. (2001). What do we owe the next generation(s)? *Loyola of Los Angeles Law Review*, 35, 293–355.

Heyd, D. (2009). A Value or an Obligation? Rawls on Justice to Future Generations. In A. Gosseries and L. H. Meyer (eds), *Intergenerational Justice* (167–188). New York: Oxford University Press.

Hojem, P. (2013). *På vägen till en grönare framtid – utmaningar och möjligheter*. Stockholm: The Commission on the Future of Sweden (Framtidskommissionen).

Keynes, J. M. (1936). *General Theory of Employment, Interest, and Money*. New York: Harcourt Brace Jovanovich.

Mill, J. S. (1985 [1848]). *Principles of Political Economy: With some of their Applications to Social Philosophy*. Harmondsworth: Penguin Classics.

Mulgan, T. (2011). *Ethics for a Broken World: Imagining Philosophy after Catastrophe*. Durham: Acumen Publishing.

Mulgan, T. (2014). Theory and Intuition in a Broken World. In M. Di Paola and G. Pellegrino (eds), *Canned Heat. Ethics and Politics of Global Climate Change* (44–60). Delhi/London: Routledge.

Naturvårdsverket (2012). *Uppföljning av generationsmålet. Underlag till den fördjupade utvärderingen av miljömålen.* Stockholm: Naturvårdsverket.

Randall, J. H. (1939). On understanding the history of philosophy. *The Journal of Philosophy*, 36(17), 460–474.

Rawls, J. (1971). *A Theory of Justice.* Cambridge, MA: Harvard University Press.

Rawls, J. (2001). *Justice as Fairness. A Restatement.* E. Kelly (ed.). Cambridge, MA: Belknap Press of Harvard University Press.

Rawls, J. (2005 [1993]). *Political Liberalism.* Expanded edn. New York: Columbia University Press.

Simmons, J. (2010). Ideal and Nonideal Theory. *Philosophy & Public Affairs*, 38, 5–36.

Smith, A. (1904 [1776]). *An Inquiry into the Nature and Causes of the Wealth of Nations.* London: Oxford University Press.

Tillväxtverket (2013). *Vision: hållbar tillväxt. Hur kan kvinnors företagande integreras i tillväxtarbetet?* Stockholm: Tillväxtverket.

Part II

Policies towards establishing sustainable welfare

5   Green political economy
Policies for and obstacles to sustainable welfare

Jamil Khan and Eric Clark

Introduction

Clean air; clean water; nutritious food; health; education; adequate housing; meaningful work; security: welfare brings these to mind. Climate change; land degradation; the 'sixth mass extinction' of life forms; premature deaths caused by pollution and inequality; extravagant consumption and accumulation of wealth for the few while many do not have adequate water, food, healthcare, education, or secure housing and livelihoods: sustainability brings these challenges to mind. Green political economy aims to grasp the complex social relations that generate sustainability challenges, and uses this understanding to form policies conducive to sustainable welfare. That the issues are politically potent bears repeating (Asara *et al.*, 2015), as 'green', 'eco' and 'sustainable' have become highly diluted value-enhancing signifiers. In this chapter we first summarize the dominant strands of green political economic thought, then present an analysis of obstacles to implementation of their core policies and finally evaluate their potential for achieving sustainable welfare.

Policy narratives for a sustainable economy

There are currently two predominant perspectives on transitioning to a sustainable economy and society: pro-growth and no-growth. These perspectives differ fundamentally in their views on the possibility of combining economic growth with sustainability. According to the pro-growth perspective, absolute decoupling between environmental impacts and economic growth can be achieved through investment in green innovation and technology and by regulating polluting technologies and by changes in environmental behaviour. The economy can continue to function much as it does today, as policies for meeting sustainability challenges make market forces compatible with ecological concerns. The no-growth perspective argues that sustainability requires social and economic relations of production and consumption that can secure stable throughput of materials, and energy that is capable of providing welfare within ecologically determined limits, and that this, in turn, requires zero economic growth. While the pro-growth perspective suggests 'a reconfiguration of the current global economy', the no-growth perspective 'implies a total transformation of the global economic system' (Urhammer and Røpke, 2013: 62).

Casting a wide net, Urhammer and Røpke conducted a discourse analysis of green macroeconomic narratives, based on policy documents from leading international organizations and associated research literature. Within the pro-growth perspective, they distinguish between 'green growth' and 'green economy' narratives, represented by the Organisation for Economic Co-operation and Development (OECD, 2011a, 2011b) and the United Nations Environment Programme (UNEP, 2011), respectively. They share a positive view on the possibilities of combining economic growth with long-term ecological sustainability, while they differ on issues such as government intervention and poverty reduction. Four distinct no-growth narratives are identified: the great transition (New Economics Foundation, NEF, 2010), prosperity without growth (Sustainable Development Commission, see Jackson, 2009), steady-state economy (Centre for the Advancement of the Steady State Economy, CASSE, see Dietz and O'Neill, 2013) and degrowth (see Assadourian, 2012; Martinez Alier, 2009; Kallis, 2011). Although they differ in some respects, they share an underlying critique of economic growth and seek to achieve similar systemic change.

Urhammer and Røpke relate a diverse set of policies and measures advocated by each perspective, bringing these together under the two main directions of pro-growth and no-growth. We build on this work, focusing our analysis of policy measures into five spheres: mitigation and technology development, financial and business sector, distribution of income and wealth, labour and work, and consumption. Policies of the pro-growth and no-growth perspectives are presented below and summarized in Table 5.1.

Of these five spheres, policies for mitigation and technology development appear to be those about which there is most consensus across pro-growth and no-growth perspectives. Both perspectives call for price-based instruments (taxes, cap and trade) and more specific technology policies (subsidies, public procurement, favourable loans), but weigh these differently. The OECD emphasizes market-based instruments, which are deemed most cost effective and least intrusive on markets (OECD, 2011b); other instruments can be necessary but should be used with care. The UNEP presents a more balanced focus on market-based instruments and more active government intervention, signalling the view that market mechanisms are not sufficient to secure green transition (UNEP, 2011). No-growth perspectives also emphasize the need for measures such as taxes, cap and trade and green technology incentives, but place this in the context of the need for much more fundamental change. A common view among no-growth proponents is that there should be scientifically determined caps on emissions and on the use of natural resources, and that these should be distributed equally among citizens (Jackson, 2009; Kallis *et al.*, 2012; Dietz and O'Neill, 2013).

Consistent with ascribing leading roles in green transitioning to private enterprise and finance capital, pro-growth perspectives argue that the

Table 5.1 Policy focus of pro-growth and no-growth perspectives

	Pro-growth	No growth
Mitigation and technology development	– Market-based instruments (green taxes, cap and trade) – Technology policies – Government intervention	– Market-based instruments (green taxes, cap and trade) – Technology policies – Government intervention – Caps should be distributed equally
Financial and business sector	– Financial sector plays a major role to invest in green technology – Policies to give incentives to green investments – Development of property rights, from undefined and incomplete to fully defined and complete	– Financial sector fuelling debt-financed economic growth is the root cause of environmental problems – Policies to control financial sector and reduce economic growth – Non-profit business models – Strengthening commons and alternatives to private property
Distribution of income and wealth	– Distribution not a main issue – Poverty reduction important but not equal distribution	– Equal distribution a basic precondition for no-growth economy – Minimum income; maximum income; redistributive taxes
Labour and work	– Policies to prepare labour market for changes in economy	– Reduction in labour time is the central policy to share work and reduce material consumption
Consumption	– Policies to change consumer behaviour towards green products and services – Information; economic incentives; labelling – Weak sustainable consumption	– Reduced consumption a major goal – Non-materialist lifestyles; regulation of advertising; sharing economy – Strong sustainable consumption

Sources: Synthesis based on Dietz and O'Neill, 2013; Jackson, 2009; Kallis *et al.*, 2012; Martinez Alier, 2009; OECD, 2011a, 2011b; UNEP, 2011; Urhammer and Røpke, 2013

substantial financial resources required for transitioning should come primarily from private funding. From this perspective, the main challenge is redirecting financial flows towards green investment. The UNEP report, for instance, refers to the last two decades as an era of 'gross misallocation of capital', financial investments pouring 'into property, fossil fuels and structured financial assets with embedded derivatives' and relatively little into 'renewable energy, energy efficiency, public transportation, sustainable agriculture, ecosystem and biodiversity protection, and land and water conservation' (UNEP, 2011: 14). Suggested policy measures include green bonds, public–private partnerships and concessionary financing (OECD, 2011b; UNEP, 2011). Measures are limited to enabling and facilitating, while more direct control over and the regulation of financial resources and activities are not considered. The strong regulation of property rights, however, is considered essential for resource efficiency. 'Undefined' or 'incomplete property rights' (OECD, 2011a: 27, 29) and 'lack of full property rights' are seen as barriers to green growth, and there are calls for 'development of property rights' to facilitate the 'emergence of green property as an asset class' (UNEP), thereby providing financial institutions with incentives to invest in 'responsible property' (UNEP, 2011: 97, 139, 596, 362).

No-growth perspectives see the current financial system as a root cause of ecological problems. Debt-fuelled economic growth, driven by a financial sector swelling well beyond the productive capacities of the 'real economy' (production of goods and services), is seen as underpinning unsustainable resource extraction and exploitation of what ecological economists call the 'real-real economy' – flows of energy and materials (Kallis *et al.*, 2009; Martinez Alier, 2009). Policies proposed from this perspective include measures to regulate finance (e.g. state monopoly on money creation, taxes on financial transactions, barriers to tax evasion in tax havens) and to design a financial system conducive to a steady-state or no-growth economy in the long run. Another focus of no-growth policies is on supporting alternative business models such as cooperatives and non- or low-profit liability companies (see Chapter 10) and strengthening legal and institutional conditions to support alternatives to private property, such as communal property, land trusts and other forms of commons (Kallis *et al.*, 2012; Bollier, 2003, 2014).

Pro-growth narratives include discussion on the need to address the distributional impacts of policies that adversely affect the poor. However, distribution of income and wealth is not seen as an essential issue for green transition. Adverse impacts on distribution are best addressed by general tools such as lower income tax, tax credits and social benefits (OECD, 2011b: 25). Reducing poverty is a major goal for the UNEP, claiming that 'pro-poor orientation must be superimposed on any green economy initiative' (UNEP, 2011: 20). The focus is on poverty eradication, and there is little recognition of the wider issues and impacts associated with inequalities.

This contrasts starkly with no-growth perspectives, which see policies geared to equalizing distribution of income and wealth as crucial to a sustainable economy. In order to curtail growth, it is necessary to establish incentive structures that limit concentrations of wealth and gaps in income. No-growth is seen as necessitating a more egalitarian sharing of resources. Extensive research suggests that more equal societies fare better than unequal societies across a broad register of variables associated with welfare and with sustainability (Wilkinson and Pickett, 2009). Suggested policies include classical social democratic measures such as redistributive taxes, as well as more radical measures such as basic income, maximum income and maximum pay differentials (Jackson, 2009; Dietz and O'Neill, 2013).

In the pro-growth perspective, labour and work policies focus mainly on how to prepare labour markets for changes brought about by the transition to a green economy, whereby some jobs are lost and others are created. Flexible labour markets are considered important. Policies are geared for labour market inclusiveness (e.g. re-employment support, vocational training), labour market dynamism (e.g. moderate employment protection and labour taxes, strong product market competition) and adapting workforce skills (e.g. new skills in education) (OECD, 2011b).

No-growth perspectives acknowledge the major challenge of maintaining full employment in a steady-state economy. Channelling gains from technological progress and increasing efficiency and productivity of labour towards reducing work time – rather than increasing wages and profits – facilitates work sharing, a key policy for reducing unemployment. Another policy is that the state should be the employer of last resort in order to reduce labour insecurities (Dietz and O'Neill, 2013). This is linked to the proposal for a guaranteed basic income. No-growth narratives seek to redefine the meaning of work and advocate less division between paid and non-paid work.

Regarding consumption, pro-growth perspectives emphasize policies for changing consumer behaviour towards reduced wastefulness, for example more energy-efficient appliances and transport modes with lower emissions. Again, price-based measures in combination with softer policies such as labelling, information and education are the main policies on the agenda for ensuring that consumption stays within the limits of sustainability (OECD, 2011b; UNEP, 2011).

No-growth perspectives see substantial reductions in material consumption in rich countries as necessary, especially in view of the prospect of these consumption patterns on the global scale. Lorek and Fuchs (2013) distinguish between weak and strong sustainable consumption, whereby weak sustainable consumption corresponds to the pro-growth approach of the OECD and the UNEP, and strong sustainable consumption is associated with radical changes in consumption patterns. Policies that are advocated to reduce consumption include the promotion of non-materialistic lifestyles (Dietz and O'Neill, 2013), regulation of advertising (Jackson, 2009), regulation of product durability (Jackson, 2009) and promotion of social innovations that are conducive to a sharing economy.

Obstacles to sustainable welfare

These policy perspectives are examples of humankind's capacity to engage in cognitive niche construction: imagining how things could be and should be (Terrell, 2015). Realizing such imaginations meets friction. Our interventions in the environment are inherently political, and any semblance of order reflects power relations. Intended or claimed outcomes do not always match real or feasible outcomes. In this sense, there are always obstacles to changes of the magnitude implied by 'transitioning'. The obstacles to sustainable welfare that we highlight here are of more contextual nature, rooted in recent history and current conditions, from which any move towards sustainable welfare must commence. There is no neutral ground: any description or analysis reflects the position and understanding of the fundamental relations involved, and ours is no exception. We suggest that the main obstacles to achieving a green political economy conducive to sustainable welfare are:

- the growth imperative driving careless consumption and excessive production
- inequalities in economic and political power
- functionless private property displacing the commons, and
- financialization of ever more spheres of natural and social life.

This is not an exhaustive list, and each obstacle is entangled with the others in various ways. Yet we suggest that these processes and conditions work against and stand in the way of transitioning towards sustainable welfare.

The growth imperative driving careless consumption and excessive production

Capitalist economies are dependent on growth. This holds at all levels. Individual capitalist enterprises are subject to the growth imperative as they are compelled to grow in order to survive market competition (Gordon and Rosenthal, 2003). Geopolitical entities (e.g. local governments, nation states) are dependent on growth in order to secure employment and tax revenues for public expenditures, in competition with other geopolitical entities. The lack of economic growth under capitalist relations – recession – causes social problems such as rising unemployment, cuts in welfare provision and increasing poverty, as witnessed in many countries today amid the ongoing economic crisis.

Relations between consumption, production and economic growth are complex. Røpke (2010) places consumption at the core of the growth engine, as the main driver of economic growth. Mass consumption is made possible by cheap access to fossil fuels and unequal relations between and within countries in the global economy. Costs are cut by technological innovations and associated increases in labour productivity, making material goods relatively cheaper while services become relatively more expensive. Consumers are consequently induced to consume more material goods. Technological change constantly provides new consumer goods, while consumption is further fuelled by an ever growing advertising industry and the commercialization of public space. A process of normalization and lock-in involves a shift whereby goods initially deemed as luxury consumption come to be considered normal necessities (Shove, 2003).

From a different angle, Galbraith (1958) positioned production at the centre of the growth imperative. Increased production is, however, dependent on increased consumption; new wants are created in the process of production, through marketing and the establishment of consumption norms. Galbraith called this the dependence effect. His main concern was that increased production of consumer goods did not make people better off, but instead reduced their willingness to spend on necessary public goods, such as education, infrastructure and health. His analysis is relevant from a sustainability perspective, since it indicates the difficulties of reducing or changing consumption patterns that are intrinsically linked to the production process and economic growth.

The argument from mainstream economics is that growth can be 'decoupled' from material throughput and thereby from environmental impact. Hahnel (2012) counters this 'dematerialization' approach by honing an alternative defence of the unhealthy growth imperative hypothesis. Hahnel acknowledges that, since real gross domestic product (GDP) is a measure of value and not of material throughput, the 'decoupling' argument of reducing throughput while increasing GDP holds in theory. Accordingly capitalism can and should become greener, as economic growth (GDP) is increasingly decoupled from material throughput. The case for the unhealthy growth imperative thesis cannot rest simply on conflating real GDP with throughput, but rather on careful descriptions of 'how specific perverse incentives inherent to the capitalist economic system result in *biases*, which in turn propel increases in productivity in environmentally destructive directions' (Hahnel, 2012: 40), favouring private consumer goods over increased leisure time, public consumption and environmental conservation.

How we measure growth is basic to these issues; GDP is a political construction. Only recently have changes been made in the metrics, 'making finance productive' by including forms of financial gains that had previously not been included (Christophers, 2011). Widely used and entrenched as political lodestar, though disqualified as a meaningful measure of welfare and social progress (Stiglitz *et al.*, 2010), GDP is built on a lie that provides an illusion of growth in what could be described as 'the most disastrous Ponzi scheme of history' (Fioramonti, 2013: 157).

Inequalities in economic and political power

Oxfam calculated that in 2013 the richest 85 people on the planet possessed as much wealth as the poorer half of the global population: 3.5 billion people. A few weeks later this calculation was updated based on the 2014 *Forbes'* Billionaires list, under the headline 'The 67 people as wealthy as the world's poorest 3.5 billion' (Moreno, 2014). Remarkably the article concludes by stating that *Forbes* has introduced constant updating of the list in real time and that the number had already fallen to 66. Fully grasping this statistic, let alone its pace of change, is difficult. Fully grasping the consequences of this growing gap is even more challenging. With some notable exceptions, inequalities have been increasing in recent decades across all geopolitical scales from urban to global. Life expectancy gaps within many 'developed' metropolitan areas are comparable to those between rich and poor countries (Wilkinson and Pickett, 2009). This polarization is a result of political reforms designed and promulgated for the very purpose of opening up opportunities for financial 'investment', that is, for the wealthy to rapidly get wealthier. For every instance of news reporting on increasing inequalities there is an economic commentator applauding this development, since inequalities, so the story goes, generate the very incentives so fundamental to economic growth.

Polarization of wealth and income has gone hand in hand with the political reforms associated with neoliberalization, spawning critical analyses and enhanced awareness of the costs of inequalities in terms of human suffering and environmental degradation. The accumulated research reveals that the degree of (in)equality has considerable bearing on a wide spectrum of social, economic and environmental issues, with inequality consistently coming out as deeply problematic (Dorling, 2014; Sayer, 2015; Stiglitz, 2012; Therborn, 2013; Wilkinson and Pickett, 2009). Practically all negative impacts of inequalities – poor physical and mental health, high mortality and low life expectancy, high rates of violent crime and theft, low social mobility and low voting rates, to name a few – clearly relate to human welfare, and most can be seen to relate to sustainability, especially the social dimensions of sustainability. Here we emphasize how inequalities constitute obstacles to sustainable welfare, and this is primarily through its impact on trust and democracy.

The difficult political decisions that need to be made in order to transition to a green political economy would be greatly facilitated in societies characterized by high levels of trust and a well-functioning democratic political culture. There is a clear correlation between these characteristics and the degree of (in)equality: inequality breeds distrust and weakens democracy (Rothstein and Uslaner, 2005; Stiglitz, 2012; Wilkinson and Pickett, 2009). The weakening of democracy results not only from distrust and low participation in elections, but more directly from the sheer power of the super-rich over policy formation, governments and entire political machines. The 1 per cent have captured not only media and think-tanks (outsourced politics), but governance structures as well. Increased inequality in the US has meant the demise of democracy and given rise to a plutocracy in which the wealthy have immense influence over policy formation, while the common people have barely any influence at all (Gilens and Page, 2014).

The obstacle is that this political power is concentrated in the hands of the wealthiest who will not quietly watch while political economic reforms for securing sustainable welfare are installed and institutionalized. Policies geared to remedy inequalities, such as the universal provision of basic income, coupled with regulations on maximum income (Daly, 1996), set in relation to basic income and maximum inequality (e.g. 20 to 1, see Dorling, 2014), are anathema to capitalist social relations. As Callinicos (2000: 117) points out, were such a proposal to be seriously proposed by any major party 'with a serious prospect of holding office anywhere in the advanced world, the reaction of the privileged would be extravagantly ferocious'. Having succeeded in changing policies to favour them, the rich have gained the power to stand in the way of policies favouring levels of equality commensurate with sustainable welfare.

Functionless private property displacing the commons

'Property is the most ambiguous of categories', claimed Tawney (1920), who critiqued the expansion of 'proprietary rights which entitle the owners to payment without work' and the diminishing of 'those which can properly be described as functional ... the significance of which it is hardly possible to over-estimate' (Tawney, 1920: 54, 66). Echoing Aristotle's distinction between the art of acquisition and the art of householding, Tawney insisted on the importance of distinguishing functionless property – 'passive property, or property for acquisition, for exploitation, or for power' – from functional property – 'actively used by its owner for the conduct of his profession or the upkeep of his household' (Tawney, 1920: 63–64). All forms of private property are not problematic, but functionless forms are. Thus, undiscriminating attacks on private property make as little sense as the undiscriminating defence of 'the dogma of the sanctity of private property' (Tawney, 1920: 54).

Yet this is commonly what happens when private property is pitted against the state as if only these two property institutions existed, and as if each were internally uniform. Not only do private and state property manifest themselves in very different ways, there are other forms of property altogether that have deep historical roots: the commons and open access resources (Bromley, 1992). Confusion about important distinctions between these two underlies 'the tyranny of the "tragedy" myth' (Bollier, 2014: 24), namely the tyranny of a generation of economists and ideologues misguided by the fundamentally flawed story of 'the tragedy of the commons'. Open access presents problems in terms of the overexploitation of resources. The commons are not open access, but rather a form of common property collectively managed through cooperation, and based on ancient principles of public trust and inherently public property (Bollier, 2003). Like private and state property, the commons have historically taken many forms: 'for thousands of years people have self-organized to manage common-pool resources, and users often do devise long-term, sustainable institutions for governing these resources' (Ostrom *et al.*, 1999: 278).

In recent decades, states have organized large-scale handouts and sell-outs of common wealth, as the commons have been turned into functionless private property. This constitutes an obstacle to sustainable welfare in that the expansion of the institutions of functionless private property – displacing and replacing the commons – is part and parcel of increasing inequalities in income and wealth, and lays the foundation for the financialization of our natural and built environments and our socially produced knowledge and cultural wealth. Together, these are neither conducive to sustainability nor to welfare.

Financialization of ever more spheres of natural and social life

Establishment of functionless private property relations in land – in its broadest sense including bodies of water and elements of land commonly called natural resources – creates a foundation for the commodification of environments by judicially and administratively rendering specified parts tradable on markets, where their exchange value can be expressed as a price and used to guide decisions on investment. The profit- and rent-seeking behaviour of finance capital and landed-developer interests drive the formation of market relations through the privatization and commodification of built and natural environments, extending the process wherever property relations retain the characteristics of commons that hinder the free flow of capital investment. Environments are securitized and, treated as pure financial assets, enter the orbit of finance capital as potential sites for investment, or disinvestment, depending on their expected yield to shareholders.

Financialization is a process whereby the privatization, commodification and securitization of the environment allow for the penetration of financial control and decision-making into the fabric of socio-ecological systems. It has involved 'the phenomenal expansion of financial assets relative to real activity (by three times over the last 30 years)' and 'the absolute and relative expansion of speculative as opposed to or at the expense of real *investment*' (Fine, 2013: 6, emphasis added). Ever in search of new fields to securitize and invest in, the financial sector actively engages in the creation of conditions allowing nature 'to circulate as financial capital' (Prudham, 2007: 259), entailing enclosures of resource commons and the displacement of people, their livelihoods, knowledge and practices (Clark and Hermele, 2014).

We emphasize investment because, as Sayer (2015: 34) convincingly argues, it is 'the most dangerously ambiguous word in our economic vocabulary'. Masking the difference between wealth extraction and wealth creation, it camouflages the former as the latter. Sayer distinguishes object-focused definitions that focus on what is invested *in*, thereby enabling the production of new use values in goods, services and skills, from 'investor'-focused definitions that focus on 'the financial gains of the "investor" from any kind of spending, lending, saving, purchase of financial assets or speculation – regardless of whether they contribute to any objective investment, or anything socially useful' (Sayer, 2015: 34–35). The slippage between these usages is a source of mystification, concealing 'not only a difference in functions, in how things work, but a moral difference – between contributing to the creation of something useful and just getting a return, no matter what' (Sayer, 2015: 36). Sayer associates the rise of exchange value-oriented 'investment' relative to use value-oriented investment to

> the emergence of "financialised" capitalism, which prioritises making money out of money, instead of the tricky business of organising people to produce goods and services. It's truly extraordinary that we treat these different things as one and the same without even noticing.
>
> (Sayer, 2015: 36)

Financialization reaches into everyday life as we increasingly consider our homes, our education and even ourselves as financial assets that we 'invest' in for the sake of financial returns (Martin, 2002). It reaches into education systems, healthcare, infrastructure of various kinds, urban planning and political life: wherever exchange value-driven decision-making displaces and replaces use value-oriented decision-making.

Financialization is tightly entwined with the previously considered obstacles. It constitutes a major obstacle to sustainable welfare in that it institutionalizes the growth imperative through establishing the logic of shareholder governance, exploiting while intensifying inequalities in economic and political power, and driving the privatization of the commons in order to expand the sphere of functionless private property upon which it 'invests' and secures speculative return on 'investment'. It is a remarkable paradox that the same period of intensified growth in knowledge on and concern for environmental problems and sustainability issues, which one would think could fuel political action and legitimize policies for sustainable welfare, is a period of rampant financialization.

Policies meet obstacles, policies as obstacles

The obstacles that we emphasize reflect our take on the various narratives within green political economy. Our brief presentation of the policies and obstacles reveal some key tensions between the perspectives. Most glaring is the growth imperative, which is actively endorsed by the pro-growth narratives, while considered a major obstacle by the no-growth analyses. Almost as pronounced is the contrast between the two main directions regarding property relations: with pro-growth viewing the commons as fundamentally flawed, and private property rights as necessary for securing levels of 'resource efficiency' that is conducive to sustainability, and no-growth regarding privatization as the basis for commodification, commercialization, financialization and, in the end, destructive overexploitation of our common environment. Clearly, it would be foolish to attempt to identify a set of obstacles equally relevant to all perspectives. Our exercise unavoidably reflects our understanding of green political economy and sustainable welfare.

Pro-growth policies and obstacles

The green growth and green economy programmes of the OECD and UNEP envision a future that builds on an extension of established political economic conditions, modified to solve environmental problems. They seek to use mechanisms founded on capitalist social relations of production to redirect financial 'investments' into green technologies and a green transition of the economy. Market mechanisms and incentives to green financial 'investments' are consequently at the core of their policy visions, and they put faith in technological solutions to environmental problems. In light of the above discussion on the main obstacles to sustainable welfare in the global political economy, three major issues present themselves regarding the feasibility of pro-growth policies for a green transition.

First, pro-growth perspectives assume the possibility of adequately addressing sustainability challenges without any major changes in the underlying logic of capitalist economies. More specifically, long-term absolute decoupling on the global scale between economic growth and environmental pressure (resource use and environmental degradation) is considered feasible. Jackson (2009) and others have convincingly shown that the case for absolute decoupling is fundamentally flawed and that no credible signs of decoupling are emerging out of present-day economic activities. Much of the growth in value ascribed to greening economies, supposedly in the process of decoupling, is rather associated with speculative financial 'investment' reflecting increases in exchange values with little or no connection with use values – the 'bubble' effect of speculation. In the terms of ecological economics, this is growth of the financial sector borrowing against the future, without any corresponding growth of the real economy (material and immaterial use values), much less of the underlying 'real-real economy' that constitutes our environment.

These are issues that pro-growth perspectives do not engage in. They fail to provide substantial and theoretically persuasive arguments for how their proposed arsenal of policies will succeed in securing both long-term growth and sustainability. They fail to address issues surrounding unsustainable patterns of consumption and production driven by the growth imperative, or how this destructive logic can be effectively countered within growth economies. As long as pro-growth perspectives limit the agenda to supporting greener technologies and greener consumer choices, without tackling the core question of how growth can be combined with sustainable throughput of natural resources, they fail to provide a viable solution for a sustainable political economy.

Second, pro-growth perspectives place faith in green financial 'investments'. The assumption is that financial 'investments' can be redirected into green technologies through incentives and facilitating policies, without any stronger regulation of or control over the financial sector. Considering the financial sector's track record of recent decades, it is highly questionable that sustainable welfare can be achieved by tweaking incentives with regard to such a powerful global agent, without more fundamental reforms that reduce the power of finance and increase the power of democratically controlled institutions. A strategy that depends on the goodwill of finance capital, with governments acting merely as supporters and facilitators, appears strikingly naive. In order to be credible, pro-growth perspectives need to demonstrate increased awareness of the problems caused by the immense and growing influence of financial institutions and develop policy responses that regulate this influence in ways conducive to quite different (use value-based rather than speculative exchange value-based) forms of growth.

Third, pro-growth perspectives do not sufficiently address the causes and impacts of inequalities in the distribution of income and wealth. Focusing on poverty alleviation and protective measures to limit the negative distributional impacts of policies does little to redress the immense concentrations at the top and the problems that this generates in terms of environmental exploitation and undemocratic decision-making. In a world constrained by the sustainability proviso (see Chapter 1), great inequalities become even more problematic. There are no conclusive arguments for the right to a certain standard of living if this level is impossible to maintain sustainably were it extended to all people in the world.

No-growth policies and obstacles

No-growth perspectives and their associated policy measures challenge the core relations of the global capitalist economy. Policy-led reduction in material consumption; tight regulation of the financial sector; state monopoly on money creation; localized economies and currencies; the advancement of non-profit businesses; work-sharing and reduced work time; effective policies to shrink inequality in income and wealth and to expand forms of community ownership: all these measures go against mainstream economic policy to varying degrees and will face resistance by powerful vested interests and large parts of the population. Welfare states developed in symbiosis with capitalist social and economic relations; today economic growth has come to be seen as the mainspring of employment and the guarantor of stability and welfare. The four obstacles to sustainable welfare presented above present greater challenges to no-growth policies than to pro-growth policies. We see two main avenues of action for the promotion of no-growth policies.

First, it is necessary to develop a credible vision of how a no-growth economy capable of providing universal welfare would work. If the challenge for pro-growth perspectives is to show how economic growth can be combined with socio-ecological sustainability, the challenge for no-growth proponents is rather to show how a non-growing economy is economically and socially viable. Friction towards change is a powerful tendency rendering strength to the hegemonic position of financialized global capitalism, while the promise of 'growth' is deceptively appealing in spite of overwhelming evidence to the contrary (Douthwaite, 1999). Although no modern society has implemented the full spectrum of no-growth policies, there are many successful practices relevant to each policy that can be highlighted as examples for locally adapted emulation and implementation elsewhere. We are not left only to the power of our imagination. There are a wealth of historical and comparative analyses on the themes of no-growth policies tallied in Table 5.1 that can provide empirically robust arguments for pursuing these policies. The challenge for no-growth policy is to turn 'the critique of growth into a positive transformation program to redistribute wealth and restructure the scale of economic activities relative to global biocapacity' (Gómez-Baggethun and Naredo, 2015: 393). Propagating blank-slate revolutions will only condemn no-growth politics to the periphery to which it has systematically been pushed since the 1970s (Gómez-Baggethun and Naredo, 2015).

Second, a viable approach to advancing selected policies in a multi-flanked strategy would be to form alliances with various interest groups in order to gain broad support within each policy focus, separately, rather than pushing one complete programme. For instance, regarding policies for emissions mitigation, renewable energy, energy efficiency, changes in transport patterns and other low carbon innovations, no-growth proponents can seek common ground with actors on the pro-growth side that are less market fundamentalist in nature and which favour state intervention, such as the UNEP. Alliances with business actors at the forefront of sustainability could forward the development of new business models that are based on the logic of sufficiency (Princen, 2005), including cooperatives and public interest companies (see Chapter 10), rather than the logic of profit and growth.

Some policies will be more difficult to advance than others. Given the incredible debacle of recent history and ongoing events, one should think it would be easy to form alliances aiming to rein in the power of finance, but the power of finance has thus far held sway over political bodies, economic policies, media and the public imagination. Similarly, though reduced work time and the welfare state are historic achievements that should inspire continued movement along these lines toward sustainable welfare, the obstacles have proven immense as these two have come to a grinding standstill and in some respects even regressed. Establishing alliances in these policy spheres presents a challenge.

We should neither exaggerate nor underestimate the importance of science in these contexts. For instance, working to understand 'what can be done to make the financial system work for society, the economy and the environment and not – as has sometimes been the case – the other way round' (FESSUD, 2015) has the potential to move political agendas, not unlike the way that climate research has already succeeded in mobilizing popular support for policies to curtail global warming. Critical intellectuals have a responsibility to 'stop worrying about their reputation with those whose hegemony requires everyone to accept that "there is no alternative"' (Streeck, 2014: 160).

Conclusion

Pro-growth narratives for green political economy propose policies that are feasible with regard to being passed by legislative bodies and being implemented, but are insufficient and in some respects counterproductive with regard to achieving sustainable welfare. The pro-growth agenda currently prioritizes opportunities for profit presented by increasingly acute sustainability challenges – land degradation, climate change, loss of biodiversity, water and air pollution, global health – over effectively meeting these challenges. Success in some of these policies, especially those geared to 'development' of property rights and the handover of environmental governance to finance capital, *are* obstacles to achieving sustainable welfare. Not only are the outcomes incongruent with sustainable welfare, but by parading as green politics and as taking action for the environment, they provide the false comfort that action is being taken to solve these problems and thus distract from meaningful debate over alternatives. In this sense, pro-growth policies constitute an obstacle to no-growth policies. Having installed market incentives to producers and consumers, flexibility in labour markets, 'fully defined and complete' private property rights and some aid for the poorest of the poor, we are well on our way to a green economy and do not need to entertain discussion of difficult and unsettling alternatives. Or do we?

The no-growth narratives for green political economy propose policies that are less feasible with regard to being passed by legislative bodies, but are more compatible with the goal of achieving sustainable welfare. The obstacles to sustainable welfare are great. The more we learn about sustainability challenges, the clearer we see that the stakes are extraordinary. The question is: Will we allow the quest for endless economic growth, excessive material consumption and opportunities for profit for the few to distract us from using what we know about climate change, land degradation, severe pollution of air and water, unprecedented loss of biodiversity and the societal costs of vast inequalities, in order to effectively meet these sustainability challenges and attempt to design a future that can reasonably be described as that of sustainable welfare?

References

Asara, V., Otero, I., Demaria, F. and Corbera, E. (2015). Socially sustainable degrowth as a social-ecological transformation: Repoliticizing sustainability. *Sustainability Science*, 10, 375–384.

Assadourian, E. (2012) The path to degrowth in overdeveloped countries. In Assadourian, E. and Renner, M. (eds), *State of the World 2012: Moving Toward Sustainable Prosperity*. Worldwatch Institute. Washington, DC: Island Press, 22–37.

Bollier, D. (2003). *Silent Theft: The Private Plunder of Our Common Wealth*. London: Routledge.

Bollier, D. (2014). *Think Like a Commoner: A Short Introduction to the Life of the Commons*. Gabriola Island, BC: New Society.

Bromley, D. (ed.). (1992). *Making the Commons Work: Theory, Practice and Policy*. San Francisco, CA: ICS Press.

Callinicos, A. (2000). *Equality*. Cambridge: Polity Press.

Christophers, B. (2011). Making finance productive. *Economy and Society*, 40(1), 112–140.

Clark, E. and Hermele, K. (2014). Financialisation of the environment: A literature review. FESSUD Working Paper Series, 32. http://fessud.eu/working-papers/#WP7 (accessed 9.15).

Daly, H. E. (1996). *Beyond Growth: The Economics of Sustainable Development*. Boston, MA: Beacon Press.

Dietz, R. and O'Neill, D. W. (2013). *Enough is Enough: Building a Sustainable Economy in a World of Finite Resources*. San Francisco, CA: Berrett-Koehler.

Dorling, D. (2014). *Inequality and the 1%*. London: Verso.

Douthwaite, R. (1999). *The Growth Illusion: How Economic Growth Has Enriched the Few, Impoverished the Many and Endangered the Planet*. Cambridge: Green Books.

FESSUD (2015). http://fessud.eu/the-project (accessed 9.15).

Fine, B. (2013). Towards a material culture of financialisation. FESSUD Working Paper Series, 15. http://fessud.eu/working-papers/#WP5 (accessed 9.15)

Fioramonti, L. (2013). *Gross Domestic Problem: The Politics behind the World's Most Powerful Number*. London: Zed Books.

Galbraith, J. K. (1958). *The Affluent Society*. London: Hamilton.

Gilens, M. and Page, B. I. (2014). Testing theories of American politics: Elites, interest groups, and average citizens. *Perspectives on Politics*, 12(3), 564–581.

Gómez-Baggethun, E. and Naredo, J. M. (2015). In search of lost time: The rise and fall of limits to growth in international sustainability policy. *Sustainability Science*, 10, 385–395.

Gordon, M. J. and Rosenthal, J. S. (2003). Capitalism's growth imperative. *Cambridge Journal of Economics*, 27(1), 25–48.

Hahnel, R. (2012). The growth imperative: Beyond assuming conclusions. *Review of Radical Political Economics*, 45(1), 24–41.

Jackson, T. (2009). *Prosperity without Growth: Economics for a Finite Planet*. London: Earthscan.

Kallis, G. (2011). In defence of degrowth. *Ecological Economics*, 70, 873–880.

Kallis, G., Martinez-Alier, J. and Norgaard, R. (2009). Paper assets, real debts. An ecological-economic exploration of the global economic crisis. *Critical Perspectives on International Business*, 5(1), 14–25.

Kallis, G., Kerschner, C. and Martinez-Alier, J. (2012). The economics of degrowth. *Ecological Economics*, 84, 172–180.

Lorek, S. and Fuchs, D. (2013). Strong sustainable consumption governance: Precondition for a degrowth path? *Journal of Cleaner Production*, 38(1), 36–43.

Martin, R. (2002). *Financialisation of Everyday Life*. Philadelphia: Temple University Press.

Martinez Alier, J. (2009). Socially sustainable economic de-growth. *Development and Change*, 40(6), 1099–1119.

Moreno, K. (2014). The 67 people as wealthy as the world's poorest 3.5 billion. *Forbes*, 25 March 25.

NEF (2010). *The Great Transition, Social Justice and the Core Economy*. London: New Economics Foundation.

OECD (2011a). *Towards Green Growth*. Paris: OECD.

OECD (2011b). *Tools for Delivering on Green Growth*. Paris: OECD.

Ostrom, E., Burger, J., Field, C. B., Norgaard, R. B. and Policansky, D. (1999). Revisiting the commons: Local lessons, global challenges. *Science*, 284, 278–282.

Princen, T. (2005) *The Logic of Sufficiency*. Cambridge, MA: MIT Press.

Prudham, S. (2007). Sustaining sustained yield: Class, politics, and post-war forest regulation in British Columbia. *Environment and Planning D: Society and Space*, 25, 258–283.

Røpke, I. (2010). Consumption at the core of the growth engine. Paper for the 11th Biennial Conference of the International Society for Ecological Economics, Oldenburg and Bremen, 22–25 August 2010.

Rothstein, B. and Uslaner, E. M. (2005). All for all: Equality, corruption, and social trust. *World Politics*, 58, 41–72.

Sayer, A. (2015). *Why We Can't Afford the Rich*. Bristol: Policy Press.

Shove, E. (2003). *Comfort, Cleanliness and Convenience: The Social Organization of Normality*. Oxford: Berg.

Stiglitz, J. E. (2012). *The Price of Inequality*. London: Allen Lane.

Stiglitz, J. E., Sen, A. and Fitoussi, J.-P. (2010). *Mis-Measuring Our Lives: Why GDP Doesn't Add Up*. New York: The New Press.

Streeck, W. (2014). *Buying Time: The Delayed Crisis of Democratic Capitalism*. London: Verso.

Tawney, R. H. (1920). *The Acquisitive Society*. New York: Harcourt Brace and Company.

Terrell, J. E. (2015). *A Talent for Friendship: Rediscovery of a Remarkable Trait*. Oxford: Oxford University Press.

Therborn, G. (2013). *The Killing Fields of Inequality*. Cambridge: Polity Press.

UNEP (2011). *Towards a Green Economy, Pathways to Sustainable Development and Poverty Eradication*. Nairobi: UNEP.

Urhammer, E. and Røpke, I. (2013). Macroeconomic narratives in a world of crises: An analysis of stories about solving the system crisis, *Ecological Economics*, 96(1), 62–70.

Wilkinson, R. and Pickett, K. (2009). *The Spirit Level*. London: Allen Lane.

Eric Clark wishes to acknowledge that this research, aside from support from the Pufendorf Institute at Lund University, also benefited from funding of the European Union Seventh Framework Program (FP7/2007–2013) under grant agreement no. 266800, FESSUD (fessud.eu), and from the richly stimulating collaborations in the Linnaeus Centre LUCID at Lund University, funded by the Swedish research council Formas (www.lucid.lu.se).

6 Climate change and the welfare state
Do we see a new generation of social risks emerging?

Håkan Johansson, Jamil Khan and Roger Hildingsson

Introduction

The notion of social risk is at the centre of welfare studies. Social risks are generally seen as the result of structural transformation processes causing new problems and risks for various social groups. Unemployment, sickness, work-related injuries and old age are portrayed as classic or first-generation social risks that emerged against the backdrop of rapid industrialization and urbanization processes. A second generation of social risks has emerged in relation to individualization and changing demographic structures, giving rise to new social demands and need structures.

This chapter seeks to explore whether a new generation of social risks is emerging, potentially replacing previous social risks, and/or transforming these in unexpected ways. Although present societies are still struggling with high levels of unemployment, poor health and the need for care for the elderly, it is beyond dispute that climate change is an even greater societal challenge. The literature on climate change and its effects on human systems is extensive, but few studies have focused great interest in the ways by which climate change is a new driver for social risks. Yet, the Intergovernmental Panel on Climate Change (IPCC) reports that climate change will have serious impacts on food security, health problems and migration flows (IPCC, 2014a). Climatic changes will also be distributed unevenly around the globe and have a direct effect on poverty levels in various regions (IPCC, 2014b). Similarly, political strategies to mitigate climate change and decarbonize social structures (see IPCC, 2014c) potentially give rise to new social risks while simultaneously affecting and transforming existing ones. Thus, climate policy can augment existing inequalities or can be designed to reduce them. The overall purpose of the chapter is thus to discuss whether we see a new generation of social risks emerging and to discuss what types of welfare arrangements such novel social risks might demand.

For these purposes, we use the most recent scientific assessments of the IPCC (2014a, 2014b, 2014c) as a point of departure in order to identify how the link between climate change and social risks is being portrayed in the relevant literature and what kinds of solutions are being proposed to deal with such a challenging future. The role of the IPCC is, as a scientific inter-governmental body, to gather and synthesize the most recent scientific knowledge on various aspects of climate change. While the IPCC does not conduct its own original research, it comprises a vast group of scientists who can be said to represent current knowledge on the physical science basis (IPCC, 2013), on impacts and adaptation (IPCC, 2014a, 2014b) and on mitigation efforts and options (IPCC, 2014c). The chapter ends with a discussion about the need for a new type of eco-social insurance regime to meet the challenges posed by climate change and to deal with the (new) kind of social risks generated.

Social risks and the welfare state

The concept of risk is central in the social sciences as well as in debates on climate change. A risk can generally be defined as the damage caused by a (potential) event, in correspondence to the probability of the event occurring (Adams, 1995: 8). Risk is closely related to a set of interlinked concepts such as uncertainty, insecurity, probability and insurance. It also connotes elements of potential gains as well as dangers, or an exposure to dangers. Taking 'a risk' obviously contains both as it is a 'calculated' action based on the probabilities for the event to occur. If one expects the opportunities to overshadow the dangers or shortcomings, then it might be rational to take a certain risk. The social sciences, however, tend to differ when it comes to various approaches and conceptualizations of risks. This above all concerns differences in whether individuals are understood as active (rational) agents in relation to risks, or whether risks are understood as part of a structure that restrains action repertoires (see Taylor-Gooby and Zinn, 2006) and hence can be understood as an exogenous event that puts pressure on societies to change.

Much welfare research into social risks tends to follow the latter conceptualization of risk: as a structural and exogenous challenge that puts pressure on welfare states and individuals to change, develop new risk strategies and deal with emerging social and economic problems. The above-mentioned distinction between 'old' and 'new' social risks constitutes a key heuristic device in this research field.

Old social risks are built around a conceptualization of the welfare state as a post-war product. Bonoli argues (2007: 495) that most post-war Western welfare states were built with one key objective:

> to protect wage earners from the social risks associated with the then dominant patterns of employment and family structures. Above all, post-war welfare states were about reducing the dependency of wage earners and their families on the vagaries of markets. The social risks that were on the table were primarily caused by capitalism, the labour market and the forms of production of that time.

The modern welfare state developed alongside these challenges and developed systems of income protection, welfare services and support systems for needy groups.

New social risks are seen as the outcome of contemporary societal transformation processes. It is a widely held view within welfare state research that globalization, increasing international competition and new forms of production are putting pressure on existing welfare models and, above all, on the possibilities for countries to promote labour market participation and a stable basis for public revenues. This new set of challenges also includes increasing individualization and greater expectations for the section of the population involved to be recognized as prudent and informed consumers of welfare services. It is furthermore acknowledged that deindustrialization trends have profoundly changed the opportunities for large sections of the population to enter the regular labour market. This not only includes a decline in the industrial sector and a rise of the service sector: what previously looked like a stable career path is now much more insecure, and even a full-time job might not ensure a decent standard of living. While old social risks were mainly concentrated on 'loss of earnings capacity due to old age, unemployment, sickness and invalidity' (Huber and Stephens, 2007: 143), the new social risks are more complex (Bonoli, 2007). Discussions on marginalization and exclusion illustrate barriers to entering the labour market and note that large sections of the population are pessimistic about their prospects of entering it at all. Standing's (2011) discussion about an emerging precariat takes the debate even further, arguing that labour market exclusion is no longer a risk for certain groups, it is in fact a permanent status. At the same time, debates on destandardization, flexible working patterns, temporary jobs and atypical forms of work suggest that social risks are also being faced by those inside the labour market. The literature also pays extensive attention to the entry of women into the labour market and changing family structures. The increase in female employment, changing family structures and greater numbers of one-parent households are not a risk in themselves, but tend to increase vulnerability. Such changes give rise to a new set of social risks that relate even more to the problems of reconciling work and family life as childcare is increasingly externalized outside family structures (Bonoli, 2005).

These examples suggest that new social risks are post-industrial by definition, and that these are new in the respect that an era of full employment and continued economic growth seems unlikely. Furthermore these risks tend to be less well served by post-war welfare states as these focused their efforts on 'core workers with stable employment and uninterrupted careers … the preservation of the income of the male-breadwinner' (Bonoli, 2006: 8).

Social risks beyond the realm of the welfare state

The societal challenges caused by present climate change challenge us, however, to conceptualize social risks in a manner that goes beyond the work–welfare nexus and the post-industrial welfare state. Discussions on climate change and other sustainability challenges raise questions about whether the social risks associated with the post-industrial welfare state are the most pressing, or whether a different set of risks will be of greater importance and have direct and/or indirect effects on established forms of social risks. Climate change is often portrayed as the ultimate ecological problem that confronts modern societies with new challenges, which could generate a different and broader set of social risks. Anticipation of intensified climatic changes demands vigorous policy responses and efforts to avoid 'dangerous anthropogenic interference with the climate system' (UNFCCC, 1992: Art. 2) by means of transforming and decarbonizing societal structures and social practices. Climate change may thus constitute a major challenge for welfare arrangements that goes well beyond the kind of issues often addressed in social risks literature.

Titmuss's (1976) original essay on 'War and Social Policy' provides an opportunity to explore the link between climate change – as a challenge of paramount nature – and its 'effect' on social policy solutions. The essay proposes that war not only causes human suffering, poverty and death, but also promotes and requires a different set of actions taken by governments about how to deal with the risks faced by the population. Unlike 'normal' challenges, a war is an abnormal situation that can change previous established categories of who is affected and who makes a contribution. Titmuss considered war and, above all, the Second World War, as a social transformer that had a tremendous effect on the entire society and on social policy arrangements. Needs, previously considered as either irrelevant or a matter for private concerns, became redefined as a matter for the common good. Established boundaries between 'deserving' and 'undeserving' groups became blurred, since the Second World War affected most of the population, directly or indirectly.

Furthermore he was of the opinion that the Second World War changed the social and moral fabric of society as it required greater solidarity, but also social discipline, and challenged existing patterns of inequality. The war as an abnormal situation constituted the grounds for particular forms of social risks, which followed a certain temporal logic as 'modern war casts its shadows long before it happens and ... its social effects are felt for longer and longer periods after the armed conflict has ceased' (Titmuss, 1976: 78), as well as a specific group logic since the effects of war stretched far beyond those who were directly affected and had both direct and indirect effects.

While there are obviously many differences between a global war and the challenges of climate change, there are also interesting similarities. They contain elements that are – potentially at least – extremely paramount and require the comprehensive reorganization of society. Like acts of war, there is no dispute that current climate change is mainly anthropogenic. However, the risks of climate change become more and more evident over an extended period of time and will most likely spread across different parts of the world in unforeseen and unexpected ways. While nobody knows exactly how such a transformation will unfold, it will most likely affect all parts of society, in direct and indirect ways, and will follow a temporal logic that will continue over several generations.

In their analysis of the nature of social risks caused by severe climate change, Gough *et al.* (2008) propose that, while older social risks were largely clearly visible, with an obvious section of the population being affected, the consequences and social risks that emerge out of climate change are far less observable, are much more complex and have a much more ambiguous effect on 'the population'. In line with Titmuss, the types of social risks emerging are more diffuse, have a longer time span and are much more indirect. As a result, the social risks that emerge out of climate change will most likely challenge present institutional welfare arrangements since these are nationally bound and built upon social risks that are associated with the work–welfare nexus (see also Schaffrin, 2014). Moreover, the social risks caused by climate change will most likely raise new types of distributional issues between different sections of the population and also between different regions as well as including developing and developed countries, albeit in different ways (Gough and Meadowcroft, 2011).

This reasoning supports the argument that a new generation of social risks is emerging, yet Titmuss's essay also contained an argument that the Second World War paved the way for innovative policy solutions and new institutional arrangements. It not only created a different type of social risk, but also constituted a different social fabric and a new basic solidarity, in terms of a need and willingness among policymakers and the greater public to develop more universal social policy measures: that is, measures that targeted the entire population in a similar way, irrespective of background, based on the premise that *all were affected and all contributed*. It appears that Titmuss's argument has some relevance for the development of social welfare arrangements. The development of many central social security benefits began in the aftermath of the Second World War, for example, soldiers' pensions, financial support systems for widows and orphans, rehabilitation and medical and health services. These are all results of the ways in which the war affected social policy arrangements. Whether welfare state expansion was a direct consequence of the Second World War can, however, be debated, but it is beyond doubt that many European welfare states started to develop more inclusive, extensive and even universal social policy arrangements (e.g. healthcare services and social protection systems) in the years after the Second World War.

While Titmuss was fairly optimistic about the extent to which the effects and risks of war could be governed and was even more so about the solidarity it caused (which one, of course, could question since conflicts also give rise to inequalities), this is less evident among scholars discussing climate change. As Levin *et al.* (2012) argue, climate change constitutes a new kind of global ecological problem that could be seen as 'super wicked' by its very nature. In 1973 Rittel and Webber had already conceptualized many societal problems as 'wicked' and too ambiguous to be resolved by rational planning and public policy responses. For Levin *et al.* (2012), climate change is a super wicked problem since it comprises four additional features: 'time is running out; those who cause the problem also seek to provide a solution; the central authority needed to address them is weak or non-existent; and irrational discounting occurs that pushes responses into the future' (Levin *et al.*, 2012: 124). While their conceptualization directs attention to the diffuse, ambiguous and indirect causes and to the complex social relationships associated with such an inherently global ecological challenge, it also forms a basis for immediate and effective policy responses to the risks caused by climate change and for progressive action that, over time, might trigger transformative social change.

Arguably, climate change and the challenge of decarbonization is prompting institutional capacity-building, which will have consequences beyond the issue of climate change itself (see, for example, Gough and Meadowcroft, 2011; Hildingsson and Khan, 2015). The institutionalization of environmental governance arrangements has already advanced the welfare state's capacity to regulate and mitigate environmental change and has contributed to addressing ecological intervention as an essential objective for public power to the extent that it is 'publicly recognized as a fundamental part of what a civilized state should do' (Meadowcroft, 2012: 67; see also Duit, 2016). Environmental politics scholars have conceptualized such efforts as attempts to green society and the welfare state, and have tried to understand the capacity for developing appropriate responses to environmental change and for enabling processes of transformative social change. As a result, Meadowcroft (2005, 2012) makes an explicit link between the welfare state and the environmental state. He sees the evolutions in environmental regulation, management and policy – ever since the dawn of the modern environmental debate in the 1960s – as a gradual process that has contributed to establishing a de facto environmental state within the realm of the modern welfare state. Some view these evolutions as having made environmental policy an integrated part of contemporary welfare policy (e.g. Wurzel, 2012), while others emphasize the commonalities with social welfare policy development (e.g. Gough and Meadowcroft, 2011; Fitzpatrick and Cahill, 2002). Some scholars have also started to explore the potential for integrated policy responses that address ecological challenges and welfare issues simultaneously (see, for example, Fitzpatrick, 2011; Gough, 2013; Koch and Fritz, 2014).

Such eco-social policies are promising but need to be studied further both in terms of theoretical conceptualization and empirical research on actual policy responses (see Chapters 5, 7 and 8 in this volume) and on the kind of solidarity needed in order to develop such policy responses. Nevertheless, while social insurance regimes once developed in response to 'old' social risks and became established in the advanced welfare states, we would argue that there is a need for eco-social insurance regimes to be developed in response to the risks caused by climate change and other sustainability challenges. We return to this question in the final section of this chapter but will first examine in more detail the relations between climate change and social risks.

Climate change impacts and social risks

The IPCC was founded in 1988 and has since worked to synthesize and communicate the current state of scientific knowledge on climate change. In November 2104, the IPCC released its fifth assessment report consisting of three working group reports assessing the literature on the physical science basis (WGI), on impacts, adaptation and vulnerability (WGII) and on mitigation efforts and options (WGIII). WGII looks at how the changes in the global climate system are having impacts on human and natural systems and what adaptation measures can be taken to deal with these impacts. The concept of risk is central and there is a strong focus on how risks are distributed, how they can be managed and reduced, and what capabilities are needed to do so. The concept of *social risks*, as discussed in welfare literature, is not mentioned explicitly. Instead the IPCC talks about the societal risks of climate change, for example in the introductory chapter of the 2014 report, which states: 'identify a larger range of potential climate change impacts and *the risks they pose to society*' (IPCC, 2014a: 179, emphasis added). The report adopts a wide definition of societal/social risks, including risks that affect individuals, households, communities and economic sectors. The main societal risks identified and discussed include food security, human health, human security, migration and poverty. The report also introduces associated concepts such as vulnerability and resilience, which relate to the capability for dealing with risks. Vulnerability is defined as 'the propensity or predisposition to be adversely affected' (IPCC, 2014a: 179), while resilience describes the ability to respond to disturbances through processes of learning and adaptation.

The report demonstrates that climate change is already affecting societal risks, although it is seldom the main driver of these risks. In the short run, climate change mainly works as an aggravator of existing social risks such as health risks, poverty, inequality and human security. For example, the report concludes that today climate change-related health risks are relatively small compared with other stressors on health and, thus, climate change in the coming decades will act mainly by exacerbating health problems that already exist (IPCC, 2014a: 713). Individuals and communities who already suffer from these problems face the risk of a worsening of their situation as a result of climate-induced effects. For example, health losses due to climate change-induced undernutrition will occur mainly in areas that are already food insecure (IPCC, 2014a: 713). Climate change-related extreme weather effects are increasingly causing forced displacement and migration, mainly from rural to urban regions, and migrants tend to be more exposed to climate change effects (e.g. landslides, exposure to flooding, storms) in their new settlements, compared to permanent residents (IPCC, 2014a: 768).

However, in the long run, and especially in a situation with limited climate mitigation and increased global warming, climate change can become a main driver of social risks, with severe effects on health, livelihood and poverty. Health risks include increased risks of injury, disease and death resulting from more intense and frequent heatwaves and fires, increased risk of undernutrition from diminished food production and increased risks of food- and waterborne diseases and vector-borne diseases (IPCC, 2014a: 713). There is an increased risk of people being permanently displaced due to rising sea levels. Studies have shown that sea level rises by 2100 of 0.5 metres would displace 72 million people, while rises of 2.0 metres would displace 187 million people, mainly in Asia (Nicholls *et al.*, 2011; IPCC, 2014a: 770). This risk is, however, closely connected to adaptation policies, and the number of people displaced could be radically reduced (to less than 0.5 million with a 2-metre rise) if adaptation measures, such as protective dikes, were undertaken on all coastlines.

The social risks of climate change mainly affect less developed countries and the poor people and vulnerable communities in these countries. The main reason for this outcome is limited resources and capability for dealing with the extra stress resulting from climate change, but also, to some extent, because poorer countries tend to be situated in regions that are being harder hit by the impacts of climate change (higher temperatures, less rainfall, more severe storms). Additionally, poor countries need to use more of their national budgets on climate adaptation, leaving less room for public expenditure on social welfare such as education and healthcare. In a study by the Overseas Development Institute of three African countries (Ethiopia, Tanzania, Uganda), it is demonstrated that public expenditure on climate change (mostly adaptation) constitutes a considerable segment of the national budget and is comparable to their spending on education and healthcare (see Bird, 2014).

Although poorer countries are more affected, climate change impacts will also influence social risks in developed countries. Some developed countries are already experiencing the consequences of climate change and will face considerable impacts in the future. In Australia, heatwaves, droughts and fires are causing major social problems, and these are expected to increase over the coming decades (IPCC, 2014b: 1374–1376). Consequently, adaptation planning is starting to be embedded into institutions and decision-making, for example, through the establishment of institutional arrangements for addressing the over-allocation of water resources and for strengthened management of bushfire and flood risk (IPCC, 2014b: 1380).

In Europe the main social effects of climate change relate to more frequent and intense heatwaves, flooding from rising sea levels and increased rainfall. In general, adaptation capacity is high in Europe and the social risks from climate change are less pronounced (IPCC, 2014b: 1273). However, there are differences in both impacts and adaptive capacity between subregions, mainly between southern and northern Europe. Climate change will also have more negative impacts on economic activity in southern Europe (tourism, agri-culture), which can increase the disparity between subregions in Europe (IPCC, 2014a: 1301). Vulnerable groups are more likely to be affected by cli-mate change impacts, for example poor households that are displaced by flooding and elderly people who are more vulnerable to the effects of heatwaves.

Based on the above reasoning, what implications can we draw regarding the relations between climate change impacts, social risks and welfare arrangements? First, it is clear that the types of social risks related to climate change impacts are very different from those associated with industrial and post-industrial welfare states in the West. Climate change affects natural systems (increasing temperature, changes in rainfall, more frequent extreme weather events, etc.), which in turn has an effect on societies and may translate into social risks (spread of diseases, heat shocks, loss of agricultural land, poverty, etc.). None of these risks are new. In most developed welfare states, they have been addressed, with varying success, through universal healthcare, distributional policies and poverty assistance, for example. However, in a time of a general crisis of the welfare state, climate change can place additional stress on these systems (Fitzpatrick, 2014). In developing countries these risks are still major challenges that are further exacerbated by climate change.

Second, there is a strong distributive and geographical dimension to the social risks caused or exacerbated by climate change. Countries, communities and individuals that are already poor and vulnerable are harder hit, while more developed countries have better capacity and resources for dealing with the risks of climate change. A crucial question is, therefore, which welfare arrangements are appropriate for dealing with the social risks triggered by climate change. Today, welfare provision is predominantly organized around the nation state. The new generation of social risks associated with individualization and globalization has proved a major challenge to state-based welfare systems. Climate change additionally challenges the credibility of state-based welfare arrangements since it leads to a situation of high institutional capacity, where the needs are lower, and low capacity, where the needs are the highest. From an equity perspective, that is questionable as the drivers of climate change come from global emissions that historically are mainly attributed to the Global North.

Third, institutional and individual capacity and resilience is a main factor in explaining whether the impacts of climate change also translate into social risks. Following on from this, and apart from dedicated adaptation measures, the main way of dealing with the social risks posed by climate change is to increase the adaptive capacity of individuals and institutions. The creation of functional welfare systems in developing countries is therefore a major goal for dealing with the negative social effects linked to climate change. Likewise, the erosion of existing welfare systems, in combination with increasing climate change impacts, could reinforce a negative link between climate change and social risks, even in developed countries.

Finally, it is clear that the social risks of climate change will be much more serious if global warming exceeds 2°C and approaches 4°C. Thus, climate change mitigation is vital in order to reduce the effects of climate change. However, mitigation policy might also have impacts on social risks, and we will turn to this issue in the next section.

Climate change policy and social risks

The societal challenges (or risks) posed by climate change is what motivates prompt and forceful climate action to avoid even greater impacts from unmitigated climate change. The essential policy objective is to mitigate climate change by reducing carbon emissions and decarbonizing energy-related societal systems and social structures, as well as by adapting to the unavoidable climatic changes that are already occurring. As stated by the IPCC WGIII, which reviews the current state-of-the-art research regarding mitigation policies and measures, 'limiting the effects of climate change is necessary to achieve sustainable development' (IPCC, 2014c: 4). However, the policy interventions required for climate change mitigation could also generate or aggravate social risks. As expressed by the IPCC, 'some mitigation efforts could undermine action on the right to promote sustainable development, and on the achievement of poverty eradication and equity' (IPCC, 2014c: 4). As is the case for any public policy efforts to address wicked problems, climate policy measures and mechanisms give rise to unintended consequences and indirect side effects, which might reinforce structures of inequality as well as generate and intensify social risks. This is, in part, related to the costs of climate action (e.g. low carbon technological investment) and in part to the capacity for addressing climate change mitigation and adaptation. The distributive impacts of policy efforts are to a large extent case- and site-specific since the costs and benefits are unevenly distributed across nations, regions, societies and social groups (see, for example, IPCC, 2014c: 472). This is also related to the specific design of policy mechanisms and to the effects of climate policy on other societal objectives and vice versa. In their contribution to the fifth assessment report, the IPCC WGIII thus argues for integrated approaches and a multi-objective perspective to design robust climate policy measures, while addressing issues of equity, justice and fairness as part of strategies for developing effective climate governance responses.

When it comes to policy-induced impacts and risks, the picture is rather mixed. First of all, climate change policies are associated with both positive and negative side effects that could be both beneficial and problematic from a social risk perspective. 'To the extent these mitigation side-effects are positive, they can be deemed "co-benefits"; if adverse, they imply "risks" with respect to the other non-climate objectives' as stated by the IPCC (2014c: 468). For instance, mitigation might generate co-benefits in terms of enhancing energy security and reducing air pollutants as well as improving associated health indicators substantially (IPCC, 2014c: 473). Such co-benefits are often important drivers for mitigation policies in rapidly industrializing countries (see, for example, Bailey and Compston, 2012). But, in other instances, policy interventions designed to reduce carbon emissions might have adverse side effects. Particularly salient issues regarding the effects emphasized in the literature are related to the social costs of mitigation policy and to investments in low carbon technologies, for which both economic costs and benefits are highly uncertain (IPCC, 2014c: 478).

Regarding the cost-related consequences of regulatory and market-based policy mechanisms, for instance, it is often argued that taxation has regressive effects on the distribution of income. Policy-induced investments and measures could lead to increasing energy costs for end users, which for the low-income strata of the population is challenging, especially for those already exposed to pressures related to energy poverty. Although lower-income groups use less energy than higher-income groups, on average, energy costs amount to a larger share of their income. However, in their review of current research on this topic, the IPCC reports that energy taxes do not always have regressive impacts as there are 'large variations in distributional impacts both within and between social groups (and) the effects range from regressive to progressive' (IPCC 2014c: 1161). On the contrary, studies demonstrate that fuel taxes are neutral or weakly regressive in developed countries, while being generally progressive in developing countries (see, for example, Sterner, 2012; Sterner and Coria, 2012) such as in India, Indonesia, China and many African countries. In the case of other taxes (e.g. kerosene, electricity or coal) regressivity can be a more serious problem and the distributional incidence largely depends on the specific design as well as on the ways in which revenues from taxes and fees are used. According to the double dividend hypothesis, such revenues could be used to reduce other distortionary taxes (e.g. income taxes) and thus improve the overall efficiency of the tax system (see IPCC, 2014c: 234). As a result, the IPCC concludes that '(c)arbon taxation can sometimes have regressive effects prior to recycling revenue, but recycling can make the poorest households better off' (IPCC, 2014c: 1162). The extent to which that is achieved is reliant on the method of revenue recycling, the progressivity of which is an essentially political and, thus, malleable, task for policymakers.

Climate change policy is also, to a large extent, geared towards transforming the generation and use of energy, in particular by promoting investment in renewable energies and other low carbon technologies. Such investments are labour intensive and, on average, expected to contribute to job creation. But, in a shorter-term perspective, this might lead to job losses in some industrial sectors and thus be challenging for certain sections of the workforce who will be exposed to job insecurity and unemployment during a transition period. This might be particularly challenging in regions highly dependent on sectors affected by more radical climate change policy efforts, for example, coal extraction, petrochemicals and other energy-intensive industries. However, the IPCC does not report any conclusive evidence of employment impacts for such sectors, nor for industrial relocation (i.e. 'carbon leakage') with regard to climate policy incentives. Rather, they emphasize subsidies for fossil fuel energy carriers, which are substantial and prevent the penetration of low carbon energies. The removal of such subsidies could result in significant emission reductions, with negative social costs (IPCC, 2014c: 1161), but could also have distributional impacts on low-income groups that benefit from lower energy prices. As with the case of taxation, these savings could be recycled for the benefit of poorer groups, which is expected to raise public acceptance for such reforms. For instance, Iran and Indonesia are reported to have successfully managed to reduce such subsidies without much unrest due to fair schemes for revenue recycling via lump-sum cash transfers to the population (IPCC, 2014c: 1162).

When it comes to the relationship between mitigation and adaptation measures, the direct links are few, due to 'the global public good nature of mitigation versus the local benefits from adaptation' (IPCC, 2014c: 1187). However, synergies and trade-offs between mitigation and adaptation policy exist in land use management. For instance, efforts to enhance carbon sequestration could contribute to afforestation, forest conservation and sustainable forestry, while increased bioenergy production could have negative impacts on biodiversity and hydrological systems unless sustainable harvesting methods are applied (IPCC, 2014c: 476). Similarly, in the agricultural sector, agroforestry, soil and water conservation may be beneficial and contribute to sustainable agricultural land management, if managed properly (IPCC, 2014c: 1186).

Overall, a main insight from the IPCC WGIII assessment (2014c) is that climate change policy can have indirect effects on social development and other societal objectives and could, thus, contribute to either ameliorating or exacerbating social pressures and inequalities. The extent to which policy interventions will generate or aggravate social risks depends on the capability for anticipating and dealing with adverse side effects, which, in turn, relies on how specific policies are designed and coordinated with policies in other sectors. A key strategy for this is the policy integration, or 'mainstreaming', of climate change concerns into development planning and of social equity and sustainability concerns into climate change policy. Effective and equitable governance responses to the challenges of climate change are thus seen as integral to the broader agenda for sustainable development, for which the institutional capacity to introduce and pursue well-designed policies and comprehensively assess packages of measures is critical. The IPCC's (2014c) call for integrated approaches is to be seen in this light, as an argument for taking a multiple set of objectives into account in the development of policy pathways towards decarbonized and sustainable futures. However, while providing a broader perspective on the embeddedness of climate change in social systems and dynamics (see, for example, Urry, 2011), their policy assessments are still predominately informed by economic approaches and do not as yet emphasize the potential of eco-social policies for dealing with ecological and social risks in an integrated fashion.

Conclusion

This chapter concludes that there is a need for a new and broader conceptualization of social risks in order to address the eco-social challenges of climate change and climate policy efforts to transform and decarbonize human societies. Whereas previous social risks were embedded in an industrial and post-industrial societal complex, it is beyond doubt that climate change changes the scope and constitution of present and emerging social risks in both direct and indirect ways. The direct effects of climate change and a warmer planet are however unevenly distributed both across and within countries, which raises new issues of equity. In poorer countries, climate change will aggravate existing problems such as poverty, loss of agricultural land and health problems. Yet there is also a connection between climate change and social vulnerability in richer countries, which will increase considerably as more severe climatic impacts become more prevalent. Countries with advanced welfare state arrangements and extensive capacity to cater for the social problems and pressures facing the population are thus expected to face a set of social risks related to climate change, resulting from changes in either their surroundings or processes at global scale.

The indirect effects of climate change policy will be equally evident, as these have indirect effects on social development and other societal objectives and could contribute to either ameliorating or exacerbating social pressures and inequalities. While adaptation measures reduce vulnerability, these might turn out to be significantly costly and at the expense of social welfare services. Similarly, while climate mitigation policies have potential co-benefits (e.g. energy security, cleaner air, health impacts, job creation), the social costs might be unevenly distributed, aggravating existing inequalities or generating new ones. The future for the 'precariat' or the 'working poor' looks gloomy if such indirect effects of climate policy are not considered and compensated for. A remaining research challenge into this field is hence eco-social policy integration, that is, evaluating developmental and social policies against their climatic and ecological impacts, while climate policies are assessed against their social impacts.

A conceptualization of eco-social risks as both reinforcing existing and creating an additional layer of new and more ambiguous social risks that are not easily detectable in either space, time or with a distinct group logic, calls for a more general debate on what are the most plausible policy responses and institutional solutions. While the welfare state rests on the work–welfare nexus, an eco-social welfare state needs to find a different logic for responding to the emerging social risks. It is evident that the separation between social risks and climate risks in policy discourse needs to be overcome, as well as more generally between sustainability and social welfare. At the same time, the immensity of climate change opens up opportunities for institutional innovation and social reform. In line with Titmuss's analogy about the impacts of war on social policy, the climate change challenge creates pressure for a comprehensive transformation of welfare state arrangements and appeals to our shared responsibility for dealing with its effects. If citizens recognize that the effects of climate change are something that will need a different type of social solidarity as *all will be affected and all will need to contribute*, and if policymakers recognize that the challenges causing social risks are not bound to any single country, then only institutional solutions that go beyond the welfare state as a national construct are reasonable.

Hence, an eco-social insurance model that goes beyond both the work–welfare nexus and the nation state needs to be put on the table for scientific and political debate.

References

Adams, R. (1995). *Risk*. London: UCL Press.

Bailey, I. and Compston, H. (2012). *Feeling the Heat: The Politics of Climate Policy in Rapidly Industrializing Countries*. Cheltenham: Palgrave Macmillan.

Bird, N. (2014). *Fair Share: Climate Finance to Vulnerable Countries*. London: Overseas Development Institute.

Bonoli, G. (2005). The politics of the new social policies: Providing coverage against new social risks in mature welfare states. *Policy & Politics*, 33(3), 431–449.

Bonoli, G. (2006). New Social Risks and the Politics of Post-industrial Social Policies. In K. Armingeon and G. Bonli (eds), *The Politics of Post-Industrial Welfare States. Adapting Post-War Social Policies to New Social Risks* (3–26). London: Routledge.

Bonoli, G. (2007). Time matters. Postindustrialization, new social risks, and welfare state adaptation in advanced industrial democracies. *Comparative Political Studies*, 40(5), 495–520.

Duit, A. (2016). The four faces of the environmental state: Environmental governance regimes in 28 countries. *Environmental Politics*, 25(1).

Fitzpatrick, T. (ed.) (2011). *Understanding the Environment and Social Policy*. Bristol: Policy Press.

Fitzpatrick, T. (2014). *Climate Change and Poverty: A New Agenda for Developed Nations*. Bristol: Policy Press.

Fitzpatrick, T. and Cahill, M. (eds) (2002). *Environment and Welfare: Towards a Green Social Policy*. Basingstoke: Palgrave Macmillan.

Gough, I. (2013). Carbon mitigation policies, distributional dilemmas and social policies. *Journal of Social Policy*, 42, 191–213.

Gough, I., Meadowcroft, J., Dryzek, J., Gerhards, J., Lengfeld, H., Markandya, A. and Ortiz, R. (2008). Climate change and social policy. *Journal of European Social Policy*, 18(4), 325–344.

Gough, I. and Meadowcroft, J. (2011). Decarbonizing the Welfare State. In J. S. Dryzek, R. B. Norgaard and D. Schlossberg (eds), *The Oxford Handbook of Climate Change and Society* (490–502). Oxford: Oxford University Press.

Hildingsson, R. and Khan, J. (2015). Towards a Decarbonized Green State? The Politics of Low-carbon Governance in Sweden. In K. Bäckstrand and A. Kronsell (eds), *Rethinking the Green State: Environmental Governance towards Climate and Sustainability Transitions* (156–173). London and New York: Routledge.

Huber, E. and Stephens, J. D. (2007). Combating Old and New Social Risks. In K. Armingeon and G. Bonli (eds), *The Politics of Post-Industrial Welfare States. Adapting Post-War Social Policies to New Social Risks* (143–168). London: Routledge.

IPCC (2013). *Climate Change 2013: The Physical Science Basis. Contribution of Working Group I to the Fifth Assessment Report of the Intergovernmental Panel on Climate Change*. New York and Cambridge: Cambridge University Press.

IPCC (2014a). *Climate Change 2014: Impacts, Adaptation, and Vulnerability. Part A: Global and Sectoral Aspects. Contribution of Working Group II to the Fifth*

Assessment Report of the Intergovernmental Panel on Climate Change. New York and Cambridge: Cambridge University Press.

IPCC (2014b). *Climate Change 2014: Impacts, Adaptation, and Vulnerability. Part B: Regional Aspects. Contribution of Working Group II to the Fifth Assessment Report of the Intergovernmental Panel on Climate Change*. New York and Cambridge: Cambridge University Press.

IPCC (2014c): *Climate Change 2014: Mitigation of Climate Change. Contribution of Working Group III to the Fifth Assessment Report of the Intergovernmental Panel on Climate Change*. New York and Cambridge: Cambridge University Press.

Koch, M. and Fritz, M. (2014). Building the eco-social state: do welfare regimes matter? *Journal of Social Policy*, 43, 679–703.

Levin, K., Cashore, B., Bernstein, S. and Auld, G. (2012). Overcoming the tragedy of super-wicked problems: Constraining our future selves to ameliorate global climate change. *Policy Sciences*, 45(2), 123–152.

Meadowcroft, J. (2005). From Welfare State to Ecostate. In J. Barry and R. Eckersley (eds), *The State and the Global Ecological Crisis* (3–23). Cambridge, MA: MIT Press.

Meadowcroft, J. (2012). Greening the State? In P. Steinberg and S. Van Deveer (eds), *Comparative Environmental Politics: Theory, Practice and Prospects* (63–87). Cambridge and London: MIT Press.

Nicholls, R. J., Marinova, N., Lowe, J. A., Brown, S., Vellinga, P., de Gusmão, D., Hinkel, J. and Tol, R. S. J. (2011). Sea-level rise and its possible impacts given a 'beyond 4°C world' in the twenty-first century. *Philosophical Transactions of the Royal Society A*, 369(1934), 161–181.

Rittel, H. W. J. and Webber, M. M. (1973). Dilemmas in a general theory of planning. *Policy Sciences*, 4, 155–169.

Schaffrin, A. (2014). The New Social Risks and Opportunities of Climate Change. In T. Fitzpatrick (Ed.), *International Handbook on Social Policy and the Environment* (3–61). Cheltenham: Edward Elgar.

Standing, G. (2011). *The Precariat: The New Dangerous Class*. London: Bloomsbury.

Sterner, T. (2012). Distributional effects of taxing transport fuel. *Energy Policy*, 41, 75–83.

Sterner, T. and Coria, J. (2012). *Policy Instruments for Environmental and Natural Resource Management*. Washington, DC: RFF Press.

UNFCCC (1992) *United Nations Framework Convention on Climate Change*, New York: United Nations.

Urry, J. (2011). *Climate Change and Society*. Cambridge, UK: Polity Press.

Taylor-Gooby, P. and Zinn, J. (eds) (2006). *Risk in Social Science*. Oxford: Oxford University Press.

Titmuss, R. M. (1976). *Essays on 'The Welfare State'*. London: George Allen & Unwin.

Wurzel, R. (2012). The Environmental Challenge to Nation States: From Limits to Growth to Ecological Modernisation. In J. Connelly and J. Hayward (eds), *The Withering of the Welfare State: Regression* (137–154). London: Palgrave Macmillan.

7 Market solutions to climate change

Examples of personal carbon-trading and carbon-rationing

Roger Hildingsson and Max Koch

Introduction

Political economists in the tradition of Karl Polanyi (1944) have interpreted the interaction between markets and society in terms of a 'double movement'. The first stage of this movement involved the creation of 'free' markets including the transformation of land, labour and money into 'fictitious' commodities in the nineteenth century. This provoked the twentieth century's countermovement for social and economic democracy and citizenship rights. Markets became embedded in a regulatory web, within which national welfare states played a prominent part. Class-based welfare arrangements gradually defused what came to be termed 'social risks' – especially unemployment, sickness and old age (see Chapter 6). However, as authors such as Harvey (2009) or Stockhammer (2008) have argued, transnationalization and financialization processes have removed major corporations from national control, while the liberalization of financial markets has been accompanied by the development of a range of new commodities including derivatives, hedge funds or private equity that Polanyi could never have dreamt of (Hyman, 2013). The gradual emergence of a transnational finance-driven accumulation regime (Koch, 2012) can therefore be understood in terms of a Polanyian 'counter-countermovement', involving the deliberate unravelling of the regulatory web constructed in the post-war context.

This chapter's point of departure is the observation that a largely disembedded and finance-driven capitalism features disruptive social and ecological consequences and that contemporary policy responses to major threats such as climate change tend to reflect the lines of policymaking that made the deregulation of financial markets possible. Alternatively, we apply a Polanyian 'double movement' approach to the opening up of new societal initiatives that aim to re-embed economic development in the ecological limits of the planet, while simultaneously addressing social risks and inequalities and designing 'eco-social' policies accordingly. Such policies would need to target the fact that responsibilities for and impacts of climate change often do not coincide and thus constitute a 'double injustice' (Walker, 2012; Gough, 2013), since the groups and populations likely to be most harmed by climate change are the least responsible for causing it and have the least resources to cope with the consequences. In this chapter we focus on the extent to which individual carbon-rationing schemes such as Personal Carbon Allowances can be regarded as eco-social policy instruments suitable for not only reducing carbon emissions but also for addressing the double injustice of climate change.

According to neoclassical economists, market solutions are those best suited for dealing with environmental issues such as climate change. This applies to the transnational, national and individual level. In relation to transnational and national levels, there is already a great deal of literature on existing carbon markets, especially on the European Union Emission Trading Scheme (EU ETS). Authors such as Lohmann (2010), Spash (2011), Böhm *et al.* (2012) and Koch (2012) have pointed to the analogy between the economic regulation of finance-driven capitalism and the preference for market solutions such as carbon trading in climate change mitigation policies. The commodification of carbon emissions and the artificial creation of private property rights, as well as emissions trading as the main policy mechanism, emerged as parts of a wider political and economic transformation, in the course of which the idea that market forces and the accompanying (re-)commodification and privatization of public goods are seen as being per se superior to state regulation. And, just as in other historical examples of the 'double movement', the transformation from state regulation to market steering in environmental governance was accompanied by the emergence of new power relationships, interest groups and actors sharing a common interest in the construction, maintenance and expansion of carbon markets (Paterson, 2011), while the question of whether carbon-trading actually contributes anything to climate protection by effectively reducing carbon emissions became a secondary issue. Given these circumstances, it is perhaps not too surprising that empirical evaluations of existing carbon market mechanisms have not provided much cheer. There is as yet no evidence whatsoever that existing regional carbon markets can be re-regulated and expanded to the global level in ways that would make a peak of global carbon emissions a realistic possibility (Koch, 2014).

While there is a great deal of literature on the EU ETS and other carbon market mechanisms at the national and transnational level, this chapter is dedicated to initiatives targeted at individuals and households. We critically discuss personal carbon allowances and their potential as an eco-social policy instrument by referring to their theoretical background, policy intentions and potential effectiveness. Though far more speculative than the EU ETS literature, as a result of the fact that personal carbon allowance schemes do not (as yet) exist in the real world, we raise the issue of the extent to which the anomalies that characterize transnational carbon markets may be reproduced at individual level and whether there are any additional ones. Indeed, the consideration of the experiences with the EU ETS may well facilitate a policy-learning process in relation to potential implementation of personal carbon allowances. We first outline three methods of environmental regulation – direct regulation,

Pigouvian taxation, and market solutions and associated eco-social policies – and then review the literature and preliminary evidence on the feasibility of personal carbon allowances as a climate change mitigation mechanism and an eco-social policy tool. Subsequently, we discuss alternative approaches such as community-based carbon-rationing initiatives.

Environmental regulation and eco-social policies

It is far from obvious that environmental regulation follows the logic of commodification and the creation of markets. Given the extraordinary ideological power of the neoliberal *pensée unique* that significantly facilitates the political preference for carbon-trading approaches, it is useful to remember that there are, in principle, three methods of environmental regulation within capitalist development that can be combined in individual empirical cases. The first method concerns directly *regulative measures*, where the government establishes restrictions on how much pollution a company or an individual is permitted to emit. Exceeding the allowed values of a particular kind of pollution identified by government authorities leads to penalties – ranging from fines for individual companies to the closure of the emitting industrial unit – so that companies and households have an incentive for reviewing their production and consumption methods. The second method is the imposition of *Pigouvian taxes* on the producers of negative external effects. Since negative externalities arising from certain economic activities lead to damages for third parties and to costs for the general public that are not already covered by the private costs of the emitter, this activity is taxed in order to 'correct' the market outcome so that efficiency is achieved and social costs are covered. Following Arthur C. Pigou (1932), governments should use the tax income raised for compensating for damage caused and for financing measures to prevent the causes of this damage. Carbon taxes are an almost ideal-typical example of Pigouvian taxation. Neoclassical environmental economists, however, criticize both direct regulative measures and Pigouvian taxation on the grounds that the government is in control of both procedures and outcomes and that its regulatory bodies intervene in markets by either restricting the quantities produced or by regulating the market price. Though scholars of 'innovation' have provided evidence that such environmental policies may drive innovation and push for industrial renewal and modernization, in line with the Porter hypothesis (Porter and van der Linde, 1995), this is seen as restricting innovation as well as being 'inefficient' in neoclassical economics.

The third method of 'internalizing' external effects therefore gives priority to the market by creating *tradable rights* or *pollution allowances*. Pollution- or emission-trading schemes are essentially an application of the ideas of Ronald Coase (1960: 15), who suggested the construction of specific property rights in order to identify and separate the affecting and affected parties in relation to ecological damage and to calculate the economic costs. Instead of a costly and cumbersome bureaucracy, the private trading of allowances would enable affected parties to decide for themselves if, how and to what extent they should restrict environmentally harmful activities. Through the internalization of previously public external costs, companies (and individuals) would be confronted with the real costs of their actions and change their production and consumption methods accordingly. For Coase, another advantage of the market over command and control regulation and taxation was that policy-makers would no longer need to decide which economic activities were to be regulated or taxed and under what conditions. The market would take care of this through the supply and demand of emissions certificates. Dales (1969), in contrast, gave this task to the government: once the state had defined the total level of emissions for a sector of the economy and a specified time period – the 'cap' – and then issued proportionate emissions allowances – the allocations – these could be traded freely between economic actors. Those who faced the highest cost of emissions reduction would have to be prepared to pay the most for the allowances. Those who had comparatively cheap opportunities for emissions reduction would opt for taking advantage of these rather than purchasing permits. In order to keep allowances scarce, Dales suggested auctioning them.

Supporters of market solutions in environmental regulation admit that the establishment of carbon markets is not cheap at the beginning, since governments have to spend money and devote resources to the definition and enforcement of progressively strict overall caps on emissions. They also have to allocate emission quotas among the industries and individuals under their jurisdiction and set up the legal and measurement machinery for making them tradable (Lohmann, 2011: 95). It is only when private property rights to contaminate the atmosphere exist that specialized platforms for emissions-trading can emerge and become accessible to holders of emissions certificates. Through the implementation of carbon-trading schemes, new business and investment opportunities arise for carbon emissions brokers, traders and bankers including those representing major finance companies and hedge funds. New actors who are becoming involved in the implementation and operation of carbon-trading schemes include market intermediaries, auditing companies, consultants, lawyers and various kinds of researchers (Paterson, 2011). Neoclassical environmental economists and climate governance theorists do not find it problematic that investors are not primarily interested in reducing atmospheric CO_2 concentrations but rather in the financial returns arising from the trading of and speculation with certificates. On the contrary, since the reduction of carbon emissions is expected to be a by-product of merely furthering individual profit interests, emissions-trading schemes are regarded as a welcome new investment opportunity, especially for financial capital.

All environmental and specifically climate policy objectives raise questions about fairness, since they have distributive consequences and hence implications for social justice and social policy (Walker, 2012). Often the responsibilities for and impacts of climate change do not coincide and may thus constitute a 'double injustice' (Gough, 2013), since the groups and populations likely to be most harmed by climate change are the least responsible for causing it and have the least resources to cope with the consequences (Büchs *et al.*, 2011). The arising distributional dilemma has so far largely been studied at global level with focus on the differentiated responsibilities of developing and developed countries. Yet this dilemma also surfaces in European countries. On average, upper-income households contribute more to carbon emissions than lower-income households, due to their higher consumption levels, while poor households suffer most from environmental degradation (e.g. through poorer housing, risk of flooding, etc.), and are disproportionally burdened by the costs of climate policies (Büchs and Schnepf, 2012). The likely social consequences of different climate change policy mechanisms and the corresponding need for countervailing social policies are therefore a key issue (see Chapter 6 in this volume). While the literature on 'eco-social policies' in general (Fitzpatrick, 2011) suggests redistribution policies of work time, income and wealth (see Chapter 9 in this volume) in order to reduce consumption, redistribute working hours more evenly across gender and age groups (see Chapter 8 in this volume) and enable a better balance between paid work, care and voluntary work, it is often argued that personal carbon-trading would have progressive redistributive effects. Some commenters have argued that such schemes would constitute a 'carbon form of the Basic Income idea' (Gough and Meadowcroft, 2011: 499), especially if the returns from the scheme were directly redistributed to individuals and/or households as lump sums (Büchs *et al.*, 2011). Indeed, most personal carbon allowance proposals assume that low-income households gain more or lose less in proportion to their income than do high-income households, since any individual who consumes less than the capped level of emissions stands to gain from the rebate. With emphasis on the likely contribution of personal carbon allowance schemes to tackle the 'double injustice', the next section addresses policy intentions and likely outcomes in more detail.

Personal carbon-trading: policy intentions and potential outcomes

Proponents regard personal carbon-trading as effective in terms of addressing climate change at individual level and socially redistributive since different income groups and lifestyles would be affected in different ways. Such personal carbon allowance schemes have been proposed to 'provide sustained reductions in national energy-related carbon emissions' (Fawcett, 2012: 283) by individuals, that is, from fuel combustion for personal transport and household energy use, while allocating the responsibility to do so on the basis of equal distribution of the right to emit carbon to the atmosphere. Hence, personal carbon allowance-trading schemes would, in one way or another, distribute emission allowances equally among eligible individuals (see Starkey, 2012a). In all schemes, the amount of allowances provided is reduced over time by lowering the cap to reflect emission reduction objectives. In contrast to 'upstream' schemes, in which emission rights are surrendered by fossil fuel energy suppliers and, as in the EU ETS, industrial production facilities, personal carbon allowances would be designed as downstream cap-and-trade schemes in which emission rights are surrendered by energy users.

Personal carbon allowances are nowhere operational and a fully worked-out policy solution does not presently exist.[1] However, personal carbon allowance schemes have been proposed and debated widely in the UK context. The introduction of a personal carbon allowance scheme was in fact considered by the last Labour government on the initiative of the then Environmental Secretary Miliband, who spurred a policy debate about its potential designs and implications beyond research circles. This led to the UK government of the time undertaking a comprehensive assessment of personal carbon allowance proposals in 2008 (Defra, 2008) as did the House of Common's Environmental Audit Committee (EAC, 2008). The Environmental Audit Committee (EAC, 2008: 3) viewed reducing the national carbon footprint as essential, but still requested further evidence and analysis before considering personal carbon allowances 'a viable policy option'. Defra (2008: 4) concluded it to be 'an idea ahead of its time', highlighting concerns that a personal carbon allowance scheme would not be socially acceptable and would be associated with high costs. More particularly, Defra (2008) estimated the costs for setting up a personal carbon allowance scheme to be in the range of £0.7–2 billion with running costs between £1 and £2 million per year. By contrast, upstream schemes were estimated to cost 'only' £50–100 million pounds to set up and £50 million per year in running costs. The report further mentions problems in relation to double-counting emissions already capped under the EU ETS (Fawcett, 2010) as well as practical issues such as deciding who should be regarded as an adult and receive corresponding emission allowances, which could increase administrative burdens and, in turn, the costs of the scheme (Starkey, 2012a). Even though UK governments did not pursue personal carbon allowances as a carbon mitigation measure any further, we will analyse in more detail the two most common policy proposals – personal carbon-trading (PCT) (see Hillman, 1998; Hillman and Fawcett, 2004) and tradable energy quotas (TEQs) or domestic tradable quotas (DTQs) (see Fleming, 1997, 2005).

In a personal carbon-trading scheme, each adult would receive a tradable carbon allowance that covers the carbon emitted from their household energy use and personal transport, including public transport and air travel. Families with children would receive a partial allowance for each child (Fawcett, 2010). This would run in parallel to policies reducing emissions in commercial and public sectors (e.g. the EU ETS and/or carbon taxation) and create a separate market for trading personal carbon allowances. A tradable energy quota scheme would be broader in scope and cover emissions from the whole economy. However, for individuals, a tradable energy quota scheme would be similar to a personal carbon allowance scheme, except that indirect emissions from public transport and air travel emissions would not be included in the personal carbon allowance,[2] and parents are not given extra allowances for their children. Instead they would be compensated via child benefits (Starkey, 2012a). Organizations such as private companies would have to buy energy quotas at the national carbon market or from individuals by means of auctioning and trade.

Still another scheme is cap and share (C&S), first proposed by the Irish non-governmental organization (NGO) Feasta in 2008 (see Starkey, 2012a; Fawcett, 2010). In contrast to personal carbon-trading and tradable energy quotas, emission rights are surrendered by fossil fuel suppliers (i.e. an upstream scheme). Cap and share covers all emissions in an economy and each adult is given an annual certificate of their share of national emissions. The certificates would be held by organizations, not individuals, and are surrendered at equal value to the carbon emissions embodied in goods and services that they provide. Other alternatives include sectoral personal carbon allowance schemes that target, for instance, the transport or residential sector. Other upstream schemes would be the cap and dividend (C&D) proposal, which entails auctioning emissions rights to fuel suppliers, and the tax and dividend approach (see Starkey, 2012a). The latter would be similar to the allocation of auctioning revenues, as in a cap and dividend scheme, to individuals, but would levy a carbon tax instead, in which the revenues collected would be returned to individuals on an equal per capita basis.

A great deal of research on personal carbon allowances has engaged with public attitudes towards and acceptance of such schemes (e.g. Bristow *et al.*, 2010; Jagers *et al.*, 2010; see Starkey, 2012b), aspects that are in turn linked to issues of equity and effectiveness. These studies report varying responses, ranging 'from enthusiasm to dislike', as Fawcett put it. Parag and Fawcett (2014) conclude a recent review by highlighting that personal carbon allowances are usually preferred to carbon taxation. However, such support relies to a large extent upon public attitudes towards taxation in general, which varies substantially across national political contexts. Not surprisingly, Jagers *et al.* (2010) found stronger public support for carbon taxation than for personal carbon allowances in a Swedish survey. Other sources of concern that may affect public acceptance negatively include the complexity and the practicalities of implementation, the risk of fraud, and civil liberty concerns, especially related to the issuing of carbon-trading ID cards (Fawcett, 2010). In addition, many respondents expressed mixed feelings about personal carbon allowances because of equity issues, a key concern associated with design and implementation of personal carbon-trading schemes.

The idea behind all personal carbon allowance schemes is based on the same egalitarian principle of equity as the 'contraction and convergence' (C&C) approach (Meyer, 2000). The latter aims at a global convergence of per capita emissions, that is, everyone has an equal right to emit CO_2. However, as emphasized by Starkey (2012a), the literature provides only limited support to the fairness hypothesis. On the contrary, it is indeed questionable whether equal per capita allocation under some personal carbon allowance designs would actually be fair. As Starkey argues, a fair allocation of emissions rights would have to be *un*equal, considering the differences in people's living conditions as well as in tastes and life choices. For instance, persons living in rural areas, in cold regions, alone or who have children would need to be entitled to consume more energy than others and, thus, should be allocated additional emission rights. Such ways of reasoning seem also to be supported by public attitudes to the allocation method in a personal carbon allowance scheme. For instance, in an online survey, the Institute for Public Policy Research (Bird and Lockwood, 2009: 8) argues that an equal per capita personal carbon allowance allocation 'would be unfair because some people need more carbon credits than others', thus recognizing 'that people in different situations have different needs for energy use'. Hence, though personal carbon allowance schemes could be 'fair', in principle, from a basic needs perspective and in order to fulfil egalitarian principles of equity, what would actually be required is a differentiated allocation of emission rights that are adapted to the needs of various social groups.

Clearly, the intention behind various personal carbon allowance proposals is to impose a climate mitigation mechanism that would be effective in regulating individual carbon emissions and at the same time address the 'double injustice' associated with the distribution of climate change impacts and the costs of climate action. Personal carbon allowance schemes based on equal per capita allocation of allowances are often portrayed as fiscally progressive. A UK government report from 2006 states that:

> 'the poor' emit less carbon dioxide than average … and 'the rich' emit more than average. On average, the rich will therefore need to buy allowances from the poor if they wish to sustain their more carbon-intensive lifestyles. However, there are nevertheless poor households who lose out and some rich households who 'win'.
> (Roberts and Thumim, 2006: 29; based on Dresner and Ekins, 2004)

Later studies confirm this statement. For instance, White *et al.* (2013; see Thumim and White, 2008) demonstrate that a modelled personal carbon allowance scheme for England is, on average, 'progressive' in its distributional impacts across income deciles of the population. However, while a majority of households are expected to benefit from the modelled personal carbon allowance scheme, certain groups would nevertheless lose out, due to large variations within income deciles (Lockwood, 2010). In particular, a personal carbon allowance scheme would have severe implications for already vulnerable groups suffering from fuel poverty (Seyfang *et al.*, 2009), as they lack the finances to invest in more efficient heating systems or energy efficiency improvements. In addition to factors such as occupancy and income that could also apply to rural households, residents in large and old properties, single adults without children and households with elderly residents are also likely to have particular needs that would have to be considered in personal carbon allowance schemes. Such implications are not very different from the distributional impacts of comparable policy options such as the upstream schemes of the cap and share or cap and dividend proposals, which, following

Starkey (2012a), are similar from an equity point of view. In order to deal with such negative distributional effects, the personal carbon allowance allocation therefore would need to be moderated; yet this would, however, raise the administrative costs and hamper the carbon efficiency of the scheme. Compared to climate policy options such as taxation, the scheme would neither generate revenues that could be recycled as lump sums or as social benefits for such purposes as compensating the 'fuel poor'.

Finally, if a personal carbon allowance scheme is to function as an ecosocial policy instrument, this would require making it not only fair and efficient but also effective in terms of reducing carbon emissions. However, this is far from certain, and most assessments have hesitated to recommend its implementation (see, for example, Starkey, 2012b). Considering the variety in implications for different household types, it is doubtful whether the universal incentives of personal carbon allowance schemes would be sufficiently effective in terms of achieving far-reaching cuts in carbon emissions and in reducing individuals' dependence on fossil fuel energy use. Even if it were possible to design strict caps and adapted allocation methods, the legitimacy of such a radical policy could be difficult to uphold, given the uncertainty regarding its public acceptance, let alone the political opposition towards any attempt for public rationing (see, for example, Corner, 2012). Proponents have therefore continued to argue for personal carbon allowances to be conceptualized, not as a purely economic instrument, but as 'a policy which operates primarily through a number of psychological and social mechanisms' (Fawcett, 2010: 6874) in order to improve the visibility of carbon emissions for individual citizens. This raises the question about alternative approaches for addressing individual climate action, including options that do not reflect the same kind of market logic as personal carbon-trading (Randalls, 2011; Paterson and Stripple, 2010).

Alternative approaches: the 'Cragger' experience

There are a number of alternatives to personal carbon allowance approaches that likewise address climate change and aim at reducing carbon emissions at the individual/household level like carbon-offsetting, carbon-dieting and carbon-rationing (Paterson and Stripple, 2010). For the argument in this chapter, the third option is particularly interesting as it relies on a collective rationality (what do *we* do about climate change?) in contrast to the individualistic logic behind carbon-dieting (what do *you* do?) and the commodification logic implied by carbon-offsetting and personal carbon-trading. Carbon-rationing (or reduction) action groups were also personal by the contraction and convergence approach and experimented with carbon calculative means of carbon footprints and measures for reducing these (Paterson and Stripple, 2010; Hoffmann, 2011; Howell, 2012; Hielscher, 2013). However, in contrast to the commodification logic of the personal carbon allowance approach, it aimed to bring together people who voluntarily and jointly agreed to decrease their carbon footprint by engaging in community energy-saving groups.

Carbon Rationing Action Groups (CRAGs) first started in the UK in 2006 and spread to Australia, Canada and the US. The CRAG model was initiated by Andy Ross, an energetic and innovative environmentalist who became instrumental in setting up CRAGs across the UK and in organizing the British CRAG network. In the mid-2000s, he started the first CRAGs, together with other citizens who were concerned about their high carbon footprints. In the CRAG guide, developed by Ross in 2006, it was envisaged that CRAGs would agree to annual equal per capita rations of carbon emissions for their members, coordinate carbon calculative practices for individual carbon foot-prints on a regular basis and share experiences of measures for reducing carbon emissions related to household energy use and personal travel (Howell, 2012; Paterson and Stripple, 2010). Originally there were also plans for introducing financial penalties for individuals whose carbon emissions exceeded the agreed annual ration. 'Over-emitters' would pay this price into a carbon fund whose distribution would be collectively decided by the group (e.g. give the equivalent to 'under-emitters', to charity or other environmental projects). In practice, however, few CRAGs implemented these penalties and in the end most opposed trade in excess emissions (Howell, 2012).

The key difference between personal carbon allowances and CRAGs is the community-based logic of CRAGs as compared to the economic rationality of personal carbon allowances. As the latter rests on a regulatory, market-based approach for imposing restrictions on individual behaviour, they 'remain colle-ctivistic, but lose their voluntary character and thus the way that the inter-subjective character of CRAGs builds on the normative identities of the participants and enables individuals to learn from and with others' (Paterson and Stripple, 2010: 358). Indeed, the main benefit of the CRAGs is the collective learning taking place among the Craggers, of which trust and reciprocity are key elements. Howell (2012) has demonstrated that CRAGs in the UK to a large extent attracted participants with egalitarian and pro-environmental attitudes wishing to improve their carbon literacy and to learn more about their carbon footprint and what they could do to reduce it. Although this facilitated trust among the members, she identifies some critical learning effects and reports how Craggers, on average, reduced their carbon emissions by as much as a third or more, thus showcasing ways of reducing individual carbon footprints.

For his part, Hielscher points to a key challenge for the CRAGs: the longevity of such civil society and community-based initiatives. The British Cragger net-work peaked in 2009 at around 25 groups and, according to Hielscher (2013), started to lose momentum in 2010. While it did spread to some other countries, it did not result in any broader engagement among the general public. However, corresponding community-based activities aimed at energy-saving and carbon emissions reductions are to be found as part of other civil initiatives, for instance, the Transition Towns movement and local carbon reduction campaigns that promote similar kinds of energy-saving practices. For our purposes, the

Cragger experience is nevertheless relevant, since these activists actually rejected personal carbon-trading (as in a personal carbon allowance scheme) in order not to reproduce and amplify the market logic of carbon commodification and instead developed different types of civil society and community-based climate action that are based on the moral obligation to reduce energy use and carbon footprints. In contrast to personal carbon allowance schemes, such a logic would encourage citizen engagement by 'nurturing a sense of collective responsibility... rather than simply addressing them as sovereign consumers in a carbon market' (Seyfang *et al.*, 2009: 14).

Discussion and conclusion

We agree with the many scholars who have suggested that the introduction of an overall cap, which gradually declines over time until a sustainable level is reached, is an efficient way of reducing carbon emissions (see Chapter 9). Neither do we deny that 'cap-and-dividend policies' could work in the way originally proposed by Dales, that is, provided emission caps are set by the state and based on scientific expertise, permits can be auctioned off to companies and individuals, while the current roads to circumvent this (e.g. through 'offsetting' via the so-called 'flexible mechanisms') are effectively blocked. And we also value the arguments of those scholars who argue for using this cap as the basis for issuing equal annual emissions permits to citizens who can then use or sell on a part of them (as in personal carbon allowance schemes). Though we are, hence, not in principle against any market solutions, we do recognize the extremely short time frame within which climate change mitigation policies must succeed in order to achieve a global peak of absolute mitigation polices (IPCC, 2014) and regard the issue of whether carbon markets will be able to function as efficient policy measures in some distant future as secondary to whether these are likely to do so in the immediate future. In this chapter, we have analysed the extent to which the anomalies that characterize and undermine carbon markets at national and transnational levels also figure at individual and household levels, and whether there are any additional anomalies.

Our conclusion is that both types of anomalies are likely to occur, severely undermining the effectiveness of individual carbon trading and rationing schemes as eco-social policy instruments. In short, any future personal carbon-trading or carbon-rationing scheme would need to deal with the following issues: first, there is not much evidence to substantiate the hope that personal carbon allowances would be fairer and more efficient than Pigouvian climate taxation solutions. A 'fair' allocation of emissions rights would indeed need to be *un*equal due to differences in geographic, social and individual circumstances. Second, the consideration of the diverse and complex circumstances of households in a personal carbon allowance scheme would necessitate a huge, 'bureaucratic' and costly administration not dissimilar to the considerable implementation and administration problems and costs reported in literature on transnational carbon markets. As with the EU ETS, authorities would need to be created to define and enforce progressively strict overall caps on emissions, divide emission quotas among households/individuals under their jurisdiction and set up the legal and measurement machinery for making them tradable. Double-counting of emissions calculated under the EU ETS would likewise need to be excluded. Though calculations for the costs of such an administrative apparatus exist only for the UK, these can reasonably be expected to be significant in other countries too. Third, a further similarity to transnational carbon markets is that, because of this new administrative machinery, new business and investment opportunities would arise for CO_2 brokers, traders, bankers, 'advisors', market intermediaries, auditing companies, consultants, lawyers and various researchers. While supporters of personal carbon allowance schemes do not find it problematic that these actors are not primarily interested in reducing atmospheric CO_2 concentrations but rather in the financial returns arising from the trading of and speculation with certificates, the experience with the EU ETS suggests otherwise. Fourth, and perhaps most significant, avant-gardists who voluntarily agree to reduce their carbon footprints – the 'Craggers' in our sample – oppose the commodification of ever more social issues and the generalization of the market logic to the private sphere and opt instead for voluntary carbon reductions without (state) control. Indeed, just as in other market-based emissions reduction schemes, personal carbon allowance schemes 'are tied up in a calculative, managerial approach to the environment' (Randalls, 2011) and are, to a significant extent, 'a logical extension of the premise of neoliberal climate governance' (Paterson and Stripple, 2010: 358). We share the Craggers' concern that the introduction of a personal carbon allowance scheme could well reinforce the deceptive appearance that it is possible to tackle climate change without also contradicting finance-driven capitalism and that this issue can be dealt with within the institutional structure thereof. Resistance and the establishment of alternative ways of working and living would become accordingly more difficult. Like carbon-offsetting schemes, personal carbon allowances could easily turn into a comfortable way of salving the consumers' guilty conscience by maintaining the illusion that climate change can be mitigated without behavioural change.

Since carbon markets of any kind, which we interpreted here as part of the 'counter-countermovement' to the crisis of Western post-war capitalism, are unlikely to result in an absolute reduction in global carbon emissions in the foreseeable future, scholarly attention should be turned to the contradictions and the associated spaces for resistance inherent to the finance-driven accumulation regime (Koch, 2012: 191–193; Ougaard, 2015). Though a 'counter-counter-countermovement' is by no means an automatic outcome, Polanyi can be read in ways that demonstrate that the latest recommodification wave of labour, money and land – and of the atmosphere in particular – could result in a new round of societal resistance and re-embedding that, in effect, could revitalize claims for a socially and ecologically progressive 'double movement'. The parallels in the emergence, expansion and functioning of financial and carbon markets and their structural interlocking suggest that effective climate mitigation policies cannot be enacted without a significant increase in public control over the finance sector. The parallel commodification of – or the development of 'market solutions' for – socio-ecological areas and issues as disparate as finances, water, electricity, health and welfare services, as well as the burning of fossil fuels, suggest supporting movements that aim for the (re)decommodification of these, particularly when these movements fight against fossil fuel extraction and advocate 'national command-and-control emissions reductions strategies plus public works investments and regional/local utility and planning controls' (Bond, 2012: 686). As Soper argues in Chapter 12, the prospects for such movements to succeed are best where state-imposed 'top-down' measures and civil society-imposed 'bottom-up' pressure interact and reinforce each other.

Our conclusion relates to a more general debate in environmental politics about the main rationalities and logics behind responses to environmental change and sustainability challenges such as climate change. In Dryzek's (2013) formulation: whether to rely on governing by the experts, the market or the people. The three kinds of policy strategies towards climate mitigation outlined above would be based at individual level on: the administrative logic of regulating and taxing the behaviour of citizens, consumers and households; the market logic of incentivizing individual actors by commodifying and allocating emission rights to be traded on some kind of market place (as in the personal carbon allowance case); or the deliberative logic of encouraging civil actors to act because of their moral obligation to do so – for instance, by engaging in community groups or, at household level, reducing their carbon footprint and dependence on fossil carbon energy (as with the Craggers' experience). Relying on civil engagement and coalition building among public interests, the latter initiatives may provide pockets of resistance to the neoliberal *doxa* that predominates environmental policymaking, showcase alternative ways of action and mobilize support for a new kind of 'double movement' for a decarbonized world.

Notes

1 The only practical experiment has so far been the voluntary NICHE test at Norfolk Island, Australia, (see Hendry *et al.*, 2013 for an assessment of the public perceptions and attitudes towards it).
2 This is due to issues of complexity in accounting for these indirect emissions.

References

Bird, J. and Lockwood, M. (2009). *Plan B? The Prospects for Personal Carbon Trading*. London: Institute for Public Policy Research (IPPR).

Böhm, S., Ceci Misoczsky, M. and Moog, A. (2012). Greening capitalism? A Marxist critique of carbon markets. *Organization Studies*, 33(11), 1617–1638.

Bond, P. (2012). Emissions trading, new enclosures and eco-social contestation. *Antipode*, 44(3), 684–701.

Bristow, A. L., Wardman, M., Zanni, A. M. and Chintakayala, P. K. (2010). Public acceptability of personal carbon trading and carbon tax. *Ecological Economics*, 69, 1824–1837.

Büchs, M. and Schnepf, S. (2012). Who emits most? Associations between socio-economic factors and UK households' home energy, transport, indirect and total CO2 emissions. *Ecological Economics*, 90, 114–123.

Büchs, M., Bardsley, N. and Duwe, S. (2011). Who bears the brunt? Distributional effects of climate change mitigation policies. *Critical Social Policy*, 31, 285–307.

Coase, R. (1960). The problem of social cost. *Journal of Law and Economics*, 3(1), 1–44.

Corner, A. (2012). Personal carbon allowances – a big idea that never took off. *The Guardian*, 30 April. www.theguardian.com/sustainable-business/personal-carbon-a llowances-budgets (accessed 30. 3. 15).

Dales, J. H. (1969). Land, water and ownership. *Canadian Journal of Economics*, 1(4), 791–804.

Defra (2008). *Synthesis Report on the Findings from Defra's Pre-feasibility Study into Personal Carbon Trading*. London: Department for Environment, Food and Rural Affairs.

Dresner, S. and Ekins, P. (2004). *The Distributional Impacts of Economic Instruments to Limit Greenhouse Gas Emissions from Transport*. London: Policy Studies Institute.

Dryzek, J. (2013). *The Politics of the Earth: Environmental Discourses*, 3. Oxford: Oxford University Press.

Fawcett, T. (2010). Personal carbon trading: A policy ahead of its time? *Energy Policy*, 38, 6868–6876.

Fawcett, T. (2012). Personal carbon trading: Is now the right time? *Carbon Management*, 3(3), 283–291.

Fitzpatrick, T., (ed.) (2011). *Understanding the Environment and Social Policy*. Bristol: Policy Press.

Fleming, D. (1997). *Tradable Quotas: Setting Limits to Carbon Emissions*. Newbury: Elm Farm Research Centre.

Fleming, D. (2005). *Energy and the Common Purpose: Descending the Energy Staircase with Tradable Energy Quotas (TEQs)*. London: The Lean Economy Connection.

Gough, I. (2013). Carbon mitigation policies, distributional dilemmas and social policies. *Journal of Social Policy*, 42(2), 191–213.

Gough, I. and Meadowcroft, J. (2011). Decarbonizing the Welfare State. In J. Dryzek, R. Norgaard, and D. Schlosberg (eds), *The Oxford Handbook of Climate Change and Society* (490–503). Oxford: Oxford University Press.

Harvey, D. (2009). *A Brief History of Neo-liberalism*. Oxford: Oxford University Press.

Hendry, A., Armstrong, B., Smart, W. and Webb, G. (2013). *Influences on Attitudes to a Personal Carbon Trading System*. Proceedings of the 24th Australasian Conference on Information Systems, RMIT University, Melbourne, Australia, 4–6 December 2009.

Hielscher, S. (2013). *Carbon Rationing Action Groups: An Innovation History*. Brighton: University of Sussex.

Hillman, M. (1998). Carbon budget watchers. *Town and Country Planning*, 67(9), 305.

Hillman, M. and Fawcett, T. (2004). *How We Can Save the Planet*. London: Penguin.

Hoffmann, M. J. (2011). *Climate Governance at the Crossroads: Experimenting with a Global Response after Kyoto*. Oxford: Oxford University Press.

Howell, R. A. (2012). Living with a carbon allowance: The experiences of Carbon Rationing Action Groups and implications for policy. *Energy Policy*, 41, 250–258.

Hyman, R. (2013). Preface: Decommodification and After. In M. Koch and M. Fritz (eds), *Non-Standard Employment in Europe. Paradigms, Prevalence and Policy Responses* (xiii–xvii). Basingstoke: Palgrave Macmillan.

Intergovernmental Panel on Climate Change (IPCC). (2014). *Climate Change 2014: Synthesis Report. Summary for Policymakers.* New York and Cambridge: Cambridge University Press.

Jagers, S. C., Löfgren, A. and Stripple, J. (2010). Attitudes to personal carbon allowances: Political trust, fairness and ideology. *Climate Policy*, 10, 410–431.

Koch, M. (2012). *Capitalism and Climate Change: Theoretical Analysis, Historical Development and Policy Responses.* Basingstoke: Palgrave Macmillan.

Koch, M. (2014). Climate change, carbon trading and societal self-defence. *Real-World Economics Review*, 67, 52–66.

Lockwood, M. (2010). The economics of personal carbon trading. *Climate Policy*, 10, 447–461.

Lohmann, L. (2010). Uncertainty markets and carbon markets: Variations on Polanyian themes. *New Political Economy*, 15(2), 225–254.

Lohmann, L. (2011). The endless algebra of climate markets. *Capitalism, Nature, Socialism*, 22(4), 93–116.

Meyer, A. (2000). *Contraction and Convergence: The Global Solution to Climate Change.* Totnes: Green Books.

Ougaard, M. (2015). The reconfiguration of the transnational power bloc in the crisis. *European Journal of International Relations.* Published online before print 26 June 2015, 1354066115589616.

Parag, Y. and Fawcett, T. (2014). Personal carbon trading: A review of research evidence and real-world experience of a radical idea. *Energy and Emissions Control Technologies*, 2, 23–32.

Paterson, M. (2011). Who and what are carbon markets for? Politics and the development of climate policy. *Climate Policy*, 12(1), 82–97.

Paterson, M. and Stripple, J. (2010). My space: Governing individuals' carbon emissions. *Environment and Planning D: Society and Space*, 28, 341–362.

Pigou, A. C. (1932). *The Economics of Welfare.* London: Macmillan.

Polanyi, K. (1944). *The Great Transformation. The Political and Economic Origins of Our Time.* Boston: Beacon Press.

Porter, M. E. and van der Linde, C. (1995). Toward a new concept of the environment–competitiveness relationship. *The Journal of Economic Perspectives*, 9(4), 97–118.

Randalls, S. (2011). Broadening debates on climate change ethics: beyond carbon calculation. *The Geographical Journal*, 177(2), 127–137.

Roberts, S. and Thumim, J. (2006). *A Rough Guide to Individual Carbon Trading: The Ideas, the Issues and the Next Steps.* Report to Defra. London: Department for Environment, Food and Rural Affairs.

Seyfang, G., Lorenzoni, I. and Nye, M. (2009). *Personal Carbon Trading: A Critical Examination of Proposals for the UK, Working Paper 136.* Norwich: Tyndall Centre for Climate Change Research.

Spash, C. (2011). Carbon Trading: A Critique. In J. Dryzek, R. Norgaard and D. Schlosberg (eds), *Oxford Handbook of Climate Change and Society* (550–560). Oxford: Oxford University Press.

Starkey, R. (2012a). Personal carbon trading: A critical survey. Part 1: Equity. *Ecological Economics*, 73, 7–18.

Starkey, R. (2012b). Personal carbon trading: A critical survey. Part 2: Efficiency and effectiveness. *Ecological Economics*, 73, 19–28.

Stockhammer, E. (2008). Some stylized facts on the finance-dominated accumulation regime. *Competition and Change*, 12(2), 184–202.

Thumim, J. and White, V. (2008). *Distributional Impacts of Personal Carbon Trading: A Report to the Department for Environment, Food and Rural Affairs.* London: Defra.

Walker, G. (2012). *Environmental Justice: Concepts, Evidence and Politics.* London: Routledge.

White, V., Thumim, J. and Preston, I. (2013). *Personal Carbon Allowances: Distributional Implications Associated with Personal Travel and Opportunities to Reduce Household Emissions*, Project Paper No. 3. Bristol: Centre for Sustainable Energy.

8 The changing landscape of work time reduction

The past and the future

Oksana Mont

Introduction

Work time reduction (WTR) became a critical and highly disputed issue in the early stages of emerging capitalism when the industrial revolution brought about not only technological advances, but also unprecedented levels of increases in work time. Improved labour productivity led to a hitherto unseen economic output, flooding markets with products and increasing material standards of living. One of the leading economists of the twentieth century, John Maynard Keynes, forecast that we would have a 15-hour work week in 2030, which would be more than sufficient to satisfy our needs. He also expected that any work needing to be done would be shared between as many people as possible. And finally, Keynes anticipated changes in the code of morals when the accumulation of wealth is no longer of high social importance (Keynes, 1930a, 1930b).

How wrong he was. Or how wrong we are. In European countries, the majority of people now work around 40 hours a week, but around 14 per cent of the self-employed in Europe work 48 hours or more every week. Standards of living expressed in terms of the incomes of workers relative to the profits of capital owners are diminishing. Many countries suffer from extremely high levels of unemployment, up to 25 per cent, especially among young people. The effectiveness of policies for work time reduction and work-sharing (where they have been introduced) seems to be rather low, and the results have usually been rather mixed. What went wrong and when? What factors affected the organization of work? What are the potential ways of organizing work in a growth-restrained society? These are the questions that this chapter will address.

The chapter starts with a historical overview of work organization strategies during the nineteenth and early twentieth century. The next section analyses the political and economic factors that affected the work time norms in the second half of the twentieth century, from around 1970 to 2000. Then I examine recent work time reduction and work-sharing policies in several European countries and evaluate their results. The final section discusses work organization in the changing world of low economic growth, decelerating increases in labour productivity and high levels of unemployment. In the conclusion, some critical questions about the role of work in our society are raised.

Historical overview of work organization and work time

Throughout history people have worked different numbers of hours. According to anthropological accounts, hunter-gatherers were able to satisfy their needs, including a sufficient diet, by working about 20 to 35 hours per week (Sahlins, 1972). In the Middle Ages, people worked less than 50 per cent of the year and work days were not as intensive as today (Beder, 2001). The number of official public holidays was 141 (Arendt, 1998: 132). In feudal societies, farmers worked according to the seasons, totalling about 120 to 150 days of work per year (Schor, 1991).

Modern work time ideology became prevalent in the early stages of emerging capitalism. The Industrial Revolution brought not only advances in technology and productivity, but also unprecedented increases in work time. In the seventeenth and eighteenth centuries, for example, early capitalist development in England was associated with both longer and more work days per year (Rule, 1981). In the nineteenth century, a typical working day lasted between 12 and 16 hours, and a work week was 6 to 7 days (Schor, 2005). Indeed, 'Après-moi le déluge! is the watchword of every capitalist and of every capitalist nation. Hence, Capital is reckless of the health or length of life of the labourer, unless under compulsion from society' (Marx, 1967: 257). In the capitalist system 'the determination of what is the working-day, presents itself as a result of a struggle, a struggle between collective capital, i.e., the class of capitalists, and collective labour, i.e., the working-class' (Marx, 1967: 225). Indeed, in many European countries, the second half of the nineteenth century was characterized by the direct struggle between the capitalist classes – that is, the factory owners – and employees, represented by increasingly powerful trade unions. The result was the development of new working hours legislation in many countries, which between 1870 and 1938 led to annual working hours decreasing from a common base of approximately 2,950 hours by 625 hours in Germany and by 720 in the Netherlands and the UK (Maddison, 1987).

Important factors that contributed to the reduction of work time during this period were Taylorism and Fordism, two systems that helped improve production efficiency and increased the specialization of the labour force. Taylorism emerged in the late nineteenth century and peaked from 1910 to 1920. It aimed to improve economic efficiency and labour productivity by scientifically studying engineering and management processes. It accelerated the transition from craft work, with humans as the only agents of production, to mechanization and automation, thereby contributing both to the increasing efficiency of production processes and the replacement of the labour force with machinery and tools (Mullins, 2007). From the perspective of the work force, the Taylorist approach was not the most successful, as it handed over much authority to management, while 'the worker was taken for granted as a cog in the machinery' (Rosen, 1993: 139). On the other hand, it helped create the market, based on economies of scale and on huge production facilities with high functional specialization of equipment as well as division of labour.

Fordism was characterized by a better balance between management (employers) and labour (employees) – the so-called class compromise or contract (Benito and Lucio, 2006). This contract meant that employees and trade unions accepted new production and management methods and, in return, management guaranteed that productivity improvements would result in wage increases for employees, the reduction of work hours and improvement in welfare services (Tolliday and Zeitlin, 1986). The goal of Fordism was to pay workers relatively high wages so that they could afford to purchase the products they were manufacturing. Thus, Fordism was a system that consisted not only of domestic mass production, but also of institutions and policies supporting mass consumption. In terms of work patterns, the Fordist social structure created a standard model of the male breadwinner, according to which male wage earners were provided with permanent work.

The mass production facilities of Taylorism and Fordism were also prerequisites for the improved organization of the European working class who organized themselves into labour unions that became a force to be reckoned with in the power struggles for the rights and welfare of workers. Indeed, since the late 1930s, working hours have been further reduced in many European countries when compared to the USA. Labour unions were also keen supporters of the main goals of the post-war Keynesian welfare state: full employment, income equality and social security.

The brief overview of the history of work time reduction shows that these efforts were vital not only for improving workers' welfare, but also for reconciling productivity gains with full employment: if there had been no work time reduction, then the productivity gains of the past 150 years would have translated into high unemployment. Fordism created a win–win situation for both the capital-owning class and for workers by creating welfare services and distributing profits more equally.

The changing landscape of work

In order to maintain and increase the level of welfare created by the Fordist social structure, and to sustain the wage and profit maximization experienced in the first half of the twentieth century, further labour productivity increases were needed. However, productivity improvements had already started changing in the 1950s, when Fordism was still the prevailing production strategy, but the typical mechanisms for boosting productivity via investments in fixed capital had been exhausted. For example, in Europe, from the 1960s onwards, labour productivity growth fell from 4.8 per cent to 0.7 per cent in the EU-15 (Koch, 2013: 31–32). The growth of gross domestic product (GDP) also followed a similar development in the EU-15 (EU members prior to the enlargement of 1 January 2004): between the 1960s and 2000, GDP fell from 4.8 per cent to 1.2 per cent (Koch, 2013: 31–32). The original Fordist balance between the interests of employers and employees had been tipped towards higher profits for capitalists and lower benefits for workers. Echoing this development, the average decline of work hours in the OECD countries in the period between 1950 and 1980 slowed down to about 18 per cent (Burgoon and Baxandall, 2004). Decreasing GDP growth and labour productivity experienced between the 1960s and 2000 had the result that work time reduction policies became increasingly difficult to implement. Indeed this is reflected in the 7 per cent average decline in work hours in the OECD countries between 1980 and 2000 (Schor, 2005). There is a consensus among scholars that Fordism as a strategy for the organization of production and work, and also as an accumulation regime, came to an end from the 1960 to the 1970s (Stockhammer, 2008). By the early 1970s, a series of forces were at work in the global economy that were calling Fordism into question. Numerous authors have examined what new sources for capitalist growth emerged as well as why and how (Schor and You, 1995). These changes obviously had a profound influence on the organization of work, employment and the distribution of welfare.

One of the important paradigms that replaced the Fordist strategy of organizing production was flexible production, which had become a prevailing mode of organizing production and work and of how people lived and consumed during the second half of the twentieth century. Flexible production is based on such processes as lean manufacturing, just-in-time delivery, total quality management and price-based costing, all of which have implications for the role of workers. While workers were relatively unskilled and highly specialized at carrying out simple, repetitive tasks in Taylorism and Fordism, in the case of flexible production, workers have to be highly skilled to be able to perform every step of the production process to perfection (total quality management), thereby reducing the need for stocks (i.e. just-in-time delivery) of high-quality products. This has led to a drastic reduction in the demand for unskilled labour over the past 30 years, and unskilled labour no longer has its previous prominent position in the labour union movement. As a consequence, we have witnessed, in some cases, a reduction in real wages for unskilled labour. Subsequently a new class of people called the precariat has been emerging, which comprises workers who lack predictability and security in their work life, whose wages are low and whose material and psychological welfare is significantly affected (Standing, 2011). In addition, the growing number of flexible workers in the labour force helps companies to respond to the fluctuations in markets for product and to deliver goods 'just in time'. Although flexibility can mean control over working time and influence over the content and the performance of their jobs, for employees, it can also lead to more unpredictable demands on and expectations of performance, less security and longer working hours (Albertsen *et al.*, 2007). The division of the labour force into those with standard employment contracts and those with non-standard ones – for example, flexible work, fixed-contract working, etc. – makes it more difficult for labour unions to represent the interests of such a diverse group of workers. Usually those with standard employment enjoy better union support and those with non-standard types of employment are often paid considerably less (Koch, 2013), which creates tensions between the two types of employees. At the same time, non-standard work opens up possibilities for participation in the labour market for other types of workers, who had been excluded by the traditional male breadwinner model. The rise of precariat and flexible work is also being ascribed to the entrenchment of neoliberalism, which can be traced in the deregulation of markets, the privatization of publicly owned utilities and services and in the withdrawal of the state from many areas of social provision since the 1970s (Harvey, 2005).

Robotization is another trend that was mentioned by Keynes as early as the 1930s and which has recently come back into the spotlight with new force. A recent report from Deloitte found that up to 35 per cent of UK jobs, especially low-qualified and low-paid jobs, are at risk of being replaced by robots by 2035. The report forecasts that many companies will employ more people with digital expertise in order to manage increasing technological demands (Frey and Osborne, 2014). Indeed, information and communication technology (ICT) has already played an important role both in flexible production and in non-standard employment. It has given rise to new modes of work organization, including mobile work places, project-based work in multidisciplinary teams and the general higher intensity of multitasking at work. So, on the one hand, these more democratic work processes, where employees are engaged in how the work is organized, are positive as they lead to a more equal distribution of knowledge, authority and responsibility. On the other hand, when one looks at the distribution of profits, then financial benefits for workers are less obvious. The increased focus of companies on short-term profits drives them to reduce costs, optimize processes and, as a result, reduce the workforce. Work itself has become more flexible, blurring the boundary between work and leisure time. At the same time, ICT enables new groups of people, for example, the disabled, to join labour markets in more flexible ways. The emerging Internet of Things promises great leaps in productivity by connecting all products, infrastructure, cars, etc. into an intelligent web of smart infrastructure comprising the communications internet, energy internet and logistics internet (Rifkin, 2014). The impact of these developments on employment have been discussed in depth; yet it is hard to foresee what exactly will happen since, while ICT brings in flexibility to work and everyday life, robotization questions the very need for workers at all, especially low-skilled ones.

Globalization is another development of the past 40 years that affects the organization of work and the welfare of workers. It includes increased economic transactions in global supply chains and between nations (Epstein, 2005), a growing global integration of capital, an expansion of international financial flows and dramatic increases in cross-border trade. As Harman comments,

If the typical capitalist firm of the 1940s, 1950s or 1960s was one which played a dominant role in one national economy, at the beginning of the 21st century it was one that operated in a score or more countries – not merely selling outside its home country but producing there as well.

(Harman, 2009: 257)

The globalized market led to the outsourcing of production facilities from Europe to countries with cheaper labour, be it Asia or Eastern Europe and more recently Africa. The availability of a cheaper workforce elsewhere on the globe makes European workers and their labour unions less powerful in negotiations with employers. 'Capital can withdraw from negotiation with a given local population by moving its site to another point in the global network' (Hardt and Negri, 2000: 297). Thus, multinational corporations can play different locations against each other and force labour unions to accept worse conditions than before.

A relatively new phenomenon that affects work time and work organization is financialization: the finance-driven accumulation regime that relies on increasing domestic and international financial transactions. More specifically it comprises a range of understandings, from the deregulation of the financial sector to the proliferation and profitability of new financial instruments and investors, from the rise of 'shareholder value' as a mode of corporate governance to the increasing political and economic power of the rentier class, from investments in the real economy to the growing importance of investments in financial markets (see Chapter 5 in this volume). The consequences of these changes are profound. The liberalization of international financial flows and the deregulation of financial markets lead to increased instability in currency markets (Koch, 2013). At the same time, the profitability and sheer number of different financial instruments, together with a long period of fixed capital amortization, undermines the willingness of companies to invest in the real economy that produces goods and services as opposed to the one that is based on financial services. Not surprisingly, while the volume of financial assets and nominal GDP were approximately of equal size in 1980, by 2006 the size of financial stock was 3.5 times higher (Koch, 2013: 35). This slowdown in productive investment is exacerbated by the shift in focus towards shareholder value and financial short-term profits, which often entails the outsourcing of production facilities to low-labour-cost countries. This increases unemployment, especially of factory workers in European countries, and forces workers to resort to various kinds of non-standard work, undermining their job security and welfare and reducing their income. In the finance-driven accumulation regime, the spending power of domestic wage earners is less critical for the profits of the capital owners than in the Fordist accumulation regime, since products and services are available and sold globally. In addition, the fall in the spending power of domestic wage earners is to some extent compensated by increased access to consumer loans, particularly mortgage loans. Still, it is the relative wage differences between wage earners and capital owners that is the critical indicator here, not the absolute wage levels. In the EU-15, the wage share has gone down from 73 per cent in 1970 to 65.8 per cent in the 2000s (Farrell *et al.*, 2008).

Recent national work time policies

Taking into consideration the aforementioned changes in geopolitical and socio-economic conditions, lets us now examine the policies for work organization and work time that have been implemented in several European countries over recent decades. The reasons for introducing work time reduction policies have changed drastically throughout history, as was indicated in previous sections. While in the nineteenth century work time was reduced in order to preserve the health and strength of the workforce, in the first half of the twentieth century, work time reduction was seen as a strategy for reducing the unemployment that was a result of dramatic increases in productivity (Estevão and Sá, 2008). Over the last 40 years, work time reduction has been discussed as a means of distributing available work more equitably, of reducing unemployment through work-sharing and by enabling non-standard work. Work time reduction was also used in many European countries during the Great Depression of the twentieth century and after the financial crisis of 2008 as a means of dealing with economic downturn (Negrey, 2012; Hermann, 2015). Nowadays, the average working time in many Western economies is between 30 and 40 hours per week, with annual average working hours at around 1,700 hours.

In 1998 the socialist government in France introduced legislation aiming to reduce the unemployment rate by about 12 per cent, to decrease gender inequality and to improve the work/life balance in general. This was to be achieved by reducing the work week from 39 to 35 hours: 'work less – live more' was the slogan (Fagnani and Letablier, 2004). The legislation encountered heavy opposition from business and was supplemented with a range of measures to alleviate cost increases, for example, via social security rebates. During the first five years of the policy about 350,000 new jobs were created, but after seven years the aggregate employment levels remained at approximately the same level. One of the positive outcomes reported in a trade union survey conducted shortly after the introduction of the policy was that 58 per cent of respondents said the policy had had a positive impact on their work/life balance (Perrons *et al.*, 2006). Studies reported differences in the effect of the law between men and women, with women benefiting more from the shorter work week (Fagnani and Letablier, 2004). Overall, the 35-hour week policy reduced unemployment in the short term, while no reduction in unemployment has been registered in the long term. So, while it seems to be a weak employment generation policy, as a means of improving the work/life balance it appears promising as a policy. What this case also demonstrates is the ongoing class struggle between wage earners and representatives of the capital-owning class.

The Netherlands and Belgium have taken a different approach to addressing the issue of unemployment and non-standard work than the French policy presented above. This approach builds on considering the different capacity, possibility and time availability for work that people have in various stages of their lives. This so-called 'life course approach' acknowledges and supports individual rights to flexibly reduce work time during different stages of their lives, often associated with reductions in income (Moen and Sweet, 2004). From the perspective of the policymaker, the benefit of this approach is that work time policies that were once developed separately in different policy areas are now being developed in synergy or are even being addressed by a unified set of policy instruments. The policies of relevance are: unemployment benefits, parental leave and childcare, disability and sickness benefits, work-related training, labour market participation rates and early retirement (Delsen and Smits, 2010). Getting people to actively engage in paid work throughout their lives usually involves three categories of policies being developed: increased time rights for employees to take career breaks and flexible working hours, financial instruments such as tax credits and rights for paid leave and childcare support, including measures to encourage return to paid work (Plantenga and Remery, 2005). This approach supports individualized voluntary changes in work time and is used in addition to collective work time policies.

The Netherlands is the leading country in terms of work time reduction, with average working hours of around 1,400 hours per year. However, much employment in the Netherlands is part-time or flexi-work. The flexible work time policy introduced in 2000 gave part-time employees the same rights as fully employed workers. In 2006 additional policy measures were legislated for – the so-called Life Course Saving Scheme. According to this scheme, employees can take an unpaid career break for up to three years. Employees using the scheme first save up to 12 per cent of their gross annual wage in a Life Course Savings account and then use these savings to finance periods of unpaid leave (Ministry of Social Affairs and Employment, 2011). In 2012 the scheme was closed to new users due to the low participation rate – 3.5 per cent of the total workforce (Pullinger, 2014) – which has been attributed to the difficulties of planning for the savings and the right of employers to deny employees the right to take a career break.

In Belgium a different approach to career breaks – the Time Credit Scheme – has been more successful. Employees can take a one-year full-time career break at any point in their career or work part time for two years or only 20 per cent of the normal work week for five years (Debacker *et al.*, 2004). In addition, employees can take 3-month breaks for childcare, care for the elderly or for medical reasons. During these breaks, employees receive a small but not insignificant flat-rate benefit of about €350 to €500 per month. Unlike the Netherlands, employers cannot refuse career breaks; however, in addition to the flat-rate benefit, employees have to finance the career break themselves. Although the scheme is considered more successful than the Dutch one, it too has limitations. For example, governmental expenditure on the administration of the scheme and on social security benefits is significant.

Employer support for the schemes is rather limited; it is especially problematic for employers to accommodate the model of 80 per cent of the normal work week pattern (Debacker *et al.*, 2004). Another issue highlighted by both schemes is the inequality of access – both schemes have been used mostly by high-income two-earner families who can support a career break for one of the partners (Devisscher and Sanders, 2007). The Belgian scheme has been mostly used by young women, although there is more equal distribution between genders among older employees in Belgium. The life course approach introduced in the Netherlands and in Belgium has no specific targets in terms of work time reduction, but does have goals in terms of flexibility and well-being.

These examples demonstrate that the work time reduction policies of the past three decades became much weaker and shifted focus from work time reduction towards increasing employment flexibility. In order to have a favourable effect on employment, a reduction of work time must be part of a wider set of changes including production patterns and work organization (Anxo, 1998). For work time reduction policies to become more feasible, general attitudes towards work and employment may need to change. It is not uncommon that some workers respond to the reduction of work hours by taking a second job, which undermines the goal of reduced unemployment rates. Schor (2005: 44) interprets this not as an expression of individual preferences for income over leisure time, but rather as evidence of 'a structural bias toward the translation of productivity growth into increased levels of output and income, rather than reductions in working hours'. On the other hand, there is a growing problem of in-work poverty: people cannot support themselves by working only in one place and have to find additional sources of income. Often, work time reduction policies are introduced with compensatory mechanisms that increase hourly rates and wages in order to diminish any negative effects from reduced income when work time is decreased. However, the upward effect on wages negatively affects the possibility of increasing employment in the long run through reducing work hours and sharing work among workers (Kapteyn *et al.*, 2004), although work time reduction policies do have positive direct effects on employment in the short term (Hunt, 1999; Raposo and van Ours, 2010). The work time reduction policies that aimed to increase the flexibility of people when it comes to choosing when and how much to work seem to be more successful, for example in the Netherlands and Belgium.

Working less and living more

So far we have examined effects of national European work time reduction policies on reducing unemployment and increasing flexibility for employees. However, if an absolute reduction of work time was the primary goal of the European work time reduction policies of the past 50 years, then this has failed miserably, as the reductions achieved have been nowhere near Keynes' hopes for a 15-hour week (Keynes, 1930a), or the 21-hour work week advocated by New Economics Foundation (Coote *et al.*, 2010) or even the 30-hour work week advocated by many (Sanne, 2012; Koch and Fritz, 2013). The factors described above such as increasing financialization, globalization and neoliberalism and the diminishing power of the state and the labour unions prevent society from capitalizing on the potential benefits of working less, not only in terms of employment rates, but also in terms of rebalancing paid and unpaid work and leisure time, increasing well-being and reducing environmental impacts. None of the policies examined here were devised to take into consideration the triple goal of employment, the environment and well-being (Pullinger, 2014). Indeed, there is little research exploring the relation between work time reduction and these three parameters together, and even fewer studies that analyse these parameters under conditions of decelerating economic growth. Is it even possible to devise an economic system where work time reduction can lead to an improved employment situation, an increased level of well-being and reduced environmental impacts? And, if yes, under what conditions could such a system sustain itself? In the world of increasing climate change impacts, growing scarcity of resources and ever decreasing capacity of major eco-services, on the one hand, and the decreasing speed of economic growth on the other, these questions deserve special attention.

One of the most advanced economic models in which the three parameters – employment, the environment and well-being – are analysed together while considering different assumptions about economic growth was developed by Peter Viktor (2008). Viktor examined how the Canadian economy could be sustained with a low- or no-growth scenario up to 2035. In addition to analysing economic parameters, Viktor also modelled environmental impacts and social factors, including employment. The 'business as usual' scenario assumed economic growth of 2 to 3 per cent per year and this model resulted in persistent unemployment and increasing environmental impacts. In a 'disaster' scenario, reduced investment and lower productivity were assumed, which led to the almost complete ending of growth, resulting in severe unemployment and growing poverty and governmental debt. In an alternative scenario with a slow increase in productivity, coupled with shorter working hours and an active redistribution policy, the model showed that the economy could still develop with slow income growth, reduced unemployment and public debt. Even though emissions would increase, they could be suppressed by a CO_2 tax. Using Viktor's model, Michael Malmaeus made calculations for the Swedish economy for the period of 2005 to 2035 (Malmaeus, 2011). During this period, economic growth was projected to increase by 170 per cent. Similar to Viktor's modelling exercise, one scenario showed that it was possible to maintain economic stability with a very small growth rate over the 30-year period: GDP would increase by 30 per cent and private consumption by 20 per cent. The critical factor in this scenario was the reduction of work volume by 65 per cent compared to the current level.[1]

One of the important parameters for understanding the dynamics between unemployment and economic growth is labour productivity. Indeed, the relationship between growth, productivity and work has been named as central to a new macroeconomics for sustainability (Jackson and Victor, 2011). A critical question is how to reconcile a low-growth economy with labour productivity changes and full employment. Increases in labour productivity mean that over time fewer workers are needed on the market. If the economy is growing fast enough, it compensates for this, if not, then unemployment inevitably follows. This is the so-called productivity trap. Jackson and Victor (2011) offer two avenues for solving this productivity problem: the first is work-sharing and the second is a reduction in labour productivity per se. Indeed, increases in labour productivity have been diminishing in recent years in most of the European economies. While average annual productivity growth between 1970 and 1995 across the EU-15 was 2.7 per cent, in the period from 1995 to 2005, this was reduced by half (Timmer *et al.*, 2007: 10).

To test the feasibility of combining work-sharing with reduced growth of labour productivity, Jackson and Victor (2011) developed a simulation model of the UK economy that projects growth rates, carbon reduction and shares of the employment market in three sectors: a conventional sector with labour productivity growth (1 per cent p.a.), a green infrastructure sector with labour productivity growth (1 per cent p.a.) and a 'green services' sector with 0.3 per cent p.a. labour productivity growth. The model aims to demonstrate how structural shifts towards the two green sectors could help maintain high employment and simultaneously reduce carbon emissions. Scenario 1 assumes 5 per cent annual growth in the green infrastructure sector, but no growth in the green services sector and no work time reduction. Scenario 2 combines the growth of the green infrastructure sector with a 1.5 per cent annual reduction of work hours across the economy. Scenario 3 includes 1 per cent reduction of work hours per year and a combination of the growth of the green infrastructure sector with a 6 per cent annual expansion of the green services sector. While economic output in scenario 1 is typical for a traditional growth-based model, both scenarios 2 and 3 demonstrate reduction in growth rates in GDP during certain periods. Scenarios 2 and 3 differ considerably in terms of the structure of economic activity. In scenario 2 the work week in 2050 has been reduced to about 20 hours and the service sector has not been well developed, while in scenario 3 work time has been reduced by 30 per cent and the green services sector has rapidly expanded. It is only in scenario 3 that the goal of an 80 per cent reduction in carbon emissions is reached. The model demonstrates that the best results are achieved through a combination of measures, such as work time reduction and a shift towards the service economy, while full employment can be maintained even under conditions of economic degrowth.

Thus, sustaining a growth-restrained economy requires a combination of measures. A critical question is: What measures could help balance low growth and growing unemployment, while preserving welfare? Would existing proposals for policy measures suffice or do we need a radical departure from solutions currently restricted by the neoliberal capitalist rationale? One of the policy measures that have been discussed since the early 1990s as a way of reducing the cost of labour and thereby increasing employment and preserving welfare is environmental tax reform, which reduces taxes on labour and increases taxes on resources and pollution (Patuelli *et al.*, 2005; Pullinger, 2014). Studies indicate that environmental tax reform could lead to a significant reduction in environmental impacts (up to 10 per cent) and a slight increase in employment (about 0.5 per cent), with minor effects on GDP (Bosquet, 2000; Patuelli *et al.*, 2005).

Basic income is another proposal widely discussed among academics, but largely ignored by the media and policy circles. The basic concept is the unconditional allocation of a certain sum of money by the government or a public body to each citizen, regardless of any income that these citizens may receive from elsewhere. Basic income could reduce the socio-economic problems and tensions associated with unemployment and poverty, but does not address the large income disparity that exists in many countries. Some opponents describe basic income as charity (Žižek, 2009), while proponents argue that basic income allocation in a society with high productivity, robotization and digitalization could be a viable way forward, provided that the power structures and the distribution of profits change accordingly (Marcuse, 1964).

Another proposal is the service economy, which builds on high labour-intensive activities instead of low material-intensive ones. Many scholars see this as a potential way of: (1) slowing down the increase in labour productivity, since these activities have low potential for labour productivity increases and (2) shifting consumption from materially intensive and environmentally harmful products to less materially intensive and less environmentally detrimental services, for example selling efficiency services or mobility instead of cars. The service economy already exists in numerous local and communal initiatives, including eco-social enterprises, cooperatives, repair and up-cycling shops, etc. Jackson and Victor (2011: 105) believe that:

> there is a clear opportunity here for a relatively local 'green services sector' in which lower labour productivities and slower productivity growth relieve the pressure on jobs and provide forms of meaningful work that support community and sustain people's livelihoods.

Obviously, in this scenario, other sectors of the economy, for example import and export sectors, would have to maintain high levels of growth in labour productivity in order to stay competitive on the global market.

If states, markets and service solutions cannot create enough jobs in a growth-restrained economy, then productivity improvements will need to be translated into fewer working hours and more leisure time and not into increased volumes of production and higher incomes. In this respect, many scholars call for greater support for different leisure time activities that increase well-being but have low environmental impacts. For example, Pullinger advocates the enhanced provision of serious leisure activities outside paid work, such as 'volunteer work in environmental and social projects, involvement in arts, crafts and cultural projects, and mindfulness training' (Pullinger, 2014: 16). Working less than full time may have other benefits too, such as more time spent on exercise and hobbies, which increase people's subjective well-being and have positive effects on health (Holmberg *et al.*, 2011).

Concluding remarks

Many critical questions still need to be addressed with regard to work organization and work time reduction in growth-restrained economies. The role of the welfare state also needs to be discussed further. As of now, the goal of total employment is at odds with many of the economic and societal trends and realities outlined above. Modern welfare societies revolve around social norms, institutions and political priorities centred on work and employment. The work ethic has evolved from being a religious calling towards a secular responsibility to the nation and is often a prerequisite for success in a modern society. Work has long been held as a virtue and as a social marker. It has provided us with a purpose in life and a structure for our days. However, voices are being heard that question this preoccupation with full employment (Paulsen, 2010) and with the notion that work should make us happy (de Botton, 2010). Perhaps the time has come to revisit Keynes' vision of the need for new moral codes that would normalize new ways of working and living and that could be better suited for the new realities of a growth-constrained world.

Note

1 Environmental impacts were accounted for.

References

Albertsen, K., Kauppinen, K., Grimsmo, A., Sörensen, B. A., Rafnsdóttir, G. L. and Tómasson, K. (2007). *Working Time Arrangements and Social Consequences – What Do We Know?* Copenhagen: Nordiska ministerrådet.

Anxo, D. (1998). *Working Time: Research and Development*. Gothenburg: Centre for European Labour Market Studies.

Arendt, H. (1998). *The Human Condition*. Chicago, IL and London: University of Chicago Press.

Beder, S. (2001). *Selling the Work Ethic: From Puritan Pulpit to Corporate PR*. Melbourne: Scribe.

Benito, L. E. A. and Lucio, M. M. (2006). *Employment Relations in a Changing Society: Assessing the Post-Fordist Paradigm*. New York: Palgrave MacMillan.

Bosquet, B. (2000). Environmental tax reform: Does it work? A survey of the empirical evidence. *Ecological Economics*, 34, 19–32.

Burgoon, B. and Baxandall, P. (2004). Three worlds of working time: Policy and politics in work-time patterns of industrialized countries. *Politics and Society*, 32(December), 439–473.

Coote, A., Simms, A. and Franklin, J. (2010). *21 Hours. Why a Shorter Working Week Can Help Us All To Flourish in the 21st Century*. London: NEF.

de Botton, A. (2010). *The Pleasures and Sorrows of Work*. New York: Pantheon.

Debacker, M., De Lathouwer, L. and Bogaerts, K. (2004). Time credit and leave schemes in the Belgian welfare state. Paper presented at TLM.net conference, Royal Academy of Sciences, Amsterdam, 25–26 November 2004.

Delsen, L. and Smits, J. (2010). Does the life course savings scheme have the potential to improve work–life balance? *British Journal of Industrial Relations*, 48(3), 583–604.

Devisscher, S. and Sanders, D. (2007). Ageing and Life-course Issues: The Case of the Career Break Scheme (Belgium) and the Life-course Regulation (Netherlands). In A. C. D'Addio and P. Whiteford, *Modernising Social Policy for the New Life Course* (117–132). Paris: OECD.

Epstein, G. A. (2005). Introduction: Financialization and the World Economy. In A. Epstein Gerald, *Financialization and the World Economy* (3–16). Cheltenham: Edward Elgar.

Estevão, M. and Sá, F. (2008). The 35-hour workweek in France: Straightjacket or welfare improvement? *Economic Policy*, (July), 418–463.

Fagnani, J. and Letablier, M. T. (2004). Work and family life balance. The impact of the 35-hour laws in France. *Work, Employment & Society*, 18(3), 551–572.

Farrell, D., Fölster, C. S. and Luno, S. (2008). Long-term trends in the global capital markets. *McKinsey Quarterly*, 2 (February), 8.

Frey, C. B. and Osborne, M. A. (2014). *Agiletown: The Relentless March of Technology and London's Response*. London: Deloitte.

Hardt, M. and Negri, A. (2000). *Empire*. Cambridge: Harvard University.

Harman, C. (2009). *Zombie Capitalism: Global Crisis and the Relevance of Marx*. London: Bookmarks.

Harvey, D. (2005). *A Brief History of Neoliberalism*. Oxford: Oxford University Press.

Hermann, C. (2015). *Capitalism and the Political Economy of Work Time*. London and New York: Routledge.

Holmberg, J., Larsson, J., Nässén, J., Svenberg, S. and Andersson, D. (2011). *Low-Carbon Transitions and the Good Life*. Stockholm: Naturvårdsverket.

Hunt, J. (1999). Has work-sharing worked in Germany? *The Quarterly Journal of Economics*, 114(1), 117–148.

Jackson, T. and Victor, P. (2011). Productivity and work in the 'green economy': Some theoretical reflections and empirical tests. *Environmental Innovation and Societal Transitions*, 1(1), 101–108.

Kapteyn, A., Kalwij, A. and Zaidi, A. (2004). The myth of worksharing. *Labour Economics*, 11(3), 293–313.

Keynes, J. M. (1930a). Economic possibilities for our grandchildren I. *The Nation and Athenaeum*, 48(2), 36–37.

Keynes, J. M. (1930b). Economic possibilities for our grandchildren II. *The Nation and Athenaeum*, 48(3), 96–98.

Koch, M. (2013). Employment Standards in Transition: From Fordism to Finance-driven Capitalism. In M. Koch and M. Fritz, *Non-Standard Employment in Europe: Paradigms, Prevalence and Policy Responses* (29–45). Basingstoke: Palgrave Macmillan.

Koch, M. and Fritz, M. (2013). *Non-Standard Employment in Europe: Paradigms, Prevalence and Policy Responses*. Basingstoke: Palgrave Macmillan.

Maddison, A. (1987). Growth and slowdown in advanced capitalist economies: Techniques of quantitative assessment. *Journal of Economic Literature*, 25(2), 649–698.

Malmaeus, M. (2011). *Ekonomi utan tillväxt. Ett svenskt perspektiv.* Stockholm: Cogito.

Marcuse, H. (1964). *One-Dimensional Man: Studies in the Ideology of Advanced Industrial Society.* London: Routledge.

Marx, K. (1967). *Capital. Vol. 1. A Critical Analysis of Capitalist Production.* Moscow: Progress Publishers.

Ministry of Social Affairs and Employment (2011). *Q+A Life-Course Savings Scheme.* The Hague: Ministry of Social Affairs and Employment.

Moen, P. and Sweet, S. (2004). From 'work–family' to 'flexible careers' A life course reframing. *Community, Work & Family,* 7(2), 209–226.

Mullins, L. J. (2007). *Management and Organisational Behaviour.* Maidenhead: Pearson Education.

Negrey, C. L. (2012). *Work Time: Conflict, Control, and Change.* Cambridge, Polity Press.

Patuelli, R., Nijkamp, P. and Pels, E. (2005). Environmental tax reform and the double dividend: A meta-analytical performance assessment. *Ecological Economics,* 55(4), 564–583.

Paulsen, R. (2010). *Arbetssamhället: hur arbetet överlevde teknologin.* Malmö: Gleerups.

Perrons, D., Fagan, C., McDowell, L., Ray, K. and Ward, K. (2006). *Gender Divisions and Working Time in the New Economy.* Cheltenham: Edward Elgar Publishing Ltd.

Plantenga, J. and Remery, C. (2005). *Reconciliation of Work and Private Life: A Comparative Review of Thirty European Countries.* Brussels: European Commission.

Pullinger, M. (2014). Working time reduction policy in a sustainable economy: Criteria and options for its design. *Ecological Economics,* 103, 11–19.

Raposo, P. S. and van Ours, J. C. (2010). How working time reduction affects jobs and wages. *Economics Letters,* 106(1), 61–63.

Rifkin, J. (2014). *The Zero Marginal Cost Society: The Internet of Things, the Collaborative Commons, and the Eclipse of Capitalism.* New York: Palgrave and Macmillan.

Rosen, E. D. (1993). *Improving Public Sector Productivity: Concepts and Practice.* Thousand Oaks, CA: Sage Publications.

Rule, J. (1981). *The Experience of Labour in Eighteenth-Century English Industry.* London: Palgrave MacMillan.

Sahlins, M. D. (1972). *Stone Age Economics.* Chicago, IL: Aldine-Atherton.

Sanne, C. (2012). *Hur vi kan leva hållbart 2030.* Stockholm: Naturvårdsverket.

Schor, J. (1991). *The Overworked American: The Unexpected Decline of Leisure.* New York: Basic Books.

Schor, J. B. (2005). Sustainable consumption and worktime reduction. *Journal of Industrial Ecology,* 9(1–2), 37–51.

Schor, J. and You, J. I. (1995). *Capital, the State, and Labour: A Global Perspective.* Aldershot: Edward Elgar Publishing.

Standing, G. (2011). *The Precariat: The New Dangerous Class.* London, New York: Bloomsbury.

Stockhammer, E. (2008). Some stylized facts on the finance-dominated accumulation regime. *Competition & Change,* 12(2), 184–202.

Timmer, M., O'Mahony, M. and Van Ark, B. (2007). *EU KLEMS Growth and Productivity Accounts – Overview.* Groningen: University of Groningen.

Tolliday, S. and Zeitlin, J. (1986). Between Fordism and Flexibility. The Automotive Industry and its Workers – Past, Present and Future. In J. C. Wood and

M. C. Wood (eds), *Henry Ford: Critical Evaluations in Business and Management* (226–251). Oxford: Taylor & Francis.

Viktor, P. (2008). *Managing without Growth: Slower by Design, Not Disaster.* Cheltenham, Northampton: Edward Elgar.

Žižek, S. (2009). Against charity. Lecture presented at RSA. London, Royal Society for the Encouragement of Arts. 24 November 2009.

Part III

Emerging practices of sustainable welfare

9 Transitions towards degrowth and sustainable welfare

Carbon emission reduction and wealth and income distribution in France, the US and China

Hubert Buch-Hansen, Annika Pissin and Erin Kennedy

Introduction

The mushrooming growth-critical literature notes that the current drift towards ecological collapse can only be stopped if the rich countries of the world embark upon a phase of planned economic contraction. The notion of 'planned degrowth' is commonly used to describe the desired transition process, which involves 'an equitable downscaling of production that increases human well-being and enhances ecological conditions at the local and global level, in the short and long term' (Schneider *et al.*, 2010: 512). The envisioned outcome is a non-growing economic system with radically reduced resource and energy use. For such a system to function, it would have to facilitate the satisfaction of basic human needs, meaning that sustainable welfare would need to be one of its core features (see Chapter 2 in this volume).

It goes without saying that planned degrowth transitions to non-growing economies and sustainable welfare are, at the time of writing, very far from being a reality. Existing welfare states are part of a transnational capitalist system that is firmly committed to economic growth, that is, to an endless increase in the volume of production and consumption of the planet's finite resources. Even though these national welfare systems are interconnected in numerous ways and have converged to some extent, they remain diverse. The question is how this diversity would affect degrowth transitions and the paths towards sustainable welfare. Gough and Meadowcroft (2011: 501) observe that, if 'continued economic growth in the rich world is incompatible with sustainability, then all forms of existing welfare state would need to radically transform'. While this is true, such transformations would be likely to take different forms in different countries, and it is equally unlikely that these would be so radical as to entail a clean break with currently existing institutions. Indeed, scholarship on institutional change has shown that past institutions and structures always leave an imprint on the institutions and structures that succeed them. Institutional change generally involves the combination of new practices and principles with existing ones (e.g. Campbell, 2010). As a result, if degrowth transitions were to be initiated – and that is indeed still a very big *if* – they would start out from these diverse existing institutional arrangements, including currently existing welfare systems, and then recalibrate these arrangements by combining existing practices and principles with new ones (Buch-Hansen, 2014).

As a result of the diverse institutional starting points and because of the open-ended nature of political processes, the sustainable welfare arrangements that would (ideally speaking) emerge from the transitions would also be diverse. Existing growth-critical research nonetheless generally fails to take into consideration the importance of capitalist diversity for degrowth transitions and their outcomes. The present chapter seeks to go some way towards remedying this deficiency. We take as our starting point the existing welfare regimes of three countries: France, the US and China. These countries have been selected because of their extreme differences: they belong to different regions of the world and they represent distinct forms of capitalism, with distinct types of welfare systems. Yet they also have some commonalities. The US and France are overdeveloped countries; the US and China are giants in the global economic system; China and France have a tradition of state-led economic development.[1]

Having outlined these welfare regimes in the first section, mainly by drawing on comparative political economy scholarship, the next two sections focus on some of the issues that Gough and Meadowcroft (2011: 499–500) identify as being of major importance to welfare regimes in a non-growing economy: the reduction of carbon emissions and the distribution of income and wealth.[2] We tentatively outline some scenarios of how the diversity of current institutions and practices in the three countries could translate into diverse ways of dealing with these specific issues in the context of non-growing economies with sustainable welfare arrangements. Our focus here is on the national scale but, certainly, there could be an argument for also considering (in a more comprehensive analysis) the interconnectedness of this scale with local and transnational levels. Indeed, all three scales are identified as being important in both degrowth and welfare regime research (see for example, Kallis *et al.*, 2015: 1–17; Kazepov, 2010). It should also be noted that it is neither the purpose of this chapter to discuss *whether* and, if so, *when*, transitions towards sustainable welfare are likely to occur, nor to present blueprints (or 'roadmaps') for how the transitions from current to future institutions could be accomplished. However, in the section prior to the conclusion, we do briefly reflect upon what social forces or practices could be pivotal for attaining the goal of a non-growing economic system in the three countries in question.

The welfare regimes of France, the US and China

Traditionally the centrality of a strong and interventionist state has been a defining feature of French capitalism. After the Second World War, the path chosen to bring the economy back on track was thus one of state-led growth. The state took control of key sectors of the economy, and a national planning board was created and given responsibility for the preparation of plans designed to enhance the performance of French industry (Hall, 1986: 140–41, 166–167). As Hobsbawm (1994: 274) quite bluntly put it,

> [t]his adaptation of Soviet ideas to a capitalist mixed economy must have had some effect, since between 1950 and 1979, France, hitherto a by-word for economic retardation, caught up more successfully than any other of the chief industrial countries with US productivity.

The significance of the influx of US aid through the Marshall Plan should not be overlooked in this context, nor should the introduction and/or improvement of a series of welfare programmes in the post-war decades (Dormois, 2004). France is still known for its generous welfare state. In 2012, it was the OECD country with the largest total social expenditure as a proportion of gross domestic product (GDP), at 31 per cent. In comparison, US social expenditure for that year was 18.7 per cent (OECD, 2014). The French welfare system, which is mainly financed by contributions from employers and employees (Boyer, 2002: 16), is, for instance, known for providing generous family allowances, subsidized childcare services, pensions and social transfers – and for the 35-hour work week (see Chapter 8 in this volume). As for the healthcare system, which has been rated by the World Health Organization as the best in the world, the state finances approximately 77 per cent of all treatment (McCann, 2014: 141–42). However, as is the case with all welfare regimes, the French regime is not static. A series of reforms have led to changes in the French social security system. For instance, the pension system has been reformed in recent years as a result of which the minimum retirement age has increased from 60 to 62 and the requirements for receiving an early pension have been tightened. In the face of a massive public deficit, the current socialist government is, for instance, also planning to cut family allowances considerably, while the 35-hour work week has come under attack from business interests (France24, 2014).

US capitalism is characterized by a welfare system that is far less generous than the French one. In Esping-Andersen's (1990) terminology, the US is a prime example of a liberal welfare regime that emphasizes the responsibility of the individual for his or her own welfare. Decommodification – that is, the extent to which social entitlements are provided independently of the market – is limited. Benefits are low and social rights weak in order to minimize so-called 'negative work incentives'. The system provides social assistance largely to those without jobs or any private resources and, consequently, as mentioned in the previous paragraph, relatively low levels of public money are channelled into social programmes. The US welfare regime has also undergone a major transformation over time. The New Deal regime, which emerged in the 1930s as a response to the Great Depression, and which was underpinned by a class compromise between capital and labour, involved the introduction of new social policies (e.g. McDonough, 1994). The 1935 Social Security Act created entitlements for the unemployed, the elderly, the blind and families with dependent children. In the 1960s, it seemed that the earlier New Deal policies 'would find their ultimate expression in the rise of the Keynesian social welfare state. Fiscal policy devoted to the attainment and further expansion of the welfare state allowed for impressive growth and the highest level of income equality in the postwar period' (Eisner, 2011: 35). However, the oil crisis of the 1970s and the rise and consolidation of neoliberal ideas from the 1980s onwards put an end to the development of a Keynesian welfare state. When Ronald Reagan took office as President in 1980, he implemented a comprehensive reform programme, which included a massive reduction in expenditure on social welfare programmes combined with tax relief that was especially beneficial for corporations and wealthy citizens. One of the main outcomes of decades of neoliberal policies is a system characterized by very modest social protection and, as we discuss below, massive inequality.

Defining China's capitalism, also dubbed 'capitalism-with-no-name' (Peck and Zhang, 2013: 371), is a difficult and ongoing task. The economic and welfare system has undergone several changes from a revived rural market economy during the 1980s to the aggressive neoliberal market reforms that began in the 1990s (Hung, 2013). Its most striking feature is one-party rule. Compared to the welfare states in the Global North, the Chinese state is omnipresent and more invasive (Saich, 2004: 213). Up to the end of the twentieth century, the state had a long history of treating the weak in a paternalist way (Hung, 2008). Most crucial in this system is the urban–rural household registration system (*hukou*) (Whyte, 2010), which began during the 26 years of Mao's rule (Peck and Zhang, 2013: 387). Based on the Maoist-era *danwei* (work unit) system, which provided simple healthcare and relief for rural residents and more elaborate social security for urban residents, the contemporary household registration system implies an agricultural–industrial division and an unequal distribution of taxation and social benefits, as well as differences in the implementation of family policies (Saich, 2004). The registration pass that comes along with the *hukou* system can be understood as an 'internal passport' (Fan and Sun, 2010: 96), with the result that more than 200 million migrant workers with a rural *hukou*, and especially their children (more than 100 million, known as either left-behind or migrant children), have only limited rights to healthcare and education in their urban homes (Biao, 2007: 179–191). Although changes to the system were initiated in 2014, which promise access to basic healthcare and education in the place of residence, numerous problems related to poverty and stigmatization remain. The household registration system also explains the discrepancies in the national fertility rate. Finally, family planning (the one-child family policy) has caused a great number of problems. Some of the greater social welfare problems caused by the frictions between this social engineering and the Chinese social fabric is the continuing increase in the percentage of elderly persons in the population and the accompanying problem of how to finance pensions via (for the most part) private family savings (Shi, 2006). Furthermore the implementation of the family planning policy has led to a sex ratio imbalance favouring boys, causing the social exclusion of large groups of young men and having a range of adverse effects on women.

Reduction of carbon emissions

To render the global economy – and thus also the various welfare regimes that are part of it – environmentally sustainable, a massive reduction in carbon emissions is required. Anderson and Bows (2011), who factor in the need for developing countries to increase carbon emissions over a period of time to allow for infrastructure, industry and technology to catch up, suggest that overdeveloped, often Western, countries need to reduce their annual emissions by as much as 8 to 10 per cent per year over the coming decades. This section will look at current carbon emissions and the correlating reduction goals for France, the US and China. We will examine key national policies that have been introduced with a view to reducing carbon emissions in these three countries. Based on the assumption that emission reductions of the required scale can in all likelihood only be accomplished if a contraction, as opposed to an expansion, of the economic system takes place, we then consider a mechanism for reducing emissions that is favoured by many growth critics: a cap system. Taking the existing political economies of the three countries outlined in the previous section as our point of departure, we will briefly outline possible scenarios for the different forms of such a cap system.

Of the three countries, France has the lowest CO_2 emissions per capita (5.6 metric tonnes compared to 17.6 for the US and 6.2 for China – World Bank, 2015). In addition to its extensive use of nuclear energy, what sets France apart in terms of the reduction of carbon emissions is its multi-stakeholder approach, which involves participation from five main societal groups: local governments, environmental non-governmental organizations (NGOs), unions, employers and the state (Worldwatch Institute, 2015). Environmental legislation such as *Grenelle 1* and *Grenelle 2* were developed from open debates that brought together representatives from these societal groups. This legislation focuses on creating a nation of informed consumers through product labels that include the products' carbon content, use of natural resources and/ or the environmental impact of the product during its life cycle. France is also bringing sustainability into its urban planning with its *Schéma de Cohérence Territoriale*, which is intended to reduce urban sprawl and overcrowding, as well as to improve policies that focus on land use. Buildings currently account for approximately 18 per cent of France's greenhouse gas emissions (Worldwatch Institute, 2015). Consequently, building efficiency laws now include energy consumption limits with the prospective target of buildings that produce more energy than they consume, becoming 'energy positive' by the year 2020. Many of France's current carbon emission reduction and redistribution efforts are focused on the daily energy use of citizens and work with citizens so that they become informed and active participants in the reduction of CO_2 emissions at local and national levels.

Globally, the US has the second-highest CO_2 emissions when comparing absolute greenhouse gas emissions. Most of its CO_2 emissions are created from the energy used to produce electricity (including coal, oil and natural gas) and the transport sector, which is reliant on oil. The third largest source of CO_2 emissions comes from the US industrial sector, while residential and commercial sectors consume the least amount of energy leading to CO_2 emissions. However, this 'least amount' is still one of the highest emission levels globally. The US has committed to reducing carbon emissions by an amount of between 26 per cent and 28 per cent below 2005 emission levels by 2025 (The White House, 2014). The focus of reduction efforts has been on investment in clean energy technologies, standardizing fuel efficiency in medium- to heavy-duty vehicles such as pick-up trucks, vans and tractor trucks and creating energy efficiency standards in commercial buildings. However, the question remains as to how far such efforts can lead to a CO_2 reduction of the necessary magnitude. According to the United States Environmental Protection Agency,

> The number of vehicle miles traveled by passenger cars and light-duty trucks increased 35% from 1990 to 2013. The increase in travel miles is attributed to several factors, including population growth, economic growth, urban sprawl, and low fuel prices during the beginning of this period.
>
> (EPA, 2015)

China is the leader in energy consumption and CO_2 emissions (Cai *et al.*, 2012; Jiang, *et al.*, 2010). China's goal is to achieve a reduction in CO_2 emissions of 40 to 45 per cent by the year 2020 from its 2005 emissions level and to reach a plateau in CO_2 emissions by 2030. China is in the process of completing its industrial development phase and is rapidly transitioning to an urban development phase. Its industrial sector remains the focus for carbon reduction, with improvements being made in technologies and a move away from coal to nuclear and renewable energy sources. China's high-paced development is disproportionate within the nation and contains extreme inequalities, particularly between rural and urban development. For example, rural to urban population migration, which reached 51 per cent in 2011 (National Bureau of Statistics China, 2012), and the increase in mega cities such as Shanghai have made it necessary for the government to adopt multi-modal methods of carbon reduction and to address the carbon emissions that result from the increase in construction, housing, transport, infrastructure and economic development, which are changing consumption behaviour to reflect the high-consumption patterns seen in developed countries. The coupling of these development phases, industrial and urban, may result in China having high consumption and high emissions from both industrial and economic development, a scenario that will inhibit China's ability to achieve its emission reduction goals and a scenario that requires the exploration of citizen engagement in order to create low carbon pro-environmental behaviour. In order to reach its carbon reduction goals, China also needs to address inequalities in regional economic development, which are reflected in regional differences in carbon intensity. However, increasing energy consumption, even if it has a lower carbon intensity, is not a realistic method of attaining the reduced CO_2 emission targets.

While the three countries have gone some way towards introducing measures that contribute towards a reduction in carbon emissions, these measures would need to be supplemented by much more far-reaching initiatives if reductions of the magnitude mentioned at the beginning of this section are to be achieved. A number of scholars have suggested that an efficient way of reducing carbon emissions would be to introduce an overall cap that gradually declines over time, until a sustainable emission level has been reached. The 'cap-and-dividend policy' (in one of its versions) involves three steps: first, emission caps are set with the help of scientific experts to determine the maximum quantity of fossil fuels (coal, oil and gas) that can be produced; second, on this basis, permits are auctioned each year to the companies that bring fossil fuels into the economy, whether by means of imports or by domestic extraction; third, all income derived from selling these permits is distributed equally to each citizen (Boyce and Riddle, 2007). A related proposal is to use the cap as the basis for issuing equal annual emissions permits to citizens who can then use or sell a part of these to fossil fuel producers via intermediaries (see, for example, Feasta, 2008; Gough and Meadowcroft, 2011).

Based on their existing institutions and practices, it seems likely that, if resource cap systems were introduced in the three countries discussed, these systems would take somewhat different forms. For the US, the scenario could be a highly market-based and individualist cap system. The task of determining the size of the annual cap could be outsourced to private actors. Moreover, rather than letting state institutions sell the permits and pass the income on to citizens, the permits would be provided directly to citizens, making it possible for them to determine on an individual basis how much to consume and how much to sell. Building on the current multi-stakeholder approach, the scenario for France could be a system in which annual caps were decided in negotiations between different societal groups on the basis of advice from independent experts. The state would play a central role in this system, being in charge of selling permits to companies and ensuring an equal distribution of the resulting income to citizens. As for China, the scenario could be a system in which the state, possibly with inputs from scientific experts, determines the annual cap level and subsequently distributes the income generated from selling permits to citizens. An argument could be made for distributing a larger share of this income to poor people than to those who are well off, thus making the resource cap system serve as a mechanism that contributes to redressing the aforementioned regional patterns of inequality.

The practical difficulties of implementing such systems should certainly not be underestimated (see also Chapter 7 in this volume). However, the promises of these systems are at least twofold. First, unlike the existing dysfunctional EU emission-trading system (see Koch, 2012), they target fossil fuels 'upstream' (i.e. at the point of extraction), making them a potentially potent instrument, provided that they are implemented throughout the overdeveloped countries. Second, they aim to ensure that the reduction of emissions is carried out in a socially equitable way. For these reasons, many advocates of a non-growing economy have embraced cap-based systems as the main way to limit throughput and thus emissions (e.g. Daly, 1991; Dietz and O'Neill, 2013).

Income and wealth (re)distribution

At first glance, it is perhaps not self-evident what income and wealth distribution have to do with degrowth and sustainable welfare. Yet there are some important links. Sustainable welfare entails that actual human needs are met in an environmentally sustainable manner (see Chapter 2 in this volume). As such, this can only be achieved if resources currently being used to finance the affluent (and environmentally unsustainable) lifestyles of some groups are used to meet the currently unsatisfied human needs of others. A more equitable distribution of income and wealth is thus a precondition for sustainable welfare. A related reason for this is that degrowth is only likely to attract the necessary support from the wider populations of the overdeveloped countries insofar as those with the highest incomes and greatest wealth are requested to shoulder a proportionate part of the burden. Indeed, as demonstrated by Wilkinson and Pickett (2010), the more equal a society is, the higher the degree of overall life satisfaction and well-being there tends to be. A third reason why income and wealth distribution is significant in the context of sustainable welfare and degrowth is that increased equality tends to reduce status competition, which in turn has the advantage of 'suppressing unnecessary and conspicuous consumption' (Dietz and O'Neill, 2013: 93; see also Gough and Meadowcroft, 2011: 500). In sum, there are compelling reasons for linking the issue of income and wealth in relation to sustainable welfare and a non-growing economy.

All societies are unequal, but some more so than others. France is in some respects a very elitist society (Suleiman, 1978), yet in terms of income and wealth, France is one of the most equal OECD countries. As mentioned above, total social expenditure as a proportion of GDP is greater in France than in any other OECD country. Although there has been a trend towards rising wage inequalities in recent years (Dormois, 2004), the minimum wage in France remains one of the highest in the OECD countries, second only to that of Luxembourg (Bloomberg, 2014). France is one of a relatively small number of countries in the world that taxes wealth. This taxation (*Impôt de solidarité sur la fortune*, 'solidarity tax on wealth') was originally introduced under the socialist government of François Mitterrand in the 1980s; today it is levied on wealth of €1.3 million and above. This wealth tax has its critics and has resulted in some capital flight, yet it is largely because of this tax, and also because of estate taxes, that the progressivity of the French taxation system increased between 1970 and 2005 (Piketty and Saez, 2006: 21). Another tax that points in the same direction is that on financial transactions, which was introduced by the newly elected socialist president, Francois Hollande, in 2012. It levies a 0.2 per cent tax on purchases of the stocks of large publicly traded companies. In comparison, the US currently taxes similar transactions at a mere 0.0024 per cent. Boyer (2002: 20) points out that 'French welfare and tax systems have had a positive effect in reducing inequalities at the lower end of the income scale' (see also McCann, 2014: 141).

Unlike France, the US does not tax wealth. Piketty and Saez find that the federal US taxation system is much less progressive than that of France and, moreover, it has become significantly less progressive in relation to top incomes: 'the top 0.01 percent of earners paid over 70 percent of their income in federal taxes in 1960, while they paid only about 35 percent of their income in 2005' (Piketty and Saez, 2006: 21). This development should be viewed within the context of the neoliberal change in politics in the US mentioned above. Neoliberalism is ultimately a political project that aims to concentrate wealth in the hands of the already wealthy (Harvey, 2005). The taxation system is one mechanism that can effectively facilitate this redistribution. In the US, tax reforms were combined with welfare policy reforms (see above) as well as with privatization and the introduction of a more 'flexible' labour market, that is, a labour market with fewer permanent and more precarious jobs, in many cases part time, with low wages. One unsurprising consequence of this was a massive increase in inequality in US society. The Gini coefficient is a commonly used indicator of income inequality: it ranges from 0 (perfectly equal distribution) to 1.00 (perfect inequality). By the late 2000s, the US Gini coefficient was 0.38, making it one of the most unequal societies in the OECD. In comparison, the French Gini coefficient was 0.29 (OECD, 2013). In the neoliberal era (i.e. the 1980s onwards), corporate profit rates (especially in the US financial sector) were considerable, whereas strong pressure was placed on the salaries of workers (Duménil and Levy, 2011). It is telling that the minimum wage ($7.11 per hour in 2013) is among the lowest in the OECD countries as a percentage of average wages (Woellert, 2014). Economic growth in the neoliberal era was, to no small extent, based on credit-financed consumer demand: by making it possible for households to become massively indebted, the negative economic impact of depressed wages could temporarily be neutralized (albeit not without further increasing inequality).

China's income inequality with a Gini of 0.41 by the late 2000s (OECD, 2013) is high and increasing. While much of the inequality can be explained by the rural–urban division aggravated by the household registration system, it has also partly been attributed to differences in wages between formal and informal urban employees (Xue *et al.*, 2014). The market reform changed the practice from socialism to one of 'let some people get rich first', which was argued as a means of allowing poorer people to get richer at a later date. However, although a possible improvement of social welfare in the country-side through transfer payments has been noted (Ahlers and Schubert, 2009), financing social welfare is still difficult. In fact, rural-to-urban migrants' wages pose a problem when it comes to calculating average household income in China (Gustafsson *et al.*, 2014) as migrants make up about one-sixth of the total population. Furthermore, transfer payments from migrant workers to their rural families are not viewed by all as being important contributions (Li and Sicular, 2014). By the mid-1990s, all international economic sanctions that had been imposed on China after the Tiananmen Square massacre in 1989 were removed and intense cooperation with the EU and the US commenced, while income inequality among households in China has increased rapidly (Li and Sicular, 2014). Since economic inequality has implications for educational inequality, for example, the consequences have been far-reaching. From 1 February 2015, China plans to tax citizens living abroad in order to reduce tax evasion and increase tax revenues in China (Bradsher, 2015).

As discussed above, the current institutional arrangements affecting wealth and income distribution in France, the US and China differ greatly, which in turn has major consequences for the respective levels of equality in the three countries. Daly (1991: 50–75) and other growth-critical scholars (e.g. Alexander, 2015: 146–148) propose that one way to reduce inequality in a non-growing economy would be to introduce institutions that impose minimum and maximum limits on income and maximum limits on wealth. If one imagines such an institution being introduced in our three countries, it seems very likely that this would take on different forms, owing to current national differences. In the US, with its long legacy of liberal thought and widespread suspicion towards a (welfare) state that redistributes economic resources to any great extent, it seems likely that the minimum levels would be low and combined with high maximum levels. Conceivably, the minimum levels could gradually be increased and the maximum levels decreased. In China, Daly's distributist institution could function as a powerful instrument for redistributing economic resources from urban to rural areas, a redistribution that would be essential for a non-growing economy to have any chance of succeeding. Given China's overall stage of development and given the recent poor record of redistributing economic resources via welfare policies, it seems likely that both the minimum and maximum levels would, at least initially, need be set at a lower level than in the other two countries. In France, with its rather generous welfare system and broader tradition of implementing policies aimed at reducing inequality, it is probable that the minimum income level could be set at a higher level than in the US and China, combined with lower maximum limits on income and wealth. Overall, the French tradition of reducing economic inequality by means of progressive taxation is likely to render the transition towards a non-growing economy with sustainable welfare less complicated there than in the two other countries.

Social forces

It is not only institutional and ideational legacies that determine the evolution of institutions. Agency and open-ended political struggles are equally important. In this section we will briefly identify some of the social forces and practices that could be pivotal for attaining the goal of a non-growing economic system in the three countries in question.

At the time of writing, the prospects of introducing a non-growing economic system seem comparably better in France than in the other two countries, which is not to say that the prospects are good. Given its legacy of hands-on market intervention, one could imagine the French state playing a role in steering the transition to degrowth. It is worth noting that degrowth – as a social and intellectual movement – is far stronger in France than in the other two countries. If the momentum of this movement were to continue to grow, state actors and political decision-makers may come to endorse degrowth. In France, connections already exist between degrowth activists and some of the smaller labour unions (Bayon, 2015: 189–191). If such alliances could also be formed with the larger unions (which is of course easier said than done) this could prove to be another important step.

As for the US, the prospects of a planned degrowth transition being initiated look bleak, to say the least. Aside from a widespread and deeply engrained individualist consumer culture, which in itself constitutes a formidable obstacle, it is not difficult to imagine that resourceful social forces – such as the powerful oil industry – would do a great deal to oppose degrowth, if the movement were to become powerful enough to constitute a threat to 'business as usual'. The most likely driving force behind degrowth in the US is probably a broad civil society movement that initiates the transition itself. In this context, it is significant that the international Transition movement – which experiments with home-based production, microenterprises, farmers' markets, long-term energy reduction plans and local currency systems – seems to have gained considerable momentum in the US (TM, 2015), which is not to suggest that it is yet a major social force. Also worth mentioning is the Center for a New American Dream, which aims to inspire a shift in the way in which goods are produced and consumed, and the 'voluntary simplicity' movement, which has its roots in the US (cf. Thoreau, 2004[1854]). Finally, it can also be noted that a large number of US-Americans are profoundly dissatisfied with the way that the economic system functions, as demonstrated by the rapid spread of the Occupy Wall Street protests in 2011 and 2012, for example. In other words, the degrowth movement may be able to connect to current and social forces in the US.

China's prospects of a degrowth movement are also not yet great, given local government emphasis on growth and the semi-authoritarian approach to social movements (Xue *et al.*, 2012; Ho, 2006). However, although local government is still pursuing high economic growth rates, this no longer appears to be the main emphasis of central government (Xue *et al.*, 2012:

105). Interestingly, a discourse about economic degrowth is slowly beginning. In an emerging literature, suggestions about how to move towards degrowth take the form of institutional and conceptual sketches that are based on large social engineering projects. These relate, for example, to shifting the importance of growth from the east coast cities to poorer regions (Xue *et al.*, 2012), reducing consumption (Zhao *et al.*, 2009: 141), making use of the large workforce of about 760 million people, of whom many could be engaged in social and environmental projects under the protection of a public employment programme (Li, 2014: 171), and increasing the income tax of wealthy individuals (Li, 2014: 173). Conceptually, the same authors propose placing emphasis on moral themes in Chinese history that point out that economic growth is not the most logical path to follow for a society (Xue *et al.*, 2012). Zhao *et al.* (2009: 141) more generally propose that China should consider abandoning its predilection for growth and aim instead for a steady-state economy and environmental sustainability. The degrowth discourse (if we can describe it as such) is largely restricted to academia. The formation of an outspoken civil society with political power in the semi-authoritarian political environment of China is currently not very likely (He and Thøgersen, 2010). Nevertheless, as long as they are not challenging political power, groups reminiscent of voluntary simplicity and back-to-the-land movements also start to come into existence in China (see Moore, 2014; Levin, 2014).

In addition to those social forces and practices that exist at local levels, interlocal and international cooperation is necessary in order to confront the environmental disasters that are being created on a global scale. Local disasters, devastating migration movements and environmental pollution often have multiple causes in different localities and therefore need to be tackled by people working together beyond national borders.

Conclusion

This chapter has tentatively considered how the diversity of current institutions and practices in France, the US and China could translate into different ways of dealing with the issues of carbon emission reductions as well as income and wealth distribution within the context of a non-growing economy. We noted that various mechanisms have already been introduced in these three countries with a view to reducing carbon emissions, yet we also noted the need to supplement these with other mechanisms. In this context, we considered the instrument favoured by many growth critics – a cap-based system – and considered the different forms that this would be likely to take in the three countries, given their different legacies. Similarly, we noted that, if a distributist institution of the kind envisaged by growth-critical scholars were to be introduced in the three countries, it is likely that the minimum and maximum income levels and the maximum limit on wealth would be shaped by the different institutional, economic and ideational legacies of these countries.

Notes

1 For an empirical analysis considering a much larger sample of countries (see Fritz and Koch, 2014).
2 It can be noted that both dimensions relate directly to institutions that were pointed out by Daly (1991) as being of great importance to the functioning of a steady-state economy.

References

Ahlers, A. and Schubert, G. (2009). 'Building a new socialist countryside' – Only a political slogan? *Journal of Current Chinese Affairs*, 38(4), 35–62.

Alexander, S. (2015). Basic and Maximum Income. In G. D'Alisa, F. Demaria and G. Kallis (eds), *Degrowth: A Vocabulary for a New Era*. London and New York: Routledge, 146–148.

Anderson, K. and Bows, A. (2011). Beyond 'dangerous' climate change: Emission scenarios for a new world. *Philosophical Transactions of the Royal Society*, 369, 20–44.

Bayon, D. (2015). Unions. In G. D'Alisa, F. Demaria and G. Kallis (eds), *Degrowth: A Vocabulary for a New Era*. London and New York: Routledge, 189–191.

Biao, X. (2007). How far are the left-behind left behind? A preliminary study in rural China. *Population, Space and Place*, 13, 179–191.

Bloomberg (2014). Highest minimum wage: Countries. www.bloomberg.com/visual-data/best-and-worst/highest-minimum-wage-countries (accessed 16. 1. 15).

Boyce, J. K. and Riddle, M. (2007). *Cap and Dividend: How to Curb Global Warming While Protecting the Incomes of American Families*. Amherst: Political Economy Research Institute Working paper series, No. 150.

Boyer, R. (2002). *Is There A Welfare State Crisis? A Comparative Study of French Social Policy*. Geneva: International Labour Office.

Bradsher, K. (2015). China wants taxes paid by citizens living far away. *New York Times*, 7 January.

Buch-Hansen, H. (2014). Capitalist diversity and de-growth trajectories to steady-state economies. *Ecological Economics*, 106, 173–179.

Campbell, J. L. (2010). Institutional Reproduction and Change. In G. Morgan, J. L. Campbell, C. Crouch, O. K. Pedersen and R. Whitley (eds), *The Oxford Handbook of Comparative Institutional Analysis* (87–116). Oxford: Oxford University Press.

Cai, B. F., Wang, J. N., Yang, W. S., Liu, L. S. and Dong, C. (2012). Low carbon society in China: Research and practice. *Advances in Climate Change Research*, 3(2), 106–120.

Daly, H. E. (1991). *Steady-State Economics*. Washington: Island Press.

Dietz, R. and O'Neill, D. (2013). *Enough is Enough*. San Francisco, CA: BK Publishers.

Dormois, J. P. (2004). *The French Economy in the Twentieth Century*. Cambridge: Cambridge University Press.

Duménil, G. and Lévy, D. (2011). *The Crisis of Neoliberalism*. Cambridge, MA: Harvard University Press.

Eisner, M. A. (2011). *The American Political Economy*. London and New York: Routledge.

EPA (2015). Sources of greenhouse gas emissions, www.epa.gov/climatechange/ghgemissions/sources/transportation.html (accessed 22. 10. 15).

Esping-Andersen, G. (1990). *The Three Worlds of Welfare Capitalism*. Cambridge: Polity Press.

Fan, C. and Sun, M. (2010). China's permanent and temporary migrants: Differentials and changes. *The Professional Geographer*, 63(1), 92–112.

Feasta (2008). *A Fair Way to Cut Greenhouse Emissions*. Dublin: Feasta.

France24 (2014). French business leaders target minimum wage, public holidays. 24 September. www.france24.com/en/20140924-minimum-wage-public-holidays-france-business-leaders-crosshairs-medef-unemployment (accessed 7. 4. 15).

Fritz, M. and Koch, M. (2014). Potentials for prosperity without growth: Ecological sustainability, social inclusion and the quality of life in 38 countries. *Ecological Economics*, 108, 191–199.

Gough, I. and Meadowcroft, J. (2011). Decarbonizing the Welfare State. In J. S. Dryzek, R. B. Nørgaard and D. Schlosberg (Eds.), *The Oxford Handbook of Climate Change and Society* (490–503). Oxford: Oxford University Press.

Gustafsson, B., Li, S. and Sato, H. (2014). Data for studying earnings, the distribution of household income and poverty in China. *China Economic Review*, 30, 419–431.

Hall, P. (1986). *Governing the Economy: The Politics of State Intervention in Britain and France*. Cambridge: Polity Press.

Harvey, D. (2005). *A Brief History of Neoliberalism*. Oxford: Oxford University Press.

He, B. and Thøgersen, S. (2010). Giving the people a voice? Experiments with consultative authoritarian institutions in China. *Journal of Contemporary China*, 19(66), 675–692.

Ho, P. (2006). Trajectories for greening in China: Theory and practice. *Development and Change*, 37(1), 3–28.

Hobsbawm, E. (1994). *Age of Extremes: The Short Twentieth Century 1914–91*. London: Michael Joseph.

Hung, H. (2008). Agricultural revolution and elite reproduction in Qing China: The transition to capitalism debate revisited. *American Sociological Review*, 73, 569–588.

Hung, H. (2013). Labor politics under three stages of Chinese capitalism. *The South Atlantic Quarterly*, 112(1), 204–212.

Jiang, B., Sun, Z. Q. and Liu, M. Q. (2010). China's energy development strategy under the low-carbon economy. *Energy*, 35, 4257–4264.

Kazepov, Y. (ed.) (2010). *Rescaling Social Policies: Towards Multilevel Governance in Europe*, Surrey: Ashgate.

Kallis, G., D'Alisa, G., Demaria, F. (2015). Introduction: Degrowth. In G. D'Alisa, F. Demaria and G. Kallis (eds). *Degrowth: A Vocabulary for a New Era* (1–17). London and New York: Routledge.

Koch, M. (2012). *Capitalism and Climate Change*. New York: Palgrave.

Levin, D. (2014). Communism is the goal at a commune, but Chinese officials are not impressed. *New York Times*, 12 March 2014.

Li, M. (2014). *Peak Oil, Climate Change, and the Limits to China's Economic Growth*. London and New York: Routledge.

Li, S. and Sicular, T. (2014). The distribution of household income in China: Inequality, poverty and policies. *The China Quarterly*, 217, 1–41.

McCann, L. (2014). *International and Comparative Business. Foundations of Political Economies*. Los Angeles and London: Sage.

McDonough, T. (1994). The Construction of Social Structures of Accumulation in US History. In D. M. Kotz, T. McDonough and M. Reich (eds) *Social Structures of Accumulation: The Political Economy of Growth and Crisis* (101–132). Cambridge: Cambridge University Press.

Moore, M. (2014). Young Chinese Maoists set up 'hippy' commune. *The Telegraph*, 24 April.

National Bureau of Statistics China (2012). *China Statistical Yearbook 2012. Total population by urban and rural residence and birth rate, death rate, natural growth rate by region (2011)*. www.stats.gov.cn/tjsj/ndsj/2012/html/D0305c.htm (Chinese) www.stats.gov.cn/tjsj/ndsj/2012/indexeh.htm (English) (accessed 5. 5. 15).

OECD (2013). *OECD Factbook 2013. Income Inequality*. Paris: OECD Publishing.

OECD (2014). *Social Expenditure Update*. Paris: OECD Publishing.

Peck, J. and Zhang, J. (2013). A variety of capitalism ... with Chinese characteristics? *Journal of Economic Geography*, 13(3), 357–396.

Piketty, T. and Saez, E. (2006). *How Progressive is the U.S. Federal Tax System? A Historical and International Perspective*. Cambridge, MA: National Bureau of Economic Research.

Saich, T. (2004). *Governance and Politics of China*. New York: Palgrave.

Schneider, F., Kallis, G. and Martinez-Alier, J. (2010). Crisis or opportunity? Economic degrowth for social equity and ecological sustainability. *Journal of Cleaner Production*, 18(6), 511–518.

Shi, S. (2006). Left to market and family – again? Ideas and development of the rural pension policy in China. *Social Policy & Administration*, 40(7), 791–806.

Suleiman, E. (1978) *Elites in French Society: The Politics of Survival*, Princeton, NJ: Princeton University Press.

The White House (2014). Fact sheet: US-China joint announcement on climate change and clean energy cooperation. Office of the Press Secretary, 11 November, www.whitehouse.gov/the-press-office/2014/11/11/fact-sheet-us-china-joint-announ cement-climate-change-and-clean-energy-c (accessed 11. 11. 14).

Thoreau, H. D. (2004[1854]). *Walden and Other Writings*. New York: Bantam Dell.

TM (2015). Transition initiatives map. www.transitionnetwork.org/initiatives/map (accessed 7. 4. 15).

Wilkinson, R. and Pickett, K. (2010). *The Spirit Level: Why Equality is Better for Everyone*. London: Penguin Books.

Woellert, L. (2014). Minimum Wages. Bloomberg, www.bloombergview.com/quickta ke/minimum-wages (accessed 6. 11. 14).

World Bank (2015). CO2 emissions 2010–2014 (metric tons per capita). http://data. worldbank.org/indicator/EN.ATM.CO2E.PC (accessed 11. 11. 14).

Worldwatch Institute (2015). An analysis of France's climate bill: Green deal or great disillusion?www.worldwatch.org/analysis-france's-climate-bill-green-deal-or-great-dis illusion (accessed 11. 11. 14).

Whyte, M. K. (ed.). (2010). *One Country, Two Societies? Rural–Urban Inequality in Contemporary China*. Cambridge, MA: Harvard University Press.

Xue, J., Arler, F. and Naess, P. (2012). Is the degrowth debate relevant to China? *Environment, Development and Sustainability*, 14(1), 85–109.

Xue, J., Gao, W. and Guo, L. (2014). Informal employment and its effect on the income distribution in urban China. *China Economic Review*, 31, 84–93.

Zhao, S., Wu, C., Hong, H. and Zhang, L. (2009). Linking the concept of ecological footprint and valuation of ecosystem services – A case study of economic growth and natural carrying capacity. *International Journal of Sustainable Development & World Ecology*, 16(2), 137–142.

10 Social economy and green social enterprises

Production for sustainable welfare?

Eric Clark and Håkan Johansson

Introduction

Human welfare requires the production of goods and services for the satisfaction of human needs. The tensions inherent to sustainable welfare (see Chapters 1 and 5 in this volume) have intensified with the expansion of capitalist social relations of production and the growth imperative playing out at ever greater scales. Aristotle's distinction between the art of householding resources – *oikonomia* (economics, or 'householding proper') – and the art of acquisition – *khrematistiké* (chrematistics, or 'moneymaking') – 'probably the most prophetic pointer ever made in the realm of the social sciences' (Polanyi, 2001 [1944]: 56), has become more relevant than ever (Stahel, 2006; Cruz *et al.*, 2009; Daly, 2009). With increasing evidence of the unsustainability of profit-oriented relations of production that have naturalized the norm of compound growth, questions concerning alternative systems of provision and forms of economic integration are becoming ever more pressing. The recent surge of interest in researching and developing cooperatives, non-profit organizations, social practices of 'commoning', social enterprises and related forms of third-sector (non-state and non-market) organizations has deep roots in social and economic thought, reflected in currents of thought associated with the notion of social economy (Amin *et al.*, 2002; Moulaert and Ailenei, 2005).

This chapter engages with issues concerning the current and potential role of 'green social enterprises' in promoting solutions to the challenges of achieving sustainable welfare. The first section sketches an analytical framework, drawing primarily on the work of Karl Polanyi on social economy and forms of economic integration. We then provide a brief critical overview of social enterprises, relating the rise and proliferation of the concept and associated phenomena to broader shifts in politics and political economy. In the following section, we then consider the notion of 'green social enterprises' from radical versus mainstream perspectives (Johanisová and Fraňková, 2013), emphasizing the role of use value-oriented versus exchange value-oriented investment and decision-making (Sayer, 2012, 2015). We conclude that 'fostering social enterprise' (Doeringer, 2010) without effective constraints on exchange value-oriented decision-making with regard to investment in systems of provision can at best only marginally contribute to sustainable welfare, and quite possibly even work against this elusive goal. Sustainable welfare requires political, economic and judicial reforms geared to foster use value-oriented decision-making processes in all spheres of investment, and not only in a marginal sector of an otherwise market- and state-dominated economy.

The social economy and economic integration

The concept of social economy has a long history, especially in the European context, where early-twentieth-century usage by political economists emphasized the social embeddedness of economic relations and processes, countering tendencies to conceptualize the economy as being separate from politics and disembedded from society. This emphasis has diminished as social economy has come to be understood more in terms of a distinct sector of economic activity arising where goods and services 'are not provided for by the state or the private sector' (Amin *et al.*, 2002: vii). From this narrower perspective, social economy is an umbrella concept covering a diverse set of practices variously known as: solidarity economy, alternative economy, non-lucrative sector, non-profit sector and, more recently, social enterprises (Galera and Borzaga, 2009; Defourny *et al.*, 2014; Laville *et al.*, 2015). Tensions between the social economy as a discrete sector and the social economy as a broader conceptualization of economies (emphasizing the social embeddedness of markets and the state as well as civil society) remain, while political economists, economic geographers and economic sociologists, drawing on Marxian, Polanyian and heterodox economic traditions, hold onto the broader understanding of social economy amid a predominant mainstream view of social economy as a third sector separate from market and state, between the private and public sectors.

Based on studies of primitive, archaic and modern economies, the economic historian Karl Polanyi critiqued the formalism of contemporary economic theory and developed a 'substantivist' alternative in which the economy is understood as an 'instituted process' involving 'mechanisms of integration'. This substantivism involves a focus on materiality such that instituted processes consist of movements of people and material things, whereby relations between things and persons are manifested in time–space. The patterns of movement generated in the specific contexts of economic integration reflect societal metabolism in that the movements serve to supply people with flows of material goods; '[the] social relations in which the process is embedded invest it with a measure of unity and stability' (Polanyi, 1968: 307). Polanyi identifies three ideal patterns of movements corresponding to the configurations of economic coordination and institutional structure associated with three basic mechanisms of economic integration: reciprocity, redistribution and exchange. Dale (2010: 115) summarizes: 'The movements of redistribution are centric, its typical institutional locus is the state; those of reciprocity are symmetrical, its locus the community; those of exchange are polydirectional, its locus the market.'

These forms of economic integration are not mutually exclusive, but rather enmeshed and, 'cannot be understood in isolation from each other. Each is defined with respect to the role it plays vis-à-vis the others' (Harvey, 1973: 283). As a result, we can only imagine (and barely that) societies entirely integrated through one mechanism alone. In practice, state redistribution, market exchange and community reciprocity coexist in all societies. Historically, however, state redistribution and market exchange and their associated patterns of movements of material flows have expanded with urbanization and the increasing density and complexity of societal formations, at the cost of (though never totally displacing) community reciprocity. We recognize the now common triad of state, market and community (or civil society). But while Polanyi emphasized their intrinsic interdependencies, the error of formalist economics – still in ascendency at the time of Polanyi's writing and today a widely accepted myth – 'was in equating the human economy in general with its market form' (Polanyi, 1977: 6). Markets are, however, 'not a kind of ether but are embedded in varying degrees in social relations' (Sayer and Walker, 1992: 230).

Drawing on Tönnies, Polanyi came to equate societies based on *Gemeinschaft* with those in which the economy is embedded in non-economic institutions. 'Policy in such societies is geared to satisfying socially determined needs; their individual members tend to suppress egotistical behaviour in favour of their role within the collective whole' (Dale, 2010: 192). *Gesellschaft*, on the other hand, 'entailed an inversion of the historical norm: instead of the economy being enmeshed within society, social relationships *"were now embedded in the economic system"*' (Polanyi, 1968: 70, emphasis in original). Chrematistic moneymaking displaces householding, as socialization pressures induce individuals to act as *homo oeconomicus*, the normative lodestar of neoclassical economics.

The forms of economic integration outlined by Polanyi continue to influence thought on the social economy, even as the more limited sectorial understanding of social economy as a third sector has become dominant. Moulaert and Ailenei (2005: 2042) define social economy as 'the universe of practices and forms of mobilising economic resources towards the satisfaction of human needs that belong neither to for-profit enterprises, nor to the institutions of the state in the narrow sense'. Other scholars make similar propositions, emphasizing sectorial differences such as the social economy constituting a distinct form of societal organizing, based on principles and incentive structures different from those of state, market or family (e.g. Evers and Laville, 2004). In a similar vein, others have focused on disentangling social economy organizations from profit-driven, market-oriented companies as distinct forms for organizing economic activity (e.g. Borzaga and Tortia, 2007).

Social economy organizations differ from market-based companies in that they are grounded in social needs, rather than in the imperative to make a profit. The social history of Europe includes a plethora of such social economic activities in which cooperatives, mutual aid societies and voluntary associations have endeavoured to provide for the needs of their members, associates or beneficiaries. The social economy hence addresses a diverse set of social problems faced by individuals and communities. An important implication of putting social needs first is that contractual market relations are subordinated to social relations between actors, either between those actors engaged in the activity, or with those whom the activity might benefit. This suggests a different governance model, since power and control are not in the hands of distant owners and shareholders, or in the hands of a central state, but in the hands of the members and participants. Internal democracy is essential as individuals engaged as members or participants are invited and expected to take part in decisions and influence the course of the organization (Laville, 2014).

The rise of social enterprises and social entrepreneurship

Social economy in its narrow sense has been experiencing a renaissance as socio-ecological challenges, combined with recent and ongoing experiences of totalitarian, oligarchic or plutocratic states, predatory capital and combinations of these, have spurred interest in alternatives. The difficulties faced by welfare states in providing security for large parts of the population have escalated with the advance of neoliberal politics based on market fundamentalism (Peck, 2010; Michaels, 2011; Mirowski, 2013; Block and Somers, 2014; Brown, 2015). In traditionally social democratic welfare states, such as the Nordic countries, there has also been a marked trend towards the privatization and creation of markets in order to provide welfare services. A recent study indicates that Sweden has liberalized faster over the last two decades than any other country in the Organisation for Economic Co-operation and Development (OECD) (Eriksson, 2012; cf. Ramesh, 2012; The Economist, 2013). As Blyth (2002; cf. Harvey, 2005) shows, this has been largely the result of a concerted effort by well organized Swedish and international capital interests. Initially the sphere of housing was targeted for privatization and reforms to attain market ideals (Clark and Johnson, 2009; Hedin *et al.*, 2012), thereafter education and healthcare, in spite of solid public opinion against the reforms (Svallfors, 2011; Lundquist, 2013) and the lack of 'evidence in support of improved cost effectiveness or enhanced service quality' (Petersen and Hjelmar, 2014: 3; cf. Hartman, 2011). Similar processes have unfolded in many countries around the world (Harvey, 2005; Peck, 2010).

Under the pressure of rising unemployment and austerity politics – part and parcel of the political processes of neoliberalization – governments are seeking new ways of engaging citizens and stimulating the creation of various types of social economy organizations and citizen associations 'in the provision and governance of publicly financed welfare services' (Defourny, *et al.*, 2014: 5). The notions of social enterprise and social entrepreneurship have rapidly ascended on political agendas, promising solutions to pressing problems (Defourney and Nyssens, 2010; Kerlin, 2010), and emphasis on the third sector's productive capacity is now a core theme in political discourses (European Commission, 2014). Social enterprises are seen as valuable complements and even alternatives to publicly owned and operated services. Unlike traditional cooperatives primarily oriented towards member interests, these initiatives serve 'a broader community' and place 'more emphasis on the dimension of general interest' (Defourny and Nyssens, 2008: 204). As a result, they provide alternative safety nets that appear to be spreading out under welfare states that are being dismantled.

The relinquishment, privatization and subsequent outsourcing that is taking place in various spheres where service provision was previously carried out by the public sector constitute a significant context for the emergence of social enterprises and the enthusiastic promotion of social entrepreneurship, as does the political mobilization of citizens' discontent with the perceived rigidities and inefficiencies of public sector models of welfare services provision. Rising expectations that services should adhere to market and business models have blurred the boundary between market-based and non-profit organizations (Anheier, 2005; Eikenberry and Kluver, 2004; Weisbrod, 2000). In the process, traditional social economy organizations such as cooperatives and non-profit organizations enter into processes of marketization and commercialization as they become increasingly involved in delivering services based on competitive bidding for public contracts. The emergence of social enterprises reflects these wider processes, and this has been supported by state and local authorities, including programmes and support mechanisms designed to help people set up social enterprises in order to achieve specific policy aims.

Meanwhile, financial and corporate actors skim off the most profitable opportunities opened up by the privatization of welfare services – through both geographical selection and the selection of specific services according to returns – *and* participate in encouraging the third sector to function in a 'business-like' manner, that is, to be profit-seeking (Werne and Unsgaard, 2014). In this way, the third sector appears to have grown, all the while being increasingly squeezed between the state and market, as 'corporate support for nonprofits has a tendency to evolve into corporate dominance over them' (Jones, 2007: 163). Commercialization, managerialism and the increasing use of contractual governance models are often identified as drivers of 'mission drift' among social economy organizations, which is associated with neglect of beneficiaries and a decline in member involvement (Bennett and Savani, 2011; Hvenmark, 2015). Levitt (2013: 101–102; emphasis in original) argues that the assumption behind policies geared to increasing activities in the third sector as a means to re-embed the economy has been 'that empowerment of civil society could substitute for the traditional role of the state. In reality, the rolling back of the state has *dis*-empowered civil society'. And she concludes that 'the result has been to diminish the capacity of societies to determine the allocation of their own resources' (Levitt, 2013: 102).

There are considerable expectations placed on these 'new' organizations, currently 'accorded a status of – if not quite a panacea – then at least a significantly important emergence in the societal management of key social needs' (Dart, 2004: 413). But where some see 'the seeds' of an economy characterized by prosperity without growth (Jackson, 2009: 130), 'the principal agents of a steady-state economy' (Dietz and O'Neill, 2013: 148) and a potential path to degrowth (Johanisová *et al.*, 2013), others see a fetish (Andersson, 2012) and argue that the marketization of the non-profit sector places civil society at risk (Eikenberry and Kluver, 2004).

It can be useful to take a moment to delve deeper into the concept at hand. Webster's New Twentieth Century Dictionary (1983) informs us that 'enterprise' is of French origin, 'from *entreprendre*, to undertake; *entre*, in or between, and *prendre*, to take; *prise*, a taking'. A now obsolete verb – 'to enterprise' – meant 'to attack'. The American Heritage Dictionary (1976) appendix on Indo-European roots informs us that the etymological root of enterprise, *ghend-*, means to seize, to take, to acquire, and its Latin variant *prehendere* means to get hold of, seize, grasp (related to predatory, prey, depredate). This resonates poorly with ideas of reciprocity and provisioning for social needs. It sounds more like a concept instrumental for the engulfing of Aristotle's social economy (*oikonomía*, householding proper) by chrematistics (the art of acquisition).

Understanding social entrepreneurship as a fetish, 'an object of desire – more important for what it symbolizes than for its substance and applicability to nonprofits' Andersson (2012), finds support in the undeniable lack of any common understanding of what constitutes a social enterprise. A recent review found that 'approaches used to frame social enterprise organizations were seriously flawed and fundamentally problematic, and criteria to distinguish social enterprise from other organizations were seemingly arbitrary, unstable, or unworkable' (Dart *et al.*, 2010: 186). While social enterprises are commonly presented as a form of non-profit activity with social aims for benefiting the community, they are also presented as manifesting the 'entrepreneurial dynamics which are at work at the very heart of the third sector' (Defourny *et al.*, 2014: 3). The extent to which social enterprises remain embedded in community- and reciprocity-based forms of economic integration is disputable since these entrepreneurial dynamics can include profit-making, shareholders and dividends, leaving little to distinguish them from corporations. While some see a risk that the 'concept of social enterprise is in danger of being co-opted by the business-as-usual approach' (Johanisová and Wolf, 2012: 566), others associate the 'emergence of social enterprise with neoconservative, pro-business, and pro-market political and ideological values' (Dart, 2004: 411), suggesting that the concept of social enterprise may rather be instrumental in an ongoing co-optation of the solidarity economy, cooperatives, non-profit enterprises, community organizations and various forms of reciprocity-based economic activities.

Towards green social enterprises

The high expectations placed on social economy organizations, increasingly referred to as social enterprises, raise the question of their potential for both upscaling and 'greening' as a way of addressing sustainability challenges. Activities in the sector tend, however, to focus primarily on social and employment concerns such as the integration of the disadvantaged and unemployed through work integration programmes and sheltered employment, the provision of social services of general interest such as long-term care for the elderly and for people with disabilities, or other types of social welfare services such as education and childcare, housing the homeless, or healthcare and medical services (European Commission, 2014). Most social enterprises remain within the main framework of work integration, in which the term 'social' is equated with a complex set of socio-economic problems linked to the restructuring of the labour market and the dismantling of the welfare state. In this sense, they fall largely under what Johanisová and Fraňková (2013: 110) call the 'mainstream perspective', in which 'social enterprises are seen as complements to mainstream enterprises, mitigating poverty and inequality and enhancing employment and growth'. Against this they juxtapose a 'radical perspective' from which social enterprises 'are seen as alternatives to mainstream enterprises and as part of an alternative non-growing economy, based on co-operation, sharing and equity' (Johanisová and Fraňková, 2013).

We find the distinction between mainstream and radical perspectives on social enterprises useful, but would caution against the 'attempt to broaden the definition' (Johanisová and Fraňková, 2013: 113) of social enterprises for the reason suggested above: this can entail the co-optation of non-profit enterprises, cooperatives and reciprocity-based organizations. What is gained and what is lost in identifying a community library as a social enterprise, as does Jackson (2009: 130)? As Eikenberry and Kluver (2004: 132) suggest, the pressure to function in a 'business-like' manner and embrace market values 'may harm democracy and citizenship because of its impact on nonprofit organisations' ability to create and maintain a strong civil society'. For social economy organizations in the third sector, 'entrepreneurial activities ... can seriously challenge the way nonprofits operate, and add additional burdens and tasks to volunteers, staff and board' (Andersson, 2012).

As we see it, a more radical perspective would not merely redefine segments of market exchange forms of economic integration so that they are then considered to be third-sector community and/or reciprocity forms of economic activities. A radical perspective would seek instead to reinvigorate the dimension of reciprocity emphasized by Polanyi, potentially through state legislation and the establishment of associated institutions that not only encourage third-sector activities but also protect them from the encroachment of powerful economic and political interests. A radical perspective would simply not consider market exchange-oriented enterprises as being part of the third sector (i.e. social economy in the narrow sense).

Another issue, much less explored, is how social enterprises can potentially contribute to addressing complex environmental challenges and thereby facilitate the achievement of sustainable welfare. It is challenging to disentangle social dimensions from environmental ones. Some investigations suggest that it is more common for green enterprises to have social benefits than the other way around (Anastasias and Mayr, 2009; Johanisová and Fraňková, 2013). In a UK study, Vickers and Lyon (2012) discern three ideal-typical forms of green social enterprises. One type (small and beautiful) is the locally embedded environmental social enterprise, which relies on local ownership and control, acts close to customers and consumers, and draws on the commitment of volunteers through close connections to the local community. These are run by local activists who have a direct personal involvement in the activity. Another type (green knowledge economy) is the expertise-oriented environmental social enterprise, based on the competence and knowledge of the actors involved, for example through selling consultancy services and expertise, often working closely with clients. A third form of environmental social enterprise (green collar army) is more in line with the mainstream model of a social enterprise. These provide labour-intensive services, often based on private and/or public contracts, for instance in carrying out waste recovery.

Emphasis on paid work, formal organizations and market orientation excludes many activities that combine social and environmental concerns. A broader understanding of social economy organizations would include informal activities, unpaid work and alternative economic activities that do not seek entrance into the mainstream economy. Johanisová and Fraňková (2013) consequently critique the mainstream perspective on social enterprises for having neglected this largely unrecognized sphere of economic activities. They go on to suggest five dimensions that characterize environmental, green, or what they call eco-social enterprises (Johanisová and Fraňková, 2013: 122–124). Besides (1) an explicit green goal of the activity, product or service, they should have (2) an environmentally friendly production process and (3) a local or regional scope of their operations, with localized patterns of provisioning. Moreover, the enterprise should (4) be designed for and retain the small scale: expansion should be by replication of small-scale units rather than the growth of each unit. And finally, eco-social enterprises have (5) a financial and organizational form of governance that insulates them from the growth imperative.

Though we have made it clear that we would use a different vocabulary indicative of a perspective more consistent with our Polanyian framework (i.e. we see an inconsistency in using the term 'enterprise' for reciprocity-based civil society/community organizations), we find this analysis of Johanisová and Fraňková highly relevant to issues concerning production for sustainable welfare. We would emphasize their fifth dimension of financial and organizational forms of governance, which not only potentially insulates organizations from the growth imperative, but also insulates them from forces encouraging exchange value-oriented decision-making, while providing a basis for the flourishing of use value-oriented decision-making. This distinction was elaborated on in Chapter 5 and is especially relevant to issues surrounding production for sustainable welfare.

The argument is based on Sayer's (2015: 34–35) critique of the concept of investment as 'the most dangerously ambiguous word in our economic vocabulary'. Used with utterly different meanings, 'investment' hides the important difference between wealth extraction and wealth creation, camouflaging the former with the latter. Sayer (2015) distinguishes between a use value-oriented meaning that focuses on what is invested *in* and an exchange value-oriented meaning that focuses on 'the financial gains of the "investor" from any kind of spending, lending, saving, purchase of financial assets or speculation – regardless of whether they contribute to any objective investment, or anything socially useful'. The confusion emanating from one concept standing for such different meanings conceals 'a moral difference – between contributing to the creation of something useful and just getting a return, no matter what' (Sayer, 2015: 36). Sayer sees the rise of exchange value-oriented 'investment' to a position of dominance over use value-oriented investment as a manifestation of

> the emergence of "financialised" capitalism, which prioritises making money out of money, instead of the tricky business of organising people to produce goods and services. It's truly extraordinary that we treat these different things as one and the same without even noticing.
>
> (Sayer, 2015: 36)

Much of the mainstream social enterprise literature remains silent about this distinction, even while assuming that social enterprises have a use value orientation in their social (and/or environmental) purpose, which they some-how fulfil more adequately by acting in a business-like manner – in practice by making decisions on the basis of exchange value considerations. Rationalizing a shift in the third sector and civil society towards exchange value-oriented decision-making obfuscates the historically significant role that they play in cultivating and maintaining conditions favourable to use value-oriented decision-making. This is conducive neither to sustainability (Clark and Hermele, 2014) nor to welfare (Sayer, 2015).

Conclusion

The remarkable rise of social enterprises and social entrepreneurship must be understood against the backdrop of decades of neoliberalization, which has brought rising and ostensibly permanent unemployment, austerity politics, the dismantling of welfare institutions and the outsourcing of public services, rampant financialization and seemingly intractable problems in the wake of severe economic, social and environmental crises. As public authorities have sought to adapt to neoliberal regimes, including the devolution of responsibilities combined with reduced transfers through national governments, it becomes more 'efficient' to be flexible and outsource services to social entrepreneurs on a contractual basis, rather than maintain the organization of such services: social enterprises are filling in the cracks of welfare states in decline. From a related, if more positive, perspective the rise of social enterprises should also be understood as being based in grassroots responses to a crisis that has left large swathes of society searching for alternatives to the politics and institutions that led to the crisis in the first place.

In the early 1950s, Karl Polanyi saw a 'change in the *institutional reality*. Exchange – the dominant form of integration – is receding, and reciprocity and redistribution are coming to the fore' (Polanyi, 2014: 136; emphasis in original). This may well have been accurate at the time, and in many places during the early post-war period. But, since the 1970s, market exchange is back on the throne, subordinating the state and civil society to the logic of market fundamentalism. Fostering the entrepreneurialism of social enterprises runs the risk of diminishing community reciprocity in order to solve problems in the spheres of market exchange (the 'market imperfection' of exclusion – especially visible in housing – and the incessant need for new fields of profitable 'investment') and state redistribution (democratic deficits and demise of welfare state provision).

Without effective constraints – in all three modes of economic integration – on exchange value-oriented decision-making over investments in systems of provision, the expansion of the green social enterprise sector can at best only marginally contribute to sustainable welfare and quite possibly even work against this elusive goal. Sustainable welfare requires political, economic and judicial reforms geared to foster use value-oriented decision-making processes in all spheres of investment, not only in a marginal sector of an otherwise market and state-dominated economy.

Polanyi (1968: 149) also argued that 'the different patterns of integration [market exchange, state redistribution and community reciprocity] assume definite institutional supports'. Effectively moving toward systems of provision and production for sustainable welfare will require strengthening institutional supports for state redistribution and community reciprocity. This direction will also require changing institutional supports for market exchange so that local and regional markets in the service of providing for needs and welfare are strengthened, while the currently excessive institutional supports for chrematistic moneymaking are radically reduced. Finance and markets need to be brought into the service of production for sustainable welfare. For this, the state must play a key role. Sustainable welfare cannot be reached by community reciprocity alone.

References

American Heritage Dictionary (1976). Boston, MA: Houghton Mifflin.
Amin, A., Cameron, A. and Hudson, R. (2002). *Placing the Social Economy*. London: Routledge.
Anastasias, M. and Mayr, A. (2009). The role of ECO-WISEs in sustainable development: Results from a research-project on ECO-WISEs in Austria, SERC-ISERC Conference, Oxford University, 14–16 September 2009.
Andersson, F. O. (2012) Social entrepreneurship as fetish. *Nonprofit Quarterly*, 11 April.
Anheier, H. (2005). *Nonprofit Organizations: Theory, Management, Policy*. Abingdon: Routledge.

Bennett, R. and Savani, S. (2011). Surviving mission drift. How charities can turn dependence on government contract funding to their own advantage. *Nonprofit Management & Leadership*, 22(2), 217–231.

Block, F. and Somers, M. R. (2014). *The Power of Market Fundamentalism: Karl Polanyi's Critique.* Cambridge, MA: Harvard University Press.

Blyth, M. (2002). *Great Transformations: Economic Ideas and Institutional Change in the Twentieth Century.* Cambridge: Cambridge University Press.

Borzaga, C. and Tortia, E. (2007). Social Economy Organisations in the Theory of the Firm. In A. Noya, and E. Clarence (eds), *The Social Economy: Building Inclusive Economies* (23–60). Paris: OECD.

Brown, W. (2015). *Undoing the Demos: Neoliberalism's Stealth Revolution.* New York: Zone Books.

Clark, E. and Johnson, K. (2009). Circumventing Circumscribed Neoliberalism: The 'System Switch' in Swedish Housing. In S. Glynn (ed.), *Where the Other Half Lives: Lower Income Housing in a Neoliberal World* (173–194). London: Pluto.

Clark, E. and Hermele, K. (2014). Financialisation of the environment: A literature review. *FESSUD Working Paper Series*, 32.

Cruz, I., Stahel, A. and Max-Neef, M. (2009). Towards a system development approach: Building on the human-scale development paradigm. *Ecological Economics*, 68, 2021–2030.

Dale, G. (2010). *Karl Polanyi: The Limits of the Market.* Cambridge: Polity.

Daly, H. E. (2009). Incorporating values in a bottom-line ecological economy. *Bulletin of Science, Technology & Society*, 29, 349–357.

Dart, R. (2004). The legitimacy of social enterprise. *Nonprofit Management & Leadership*, 14(4), 411–424.

Dart, R., Clow, E. and Armstrong, A. (2010). Meaningful difficulties in the mapping of social enterprises. *Social Enterprise Journal*, 6(3), 186–193.

Defourny, J. and Nyssens, M. (2008). Social enterprise in Europe: Recent trends and developments. *Social Enterprise Journal*, 4(3), 202–228.

Defourney, J. and Nyssens, M. (2010). Conceptions of social enterprise and social entrepreneurship in Europe and the United States: Convergence and divergences. *Journal of Social Entrepreneurship*, 1(1), 32–53.

Defourny, J., Hulgård, L. and Pestoff, V. (2014). Introduction to the 'SE field'. In J. Defourny, L. Hulgård, and V. Pestoff, (eds) *Social Enterprise and the Third Sector. Changing European Landscapes in a Comparative Perspective* (1–14). London: Routledge.

Dietz, R. and O'Neill, D. W. (2013). *Enough is Enough: Building a Sustainable Economy in a World of Finite Resources.* San Francisco, CA: Berrett-Koehler.

Doeringer, M. F. (2010). Fostering social enterprise: A historical and international analysis. *Duke Journal of Comparative & International Law*, 20, 291–329.

The Economist (2013). The next supermodel. *The Economist*, 2 February.

Eikenberry, A. M. and Kluver, J. D. (2004). The marketization of the nonprofit sector: Civil society at risk? *Public Administration Review*, 64(2), 132–140.

Eriksson, G. (2012). Den liberala revolutionen. *Svenska Dagbladet*, 24 March.

European Commission (2014). *A Map of Social Enterprises and their Eco-Systems in Europe. Synthesis Report.* Brussels: European Commission.

Evers, A. and Laville, J. L. (eds) (2004). *The Third Sector in Europe.* Cheltenham: Edward Elgar.

Galera, G. and Borzaga, C. (2009). Social enterprise: An international overview of its conceptual evolution and legal implementation. *Social Enterprise Journal*, 5(3), 210–228.

Hartman, L. (2011). Privatiseringar i välfärden har inte ökat effektiviteten. *Dagens Nyheter*, 7 September.

Harvey, D. (1973). *Social Justice and the City*. London: Edward Arnold.

Harvey, D. (2005). *A Brief History of Neoliberalism*. Oxford: Oxford University Press.

Hedin, K., Clark, E., Lundholm, E. and Malmberg, G. (2012). Neoliberalization of housing in Sweden: Gentrification, filtering and social polarization. *Annals of the Association of American Geographers*, 102(2), 443–463.

Hvenmark, J. (2015). Ideology, practice and process? A review of the concept of managerialism in civil society studies. *Voluntas. International Journal of Voluntary and Nonprofit Organizations*, DOI 10.1007/s11266–11015–9605-z.

Jackson, T. (2009). *Prosperity without Growth: Economics for a Finite Planet*. London: Earthscan.

Johanisová, N. and Wolf, S. (2012). Economic democracy: A path for the future? *Futures*, 44, 562–570.

Johanisová, N. and Fraňková, E. (2013). Eco-social Enterprises in Practice and Theory – A Radical Versus Mainstream View. In M. Anastasiadis (ed.) *Eco-wise – Social Enterprises as Sustainable Actors* (110–129). Bremen: EHV.

Johanisová, N., Crabtree, T. and Fraňková, E. (2013). Social enterprises and non-market capitals: A path to degrowth. *Journal of Cleaner Production*, 38(1), 7–16.

Jones, B. (2007). Citizens, partners or patrons? Corporate power and patronage capitalism. *Journal of Civil Society*, 3(2), 159–177.

Kerlin, J. A. (2010). A comparative analysis of the global emergence of social enterprise. *Voluntas. International Journal of Voluntary and Nonprofit Organizations*, 21(2), 162–179

Laville, J. L. (2014). The Social and Solidarity Economy: A Theoretical and Plural Framework. In J. Defourny, L. Hulgård, and V. Pestoff (eds), *Social Enterprise and the Third Sector. Changing European Landscapes in a Comparative Perspective* (102–113). London: Routledge.

Laville, J. L., Young, D. R. and Eynaud, P. (eds) (2015). *Civil society, the Third Sector and Social Enterprise. Governance and Democracy*. London: Routledge.

Levitt, K. P. (2013). *From the Great Transformation to the Great Financialization*. London: Zed Books.

Lundquist, L. (2013). NPM och demokrati. *Futuriblerne*, 41(3–4), 53–61.

Michaels, F. S. (2011). *Monoculture. How One story is Changing Everything*. Canada: Red Clover Press.

Mirowski, P. (2013). *Never Let a Serious Crisis Go to Waste: How Neoliberalism Survived the Financial Meltdown*. London: Verso.

Moulaert, F. and Ailenei, O. (2005). Social economy, third sector and solidarity relations: A conceptual synthesis from history to present. *Urban Studies*, 42(11), 2037–2053.

Peck, J. (2010). *Constructions of Neoliberal Reason*. Oxford: Oxford University Press.

Petersen, O. H. and Hjelmar, U. (2014). Marketization of welfare services in Scandinavia: A review of Swedish and Danish experiences. *Scandinavian Journal of Public Administration*, 17(4), 3–20.

Polanyi, K. (1968). *Primitive, Archaic and Modern Economies: Essays of Karl Polanyi*. (Ed.) G. Dalton. Boston: Beacon Press.

Polanyi, K. (1977). *The Livelihood of Man*. (Ed.) H. Pearson. New York: Academic Press.

170 *Eric Clark and Håkan Johansson*

Polanyi, K. (2001 [1944]). *The Great Transformation: The Political and Economic Origins of our Time*. Boston: Beacon Press.
Polanyi, K. (2014). *For a New West. Essays 1919–1958*. (Eds) G. Resta and M. Catanzariti. Cambridge: Polity Press.
Ramesh, R. (2012). Private healthcare: the lessons from Sweden. *The Guardian*, 18 December.
Sayer, A. (2012). Facing the Challenge of the Return of the Rich. In S. Roberts, M. Savage and W. Atkinson (eds), *Class Inequality in Austerity Britain* (163–179). Houndmills Basingstoke: Palgrave Macmillan.
Sayer, A. (2015). *Why We Can't Afford the Rich*. Bristol: Policy Press.
Sayer, A. and Walker, R. (1992). *The New Social Economy: Reworking the Division of Labor*. Oxford: Blackwell.
Stahel, A. W. (2006). Complexity, oikonomía and political economy. *Ecological Complexity*, 3, 369–381.
Svallfors, S. (2011). A bedrock of support? Trends in welfare state attitudes in Sweden, 1981–2010. *Social Policy & Administration*, 45, 806–825.
Vickers, I. and Lyon, F. (2012). Beyond green niches? Growth strategies of environmentally-motivated social enterprises. *International Small Business Journal*, 32(4), 449–470.
Webster's New Twentieth Century Dictionary (1983). New York: Prentice Hall.
Weisbrod, B. (2000). *To Profit or Not to Profit: The Commercial Transformation of the Nonprofit Sector*. Cambridge: Cambridge University Press.
Werne, K. and Unsgaard, O. F. (eds) (2014). *Den Stora Omvandlingen: En Granskning av Välfärdsmarknaden*. Stockholm: Leopard förlag.

Eric Clark wishes to acknowledge that this research, aside from support from the Pufendorf Institute at Lund University, also benefited from funding of the European Union Seventh Framework Program (FP7/2007–2013) under grant agreement no. 266800, FESSUD (fessud.eu), and from the richly stimulating collaborations in the Linnaeus Centre LUCID at Lund University, funded by the Swedish research council Formas (www.lucid.lu.se).

11 What is possible; what is imaginable

Stories about low carbon life in China

Erin Kennedy and Annika Pissin

Introduction

On 17 October 2014, prompted by a question about how to deal with smog, a young female blogger shared a three-item list: (1) use public transport or walk instead of using a private car; (2) do not throw away garbage or burn it randomly, do not randomly dispose of e-waste, and (3) save paper and use fewer disposable chopsticks. The blogger, who is in the last year of primary school, explained how she personally contributes to lower carbon emissions: instead of being driven to school by her father, she walks 40 minutes to school every day. In her opinion and based on her knowledge, she comments that the worst environmental effects and practices are to be found in the countryside near her grandparents' hometown where the mountains are bare because of clear-cutting and where peasants burn straw creating thick smog. The young blogger concludes 'In order to decrease the increase of smog, let us start close to ourselves, with ourselves! Let's make an effort together for our beautiful homeland. Carry the low carbon environmental protection through to the end.'[1] During World Café discussions, held at one of China's top universities,[2] students were asked to envision the type of future environment they hope to live in, taking into consideration China's current environmental problems and how these problems impact daily life. Students were asked to discuss their visions for the future and the actions required to achieve these visions, to identify key actors, to reflect on their own lives and to consider what actions they could take towards a low carbon lifestyle. Although some of the self-reflective optimism and idealism of the young blogger's comments can be found in the university student discussions, the students also clearly state the complexities involved in dealing with environmental issues in China. Concerns over clean air, water and food, particularly in relation to health and disease were the most frequently discussed environmental problems during the World Café sessions. Images of a future low carbon life included equal access to clean air, water and food for China's population. However, in discussions surrounding the actors and actions necessary to achieve these imagined futures, the students were divided, with contrasting points of departure when it came to considering responsibility, accountability and measurable actions for achieving reduced carbon emissions. The students' discussions highlight the complexity of environmental issues in relation to social welfare and well-being in Chinese society in general.

The purpose of this chapter is to explore stories of what is possible and what is imaginable for a low carbon life in China from the perspective of today's youth. This chapter draws predominantly from World Café discussions with university students and is supported with evidence from the blogs of children from mainland China. Through these sources, we explore the current discourse on environmental issues such as climate change and carbon emissions. Pressing environmental issues, how to address these issues, the key actors involved and the visions of the desired future and environment are explored in this chapter. Understanding how today's youth envision their future can be helpful when developing more innovative and adaptive methods for achieving China's reduced carbon emissions goals by 2030. Following the introduction, this chapter has four sections. We first look at the focus population for this chapter and discuss why it is important to include youth and China in environmental discussions. The second section explores the discourse in China on the topics of sustainability and climate change. Taking the 'good life' as our point of departure, we explore how this Western concept is being conceptualized in China. Then we look at the concept of low carbon life, which is a more local concept used in discourse on climate change in China. In order to provide some insight into this generation's knowledge and use of these concepts, this section draws from interviews with university students. These university students participated in World Café discussions on the topic of low carbon life and creating a zero-emission campus. It is important to note that, of the three World Cafés held, two events consisted of students studying in fields connected to the environment such as engineering, biology, chemistry, physics, public policy and medicine. The third World Café consisted of students from an array of academic disciplines, ranging from the sciences to the humanities. The majority of these participants did not focus on environmental issues in their studies. The third section discusses how youth in China conceive the future environment they would like to live in, their current environmental concerns and their ideas on how to address these environmental issues. Drawing from these ideas, in the final section of this chapter, we conclude with proposals for sustainable development that could be taken into consideration for policy development and implementation.

The ideas, knowledge and perceptions of youth with regard to the environment are often overlooked when it comes to policy, education and industrial development. This is a shortcoming of governments and societies the world over, which exclude a large section of the population from sharing their visions and ideas about the future that they themselves will actually experience one day (Toots et al., 2014; Smith, 2015; Holzscheiter, 2010). Why is it important to consider the perspectives of children and adolescents in discussions about the environmental problems of today and tomorrow? Why is it important to focus on youth in China?

Why youth and why China?

Children and adolescents are the focus population in this chapter because this section of the population is considered to be most vulnerable to the impacts of climate change (Bartlett, 2008; IPCC, 2012; Mitchell and Borchard, 2014; Baker, 2009). The youth of today will live through the era of climate change, having the longest exposure to the effects of climate change, which puts their health, physical, mental and social development at risk. Agenda 21 (1992) from the United Nations Conference on Environment and Development in Rio de Janeiro states the following when discussing action and the inclusion of children in sustainable development:

> Children not only will inherit the responsibility of looking after the Earth, but in many developing countries they comprise nearly half the population. Furthermore, children in both developing and industrialized countries are highly vulnerable to the effects of environmental degradation. They are also highly aware supporters of environmental thinking. The specific interests of children need to be taken fully into account in the participatory process on environment and development in order to safeguard the future sustainability of any actions taken to improve the environment.
>
> (Agenda 21, 1992, Chapter 25.12)

The youth of today should be included in discussions on issues that will impact their lives such as climate change. From a human rights perspective, The United Nations Convention on the Rights of the Child (United Nations, 1989) states that children have the right to participate, speak freely and be heard in matters that affect their lives. This includes the ideas, perspectives and visions of youth, as well as recognizing that children know a great deal about their environment and the environmental problems that they are confronted with during their daily lives as well as the problems of their nation and of the world (Engdahl and Rabušicová, 2011). Children have creative ideas about sustainable development and about developing environmentally friendly behaviours and actions in different sections of society (Engdahl and Rabušicová, 2011; Malone, 2013; Mitchell and Borchard, 2014). By including children and adolescents in discussions about the environment and the future of the environment, they develop a meaningful 'relationship between human behaviour and the environment and begin to think about the impact of human behaviour on the environment' (Engdahl and Rabušicová, 2011: 172). Mitchell and Borchard (2014) take this idea one step further and find anecdotal evidence that a 'child-centered approach to community-based adaptation can build the adaptive capacity of children and also provide benefits to entire communities' (Mitchell and Borchard, 2014: 372). Admittedly, this idea is in the early stages of development and requires further attention and collaboration between researchers and practitioners. However an increasing number of cases have had success using a child-centred approach (Johnson *et al.*, 2007; Malone, 2013; Mitchell and Borchard, 2014). This is significant, as one of the greatest challenges that today's youth face are issues of environmental change, access to natural resources and food security. Including tomorrow's future leaders in discussions about environmental issues that will impact their lives assists in developing the capacity of the next generation to adapt to the changing environment and, in the best case scenario, to move towards the education, industry, economy and society that facilitate sustainable development.

In absolute terms, China has been emitting the highest level of CO_2 emissions since 2007, having surpassed the United States. It is important to study China's carbon emission targets, environmental policies and implementation methods as China's carbon emissions have environmental impacts that are being and will continue to be felt around the world, on both the environmental and economic level. China has made significant efforts to reduce its CO_2 emissions within the industrial sector, its main source of carbon emissions. Since China is still a developing nation, its efforts to reduce CO_2 emissions is different from those of more developed nations, which focus on reducing emissions in the construction and transport sectors, with an increasing focus on citizen behaviour. China has the challenge of addressing large-scale emission ineffi- ciencies within multiple sectors, including the public sector. These emission inefficiencies differ across the vast and diverse geographical, cultural, regional economies, infrastructures and developmental stages that make up China. China is therefore faced with the task of simultaneously addressing different – and often conflicting – carbon emission challenges. How China addresses its multifaceted challenges is of interest to the global population as well as to the current generation of China's youth. Engaging with today's youth can provide some important insights into the concerns and visions that China's future generation has for its country's environmental, industrial and economic development.

The good life in China

Some contributors to this volume criticize contemporary Western ideas about well-being, happiness and the 'good life' in relation to sustainable life and human needs, as well as human capacity (see Introduction). The Western model of the 'good life' is viewed as being inappropriate for a sustainable life, due to its high and increasing material and energy consumption *and* unsustainable waste creation (see Chapter 1 in this volume). In Chapter 12, Soper suggests that it will be consumers who will act as drivers of change, mostly because of their 'disenchantment with the affluent life style'. She envisions that a turn toward more sustainable conceptions of the good life by the minority world consumers (in the case of China that would mostly be citizens of 'first-tier' cities along the east coast) might influence majority world consumers to try to understand and avoid the 'worst consequences of overdevelopment'(Soper, Chapter 12).

What does the good life mean in China, a country that is an amalgamation of overdeveloped pockets alongside large developing areas and a countryside where these dichotomies are expressed in large-scale inequalities in income and access to basic human needs?

The vision and practice of the good life in contemporary China is a growing middle-class lifestyle based on the concept of a privileged Western lifestyle, which is best expressed in urban housing and lifestyle practices (Pow and Kong, 2013: 11), big-ticket item purchases such as foreign cars (Youmin, 2012: 82–83) and the ability to access all things foreign and exotic, including travel to foreign countries (Pow and Kong, 2013). In general, great emphasis is placed on urban life when studying the good life in China, as cities are perceived as offering more opportunities for maintaining a good life, such as 'accumulation, attachment, handing down and agglomeration of wealth, power, information and the whole set of human lifestyles' (Li, 2010: 134). In fact, Li equates the good life with a '"way of life" that is distinctively urban' (Li, 2010: 145) because it is predominantly in cities where the kind of social development occurs that can lead to a community beyond the connections of family and home. The aspect of community is emphasized in most studies about the good life in China. When comparing a group of Chinese and a group of Canadian students' perceptions about their 'structure of cultural visions of the good life', Bonn and Tafarodi (2013: 1852) found that of most importance to the different groups was 'being connected to other people in desirable ways'. In the World Café discussions about environmental issues such as climate change with university students in China, the importance of having meaningful connections with other people was echoed as being an important part of their future hopes and imaginings. As part of a discussion that focused on environmental issues and on creating a zero-carbon campus, students were asked about their dreams for the future. The implications of this question focused on the environmental issues of today, the environmental issues that impact the students' lives, the changes they hope to see in the future and how to achieve these changes. However, some students interpreted this question in a more personal way, considering their dreams for their future personal life, and responses included the following hopes for their future lives: 'Finding my life partner', 'Graduating with ease, and falling in love just once' and 'Better health, easier life, harmonious'. Although, this is just a small sample, these quotes demonstrate the importance of developing significant human relationships and that having meaningful relationships in the future are at the forefront of the imaginings of some students.

In their study, Bonn and Tafarodi noted a higher investment in 'security, wealth, and social success' (2013: 1853) as being a particular feature of the Chinese participants, pointing to a specific type of ambition that is thought to lead to a good life. Bonn and Tafarodi's study about the good life did not mention consumption; instead it focused on general cultural differences and commonalities. Providing a brief overview about changing ideas in southern China concerning the good life throughout the whole period of the People's Republic of China up to the present day, Youmin (2012) demonstrates that, while material goods such as cars are of great importance for social status, people's longings and efforts are turning towards community creation and community rituals. According to Youmin (2012: 97), ideas about a good life in China are interwoven with Chinese perceptions of modernity – 'including industrialization, socialist movement, economic development and urbanization'. However, she states, 'though people are wealthier than before, the good life is still not coming according to their wishes. They feel that community life is incomplete and less than satisfactory due to a lack of traditional cultural and communal cohesion' (Youmin, 2012: 97).

Although a sense of happiness was reported in other studies (Li and Raine, 2013), it remains somewhat unclear if a plateau has been reached in levels of happiness that correlates to increases in wealth. For example, people's happiness may increase to a certain level in correlation with economic improvements; however, there may be a level of economic gain after which happiness no longer continues to rise exponentially, despite continued economic growth. Li and Raine (2013) concluded their study about life satisfaction quite contrarily, finding that despite economic growth over the last two decades, life satisfaction has declined. They investigated answers from a survey to the question, 'Are you satisfied [with your life]?', which does not carry the same socio-cultural pressure as the term 'happiness'. In a long-term study about the changing meaning of 'happiness' in Chinese history from 200 BCE to the early 1970s, Bauer (1976), for example, demonstrates that historical records express 'happiness' in a diverse range of imaginings and hopes according to the prevailing context of the creators of the records. Expressions of happiness thus included characteristics of hedonism and individualism, living in harmony with the environment, different ideas about paradise, anarchy, life in correspondence with society, nature and the universe, revolution and other ideas. One of Bauer's findings is that people also need the mystical or fantastical aspects of the world, since these are much closer to reality and surely a better aid for coping with the future than rigid ideas fixed in writing, such as Confucianism (Bauer 1976: 376).

The discussions of the good life in China range from how people actually live and what they practise or strive to practise in terms of lifestyle (lavish Western-style houses, high-rise apartments, high consumption of material goods, etc.), what is missing and thus preventing them from having a good life (e.g. sense of community) and which ideas exist in Chinese history and philosophy that add to the Western debate about a good life, such as: How is the low carbon life discussed? Does this present itself as a life of self-denial, as just another boom or simply as a necessity? Would a practice of low carbon life interfere with the practice of a good life? Prior to our discussion on low carbon life in China, we will introduce the concept of low carbon and explore the meanings that this concept has adopted and how it is being used within the context of China.

Low carbon

In China, low carbon (低碳生活) is a commonly used term; it is used and produced from multiple sources within the 'greenspeak' discourse, which is a form of a 'green public sphere' (Yang and Calhoun, 2007) within China. Private citizens, for example, use the term low carbon in their blogs and on social media platforms, such as Sina blogs and microblogs (Weibo). It is also used in messages developed and distributed by non-governmental organizations (NGOs) such as the green NGO Lvngo (Lvngo, 2015). A discourse known as 'greenwashing' also exists within the green public sphere of greenspeak; here the term low carbon is used by private and state businesses. Low carbon is used in messages produced by the state and consumed through mass media, propaganda slogans and the internet. Applied mostly in combination with concepts such as the economy, cities, travel, agriculture, architecture, technology, industry, steel, or quality of life, it is sometimes used interchangeably with the prefix 'green'.

The concept of the 'Chinese Dream', a term inspired by the 'American Dream', exists within the discourse on low carbon. The concept was initially introduced by Helen H. Wang (2010) in her book *The Chinese Dream*; influential environmentalists and NGOs in mainland China have inserted environmental concerns into the concept of the Chinese Dream and developed the concept further. The Chinese Dream is now a low carbon motto that seeks to re-image prosperity and to reshape consumerism in China. In interviews with one of the influential NGOs developing the Chinese Dream concept, Joint US-China Collaboration on Clean Energy (JUCCCE), representatives and Peggy Liu outlined the goal of the Chinese Dream as that of creating a new aspirational lifestyle that is sustainable for the emerging middle class in China. This Chinese dream focuses on creating new norms for the middle class; key actors include connecting leaders from environmental groups, cultural experts, advertising agencies and leading thinkers. According to JUCCCE representatives, their concept of the Chinese Dream has reached upper levels of government and has been used in speeches by Xi Jinping since 2013. JUCCCE is taking a market approach via advertisements and branding in order to create sustainable consumption habits that will become the new norms for the Chinese middle class. However, what 'sustainable' means within the context of the middle classes in China is still unclear and undefined. Thus, we can see similarities with Western discourse that focuses on curbing consumption habits and introducing concepts of sustainability into lifestyle aspirations. In interviews with JUCCCE, it became clear that the key actors involved operated at higher levels of society such as government staff and business leaders. Local citizens were included in initial pilot projects but during the planning and implementation stages the focus has remained at upper levels that do not include the views, perspectives or interpretations of the Chinese Dream at local citizen levels. Shifting the focus to include the ideas of local citizens, we move to the concept of low carbon life and examine how youth in China are becoming informed about a low carbon life and how they envision this life.

In China's 'green' propaganda machine, the terms climate change or global warming are noticeably absent. Instead messages focus on 'low carbon' or being 'green': these are politically and socially accepted terms (Eberhardt,

2015). This chapter focuses on the concept of 'low carbon life'. We are especially interested in how young people understand, imagine and practise a low carbon life, and how this can be framed within a global discourse on sustainable lifestyles. In this sense, we ask whether the low carbon life discourse can be compared to and combined with contemporary (Western-centred) discourse about reinterpreting concepts such as 'good life', 'happiness' and 'well-being' in sustainable lifestyles.

Low carbon life

At the beginning of this chapter we quoted a young female blogger who clearly articulated her understanding of environmental issues and how these issues can be resolved through living a low carbon life. How has a child developed the ability to understand and formulate the practical everyday behavioural changes that she can practise in her daily life in order to contribute to reducing her own carbon footprint? The reasons why low carbon life is a concept that ten-year-old children know well are manifold. First and foremost are the practical reasons: over a relatively brief period of time, environmental pollution – taking on distinct forms in rural and urban areas – has reached hazardous levels in China. People living in mega cities like Beijing, Shanghai, Guangzhou, Chengdu or Nanjing and other places use mobile apps to get information about the current level of air pollution as measured in particular matters (PM), carbon monoxide, nitrogen dioxide, ozone and sulphur dioxide, etc. In a similar way to checking the day's weather, it is now common practice to check air pollution levels in the morning as this will influence the day's activities. In Beijing, for example, on more than 180 days each year, air-quality levels are deemed as being 'dangerous', 'hazardous' or, at best, a warning is issued that the elderly, young and those with weak immune systems should stay indoors with the windows shut. Children in China are directly impacted by environmental pollution and poor air quality. From a health perspective, they are at risk of developing asthma; their growth and development are also at risk of being negatively impacted by poor air quality. On a practical level, children are not allowed to go outside and play, limiting their physical activity and increasing potential for obesity and decreasing opportunities for improving physical health, including muscle and bone mass development. Lifestyle habits like regular exercise and feeling connected to nature by spending time outside are also negatively impacted. Given the wide-ranging and long-term impacts on their health and development, it is important that children become aware of the environmental issues that they are facing and have the opportunity to talk about types of behaviour that support a low carbon life.

Increasing environmental awareness and activism by celebrities and famous people in China is increasing awareness of environmental concerns. At the end of February 2015, for example, the renowned Chinese journalist Chai Jin released a haunting documentary about the intersections between air pollution, health and the limitations that pollution puts on well-being and happiness. The conclusion that Chai Jin draws is hopeful, urging people to start changing their personal habits and encouraging the public that every small step matters.

Low carbon life is now part of the elementary school curriculum and is a topic that children are tested about with regard to knowledge, discussion and writing skills. Low carbon life is also present in university environmental clubs and is a concept discussed in speciality courses designed to investigate environmental issues at national and international levels. For example, at Fudan University in Shanghai, students can study courses that look at climate change and energy that are more 'progressive' and take national and global discussions into consideration.[3] Low carbon life promotes infrastructural, behavioural and systematic change within universities. Tongji University in Shanghai, for example, is making efforts to move towards carbon neutrality (Li et al., 2015), and both Tongji and Fudan universities are developing campus sustainability infrastructures and individual behavioural changes to reduce CO_2 emissions (Li et al., 2015; Jiang et al., 2013).

Low carbon life is also taking on a political dimension. Climate change is a politically sensitive term: it is tainted by a history of unsuccessful attempts to implement carbon emission reduction policies that placed China at the centre of international tensions surrounding its initial unwillingness to cooperate with global pressures to reduce its CO_2 emissions. Beyond global level pressures, which arguably did not take China's political, environmental, social and economic intricacies into account, Eberhardt (2015) suggests that the concept of low carbon life be used to discuss the consequences of anthropogenic climate change, a connection that is often overlooked, ignored or tiptoed around within the context of greenspeak and greenwashing messages.

Interpreting and conceptualizing low carbon life

World Café discussions with university students from one of China's top universities revealed multiple conceptualizations of low carbon life; these can be grouped into the following four main categories: (1) high quality lifestyle – here we can see ideas based on the activities of the individual and the community; (2) fashionable lifestyle – wherein the focus is more on the aesthetic and trendy aspects of a low carbon lifestyle; (3) resistance or rejection of a low carbon life – here the focus is on resistance towards individual behavioural changes and a reliance on the government to address environmental issues, including a focus on technology as the main source of pro-environmental change. The final category is (4) a lack of awareness of environmental problems – here people express denial of environmental problems and a lack of experience or knowledge of environmental issues such as air quality. Each category is explored through the discourse provided by World Café participants. As the majority of the participants provided their responses in Mandarin Chinese, it is important to note that the translations have not been edited to produce polished English sentences; they remain close to the source language.

Low carbon life, when perceived as a high-quality lifestyle, includes individual and community behavioural changes that are similar to degrowth ideologies and reduced-consumption behaviour; this is evident in quotes such as the following:

> Low carbon life is a high-quality life to me, because it means that you pay more attention to energy and environmental issues instead of material enjoyment. At the same time, you must constrain some desires or high carbon habits. I hope for a better environment and that my future generations have enough resources!
>
> Low carbon life means: healthy transport (more by bicycle and foot and less by car); good living habits and consciousness; starting from details to save energy. The change I mostly want to see is that energy expenditure decreases and lifestyle becomes healthier.
>
> Low carbon life means safety and moderation. I hope the air quality improves and there won't be any extreme weather.

Within the same category of a high-quality lifestyle, a low carbon life is associated with a lifestyle that promotes environmental changes that promote improved health. A low carbon life is described as including the activities of the individual and the community. The following is a selection of the students' imaginings:

> Low carbon life is a kind of lifestyle, a sense of responsibility and sense of mission. I hope the environment becomes clean and the temperature comfortable. I hope to become a part of the change.
>
> [Low carbon life is] a healthier lifestyle. Everybody has good pro-environmental consciousness and takes the initiative to participate in energy-saving and emission reduction activities.
>
> Low carbon life means a healthier life and a clean planet.
>
> It [low carbon life] means healthy. I think it not only has benefits for saving energy, but also to make us healthy.
>
> [Low carbon life means a] lifestyle and life attitude. More people choose to live a low-carbon life and start to improve the environment from daily details.
>
> It [low carbon life] means something new to my life and the better way to live. There would be less smog and the exhaust emission from vehicles is reduced.
>
> Everybody can live a low carbon life. It starts from quantitative and would accumulate to qualitative change. And developing a low carbon habit is the key to this problem.

Finally, within the same category of a high-quality lifestyle, a low carbon life includes descriptions of living closer to nature and having the ability to enjoy a relationship with a healthy environment. Participant responses include the following:

> I want to live in a precious space, living in a small house near a lake with clean water and fish and fresh air.
> The lifestyle we prefer includes a green environment, not crowded, quiet, safe, a lot of trees.
> Air pollution disappears, fewer people (lower population) and comfortable living environment.
> Low carbon life means a nice lifestyle. I hope that nobody litters.
> Personally, low carbon life is very necessary. Saving water and energy are not a big deal, if everybody can unconsciously do these things, our environment would become better.

The second conceptualization of a low carbon life is the idea of a fashionable lifestyle. Here participants discuss low carbon life in more general terms, the focus being more on the identity of living a low carbon life and the collective inclusiveness of a low carbon life.

> Low carbon life is a life attitude and a fashionable way of life, and should be brought into every detail of daily life. For me, I'd like to comply with this notion, from transport to other aspects (but I cannot be vegetarian …). I think low carbon cannot just be a slogan, and I hope I can do some promotion work. What I want most is to see the improvement of the air quality. And I hope to see that renewable energy could be used more widely, but it seems not that practical.
> It [low carbon life] means a more healthy and fashionable lifestyle. I want to see the sky become bluer and the air become fresher.
> Low carbon life means a fashionable life. I hope to see that everybody is doing things in a low carbon way.

The third main conceptualization of low carbon life includes the resistance or rejection of a low carbon life. Some participants expressed resistance towards and rejection of lifestyle changes that are based on reducing consumption or moving to behaviours perceived as being less developed. In the following quotes, the main actors for environmental improvements remain at the government level, and solutions focus on a reliance on technology. Resistance from the individual or the community as key actors in reducing carbon emissions is expressed.

> Low carbon life is not *barbarian* life. We can never go back. We should look into the future, new clean technology i.e. solar, nuclear energy.
> No bike! Not vegetarian! That's a stupid lifestyle.
> High-tech is more important than the small low carbon lifestyle.
> Dealing with the environment is not a short-term problem. We have to spend a lot of time to balance the economy and the environment at the

same time. For example, taking the bike to work or anywhere else is inefficient and a waste of time.

The fourth category found within the World Café conversations was a lack of awareness of environmental problems. Some students did not recognize their environment as being polluted or expressed an acceptance of the pollution as a temporary condition of development.

[I don't have] much personal experience [with] environment pollution.
The following pollution is part of a developmental phase: air, water and soil pollution, food safety, factory pollution, traffic. Pollution is a phase of industrialization and has to be tolerated. China is getting false accusations from developed countries.

From the discussions with university students, we can get an idea of students' understanding of current environmental concerns and imaginings of what a low carbon life could mean and what they hope it can develop into. Of course this is not representative of all of China's youth and only provides anecdotal evidence of the imaginings of young people today about their future.

Conclusion

What can we learn from talking to China's youth? Why is engaging with China's youth and listening to the discussions they have with their peers about the future of their environment valuable? The ways that youth describe and view their current environment and the visions they have for their future environment provides anecdotal evidence of the environmental, social and economic challenges that China is facing as it works towards reducing its carbon emissions. From the children's blogs and World Café discussions, it is apparent that China's youth is capable of envisioning a low carbon future and is motivated to create pro-environmental changes at local and national levels. The resistance met from some participants could actually be perceived as a positive response: this resistance demonstrates an anecdotal attempt to challenge the value of behavioural change and its actual impact on climate change. This resistance could be understood as a request for large-scale, measurable pro-environmental action from the government. Finally, the avoidance of the need for change (although anecdotal), is a minority opinion among the participants and is perhaps a reflection of the minority opinion within China; anti-climate change discourse is not limited to China but something that many Western countries continue to face.

In China, due to fast-paced development and high levels of pollution that are a result of this development path, ignoring the environmental problems that impact people's lives on a daily basis is not an option. Children and youth in China grow up in a vastly changed natural, political, social and economic environment compared to that of their parents. Until the mid-1990s, for example, bicycles were used as a common means of transport in cities (Zhang *et al.*, 2013). By the mid-2000s, as a result of several factors such as expanded urban areas but also accelerated by policies, bicycles were largely exchanged for fuel-driven means of transport such as scooters and cars (Zhang *et al.*, 2013: 318). Diet has also changed dramatically, favouring more sugar, oil and meat, especially pork, which has not only led to food-related diseases in children but also increased CO_2 emissions within less than one generation (Zhai *et al.*, 2014). China's population has extensive experience with large-scale social, political, economic, industrial and environmental change; today's youth is adept at living within a society that is constantly changing. The most prevalent changes are deteriorating air quality, questionable food sources and poor water quality, and hazards caused by waste, including e-waste in cities and in the countryside. Many of the children who received environmental education in primary school are now studying at college and university. As Eberhardt (2015: 38–39) points out, not only are young people aware of climate change as an environmental and political issue, but also the image of young people is used as a symbol for 'the next generation' in order to prompt people into action. Although an anecdotal and possibly overly optimistic observation, it does appear that China's youth is a group that could have the ability and the desire to shift towards a low carbon future, and they also have the education and technology to make their imaginings a reality. In terms of environmental policy development, the imaginings and abilities of China's youth should be harnessed, included and implemented within policy development. If China is to reduce its carbon emissions and achieve the 2030 carbon emission goals, it needs to look to the skills and visions of its future generation.

Notes

1 She writes: 将低碳环保进行到底, which is a pun on Mao Tse-tung's talk in 1948 entitled 'Carry the revolution through to the end', 将革命进行到底 (translation by Annika Pissin).
2 In order to protect the identity of the participants, the name of the university will remain confidential.
3 The course 'Climate Change and Energy' was taught to undergraduate students by Professor Jiang Ping from March to June 2014 at Fudan University.

References

Agenda 21 (1992). United NationsConference on Environment and Development. Rio de Janeiro, Brazil, 3–14 June 1992.
Baker, L. (2009). *Feeling the Heat: Child Survival in a Changing Climate*. London: Save the Children.
Bartlett, S. (2008). Climate change and urban children: Impacts and implications for adaptation in low- and middle-income countries. *Environment and Urbanization*, 20, 501–519.
Bauer, W. (1976). *China and the Search for Happiness: Recurring Themes in Four Thousand Years of Chinese Cultural History*. New York: Seabury Press.

Bonn, G. and Tafarodi, R. W. (2013). Visualizing the good life: A cross-cultural analysis. *Journal of Happiness Studies*, 14, 1839–1856.

Eberhardt, C. (2015). Discourse on climate change in China: A public sphere without the public. *China Information*, 29, 33–59.

Engdahl, I. and Rabušicová, M. (2011). Children's voices about the state of the Earth. *International Journal of Early Childhood*, 43, 153–176.

Holzscheiter, A. (2010). *Children's Rights in International Politics*. Houndmills: Palgrave Macmillan.

IPCC (2012). *Managing the Risks of Extreme Events and Disasters to Advance Climate Change Adaptation. A Special Report of Working Groups I and II of the Intergovernmental Panel on Climate Change*. Cambridge: Cambridge University Press.

Jiang, P., Chen, Y., Xu, B., Dong, W. and Kennedy, E. (2013). Building low carbon communities in China: The role of individual's behaviour change and engagement. *Energy Policy*, 60, 611–620.

Johnson, L. R., Johnson-Pynn, J. S. and Pynn, T. M. (2007). Youth civic engagement in China: Results from a program promoting environmental activism. *Journal of Adolescent Research*, 22, 355–386.

Li, C. (ed.) (2010). *China's Emerging Middle Class beyond Economic Transformation*. Washington, DC: The Brookings Institution.

Li, J. and Raine, J. W. (2013). The time trend of life satisfaction in China. *Social Indicators Research*, 116, 409–427.

Li, X. W., Tan, H. W. and Rackes, A. (2015). Carbon footprint analysis of student behavior for a sustainable university campus in China. *Journal of Cleaner Production*, 106, 97–108.

Lvngo (green NGO) (2015). www.lvngo.com (accessed 23. 10. 15).

Malone, K. (2013). 'The future lies in our hands': Children as researchers and environmental change agents in designing a child-friendly neighbourhood. *Local Environment*, 18, 372–395.

Mitchell, P. and Borchard, C. (2014). Mainstreaming children's vulnerabilities and capacities into community-based adaptation to enhance impact. *Climate and Development*, 6, 372–381.

Pow, C. P. and Kong, L. (2013). Marketing the Chinese dream home: Gated communities and representations of the good life in (post-)socialist Shanghai. *Urban Geography*, 28, 129–159.

United Nations (1989). Convention on the rights of the child, 20 November. *Annual Review of Population Law*, 16(95), 485–501.

Smith, A. (ed.) (2015). *Enhancing Children's Rights: Connecting Research, Policy and Practice*. Houndmills: Palgrave Macmillan.

Toots, A., Worley, N., Skosireva, A. (2014). Children as Political Actors. In G. B. Melton, A. Ben-Arieh, J. Cashmore, G. S. Goodman and N. K. Worley. *The SAGE Handbook of Child Research* (54–81). London: Sage.

Wang, H. H. (2010). *The Chinese Dream: The Rise of the World's Largest Middle Class and What It Means to You*. Brande: Bestseller Press.

Yang, G. and Calhoun, C. (2007). Media, civil society, and the rise of a green public sphere in China. *China Information*, 21, 211–236.

Youmin, L. (2012). Making sense of good life: Local modernity from a traditional industrial-commercial region in Southern China. *International Journal of Business Anthropology*, 3, 82–101.

Zhai, F. Y., Du, S. F., Wang, Z. H., Zhang, J. G., Du, W. W. and Popkin, B. M. (2014). Dynamics of the Chinese diet and the role of urbanicity, 1991–2011. *Obesity Reviews*, 15, Supplement 1, 16–26.

Zhang, H., Shaheen, S. A. and Chen, X. (2013). Bicycle evolution in China: From the 1900s to the present. *International Journal of Sustainable Transportation*, 8, 317–335.

12 The interaction of policy and experience
An 'alternative hedonist' optic

Kate Soper

Introduction

Against the background of ever more confident pronouncements from climate scientists on anthropogenic global warming, and ever more urgent appeals for action to counter it (IPCC, 2014), much attention is now being paid to the economic and social measures that could avert the more catastrophic outcomes. Environmental economists (if not politicians as yet) are rightly exposing how impossible it will be to reconcile ecological sustainability indefinitely with continuing economic growth and are calling for moves towards a steady-state economy (Goodland and Daly, 1992; Jackson, 2004, 2009; Victor, 2008; Kallis, 2011; Koch, 2012; Chapters 2, 9 and 10 in this volume). There is now a growing literature on the limitations of gross domestic product (GDP) as a measurement of prosperity, and much is being written on the disconnections between increased income and enhanced happiness (Inglehart and Klingemann, 2000; Easterlin, 2001; Layard, 2005; Latouche, 2009).[1] Much attention (as other chapters here testify) is also being paid within the social sciences and human geography to the lifestyle and policy changes that will be essential to secure sustainable welfare in the future.

But the means whereby such revolutionary economic and social transformations might be accomplished also require consideration. As academics we can elaborate upon the essential preconditions of globally sustainable welfare: greater equality, dramatic reductions in work and productivity, the formation of cultures in which money and material acquisition have become subordinate to other objectives and measures of prosperity, and so forth. We can also blueprint the economic and social arrangements that would best contribute to the realization of these goals. Yet these theoretical contributions will, alas, remain too purely theoretical in the absence of the powers and pressures required to translate them into effective practice. We need therefore to pay equal attention to the possible agents and processes of transformation: to ask how the pressures might begin to build for such an unprecedented and seismic geopolitical shift.

This is partly a question about the formal political process of change at international level, the influence exercised on that by national governments, and the role that electorates might play. But it also concerns the interactions between individual experiences, on the one hand, and social structures or systemic pressures, on the other, in bringing about the kind of substantive changes in provision for health, transport, education and the like that will be needed to secure more sustainable ways of living. It concerns, for example, the respective roles of individual actions and state interventions in changing consumer behaviour, or the impact of new attitudes and motivations on shifts in policy making, and vice versa.

Both at the more formal political level and in respect of social systems and their evolution, we confront a type of 'hen and egg problem' in the sense that the necessary public support for systemic change would seem to presuppose large-scale shifts in individual attitudes, while these latter would, in turn, appear to depend on the formative impact of prior changes at systemic level. 'High' living standards as measured by GDP have generally gone together with the evolution of representative democracy. But this, in turn, means that political transformations will require enlightened electoral mandates of a kind unlikely to precede, rather than follow upon, predisposing forms of social reform. And although it is true that more recourse to deliberative democracy could help to resolve these antinomies, this is itself a procedure that presupposes the ideal conditions of discourse (freedom and equality of persons, access to all relevant information, impartiality of judgement, etc.) that existing economic and social structures currently pre-empt. So while (as argued in more detail below) it is impossible to see how, in advanced democracies, any very major structural or institutional changes could be achieved in the absence of widespread enthusiasm for such measures, one also has to acknowledge how difficult it can be for such new collective dispositions to emerge without the conditioning of prior structural and institutional changes. People, for example, are unlikely to vote in large numbers for a reduction in the working week, however well-thought out the plans for that might be, in the absence of proper understanding and experience of the advantages that this could bring. But that understanding and experience can only be attained on the basis of informed discussion and implementation. Parties in government, moreover, will seldom see fit to provide the kind of systemic changes that could shift public attitudes over time because to do so would be to risk their own popularity with the electorate in the here and now. Their dependency on the goodwill of the business community is an added disincentive to the introduction of any policies relating to sustainability that will seriously reduce profits. Food manufacturers will be requested, but not forced, to reduce salt or sugar content in their goods; legislation on costing in the environmental impacts of commodity production will remain lax for fear of cutting profits or increasing prices, and so forth.

'Alternative hedonism': an immanent critique of consumer culture?

My argument on 'alternative hedonism' has been conceived and developed with these dilemmas in mind and with a view to bolstering credence in the possibility of democratic pressures for change (Soper, 2007, 2008a, 2008b, 2009).[2] Presented as an immanent critique of consumer culture, it focuses on the forms of emerging disaffection with the consumerist lifestyle experienced by consumers themselves and relates these to the ways in which affluent consumption is both compromised by its negative by-products (stress, time scarcity, ill health, traffic congestion, noise, and so on) and closes off other sources of pleasure and well-being.[3]

The emphasis is therefore on the more self-regarding, rather than altruistic, critical responses to contemporary consumer culture, a focus justified in part by the reinforcing and overdetermining role that it may come to play in promoting sustainable consumption.[4] For in the absence of a revised conception among the already more affluent communities of their own needs, interests and pleasures, pressure to secure the necessary policy changes is unlikely to be forthcoming. A changed perception of the 'good life' (an 'alternative hedonism') is thus a vital stimulant to the future curbing of consumerist culture and its more negative social and environmental impacts. The moral and material dissatisfactions generated by the affluent lifestyle acquire in this sense a definite political dimension. Or, to put the point slightly differently: it is not at all clear that other than at the level of consumption, and through resistance generated by disaffection with consumerism, that we can discover any leverage for a democratically achieved process of change in the West today. To invoke Bauman's terminology (Bauman, 1993), these first-world actors would belong to the 'seduced' rather than the 'repressed', to the majority, that is, with access to credit and consumer goods – but to an increasingly 'disillusioned' section of that majority within which Klein's 'blockadia' protesters and the alternative globalization 'multitude' currently figure as the most explicitly disillusioned (Klein, 2014, cf. Klein, 2000; Hardt and Negri, 2002; cf. Soper, 2008b). Let us note, however, that even if it is those who have already met their more material needs who can be expected to act most immediately in response to an interest in 'alternative hedonism', its objective has a more universal reference, since it relates to the provision of conditions of sustainable well-being from which everyone will benefit, regardless of income. Where Marx spoke of the proletariat as the 'universal class of humanity', we might today suggest that it is the trans-class constituency of the 'disillusioned seduced' who – were they over time to become numerous enough and sufficiently disenchanted with the methods and provisions of their multinational seducers – have it in their power to set off a relay of pressures that could both help to rescue the 'repressed' from their social exclusion and restore lost pleasures to everyone.

My argument, then, in summary form, is that if we are to see any radical shift of political direction in the developed nations, its agents will not be confined to the traditional labour movement, but will come from a broader trans-class body of concerned producers and consumers; that the pressure for change will be fuelled in part by disenchantment with the affluent lifestyle itself; and that it will discover its 'utopian' summons in a post-consumerist vision of the 'good life': a vision in which enjoyment and personal fulfilment are linked to methods of production and modes of consumption that are socially just and environmentally protective. This is not to predict a process, only to hypothesize the likely form of its evolution, were it to come about. Nor is it to deny the complexity of human desire and the need for sustainable alternatives to accommodate the distinctively human quests for novelty, excitement, distraction, self-expression and the gratifications of *amour propre*. Indeed, the critique associated with 'alternative hedonism' is directed primarily against the resource-intensive and competitive ways in which such desires are pursued in consumer culture, rather than against the quests themselves. 'Hedonism' is not here signalling advocacy of Utilitarianism, but the pleasures of escaping the light and noise pollution, the waste and material encumbrance and sheer ugliness of much that counts as a 'high' standard of living. The 'alternative hedonist' approach thus offers a profile of the consumer that differs in some respects from more conventional accounts: consumers, it suggests, are neither as heroically autonomous in their pursuit of private needs/desires as the neoclassical model implies (Campbell, 1995, 2004: 60–86; Featherstone, 1991; Fiske, 1989), nor as duped by market manipulation of their needs/desires as the Left critiques of commodification have claimed (Haug, 1986; Lodziak, 1995; cf. Gorz, 1989; Bauman, 1998). The main focus is neither on consumption as a bid for personal distinction, nor on consumption as a form of brainwashing, but on the ways in which a range of contemporary consumerist practices are being called into question by reason of their environmental consequences, their impact on health, and their limitations on sensual enjoyment and more 'spiritual' forms of well-being. It thus presents consumer responses as rather more open to 'republican' sentiment than previously acknowledged (in the sense that self-interested needs can also come to encompass public goods and gratifications) and also more equivocal (in the sense that, even as people are subject in all their purchasing decisions to the shaping forces of the market, they are also reflexive agents who are often troubled about the powers of consumer culture to determine their lived experience, especially in respect of the time spent working and the dominance of work over life; cf. Gorz, 1999; Fevre, 2003; Chapter 8 in this volume).

This new climate of disenchantment is reflected in the now quite widely held (and discussed) view that the 'consumerist' lifestyle is in many ways bad for us as well as for the environment (cf. Schor, 2010; Levett, 2003; Bunting, 2004; Honoré, 2005; Thomas, 2008, 2009; Osbaldiston, 2013) and in the concerns of policymakers with the economic and social effects of the high-stress, fast-food lifestyle (Brown and Kasser, 2005; Kasser, 2002, 2008). And it chimes with the evidence on the links between greater equality of income and improved happiness (Wilkinson and Pickett, 2009) and with the growing demands for the GNP measure of productivity to yield to others – such as the United Nations Development Programme (UNDP) Human Development Index (HDI) and the Index of Sustainable Economic Welfare (ISEW) – which are more reflective of real levels of well-being rather than purely quantitative economic growth.

Democracy: ally or enemy of sustainable welfare policy?

The 'alternative hedonist' response is, in this sense, a recognized cultural presence, and one that should be welcomed and encouraged by policymakers claiming a concern for sustainable welfare. In the eyes of some, however, it instantiates an altogether too wishful faith in the power of democratic process to resolve the environmental crisis. Cumulative 'bottom-up' pressures, on the contrary, it is argued, almost always run counter to environmental protection and therefore only more 'top-down' autocratic interventions will suffice. While noting that the earliest advocates of eco-authoritarian policies (cf. Heilbroner 1974; Ophuls, 1977) have been robustly refuted within the environmental movement, Ingolfur Blühdorn for example, has recently questioned the effectivity of democratic systems in delivering sustainable welfare and argued that, since 'democracy is always emancipatory, that is, it always centres on the *enhancement* of rights and (material) living conditions [...] it is not really suited for any form of *restriction* of rights or material conditions affecting the majority' (Blühdorn, 2011 (emphasis in original); cf. Blühdorn, 2013). Other commentators, he notes (Westra, 1998: 53–80; Shearman and Smith, 2007: 4; Giddens, 2009: 56, 198–199, 91–128), have likewise begun to regard participatory democracy as eco-politically ineffective and to suggest that liberal democracy is part of the current problem rather than the solution to it. For this way of thinking, the emancipatory-democratic optimism that once viewed liberation as release from the alienating and unsustainable logic of growth and productivism upheld by institutional authorities and elites, has given way to a conception of emancipation as the individual freedom to pursue a consumerist lifestyle and has thus become compliant with the established capitalist system. Echoing Bauman's views on 'liquid modernity' (Bauman, 2000, 2008), Blühdorn claims that, for today's pace-setters, 'acts of consumption have become the most important means of self-construction, self-expression and self-experience' and that, as these conceptions of identity become prevalent throughout society at large, citizens will demand to see them politically fostered – with dire consequences for any prospects of ecological sustainability. Moreover, in the wake of this so-called 'post-democratic' turn, the new cultural limitations, added to existing structural restraints, will

> stifle all hopes for the profound value change that would be required for any democratic transition to sustainability [...]. Contrary to the narratives of an emerging alternative hedonism, it is to be feared that under the conditions of advanced modern societies *more democracy* could imply even *less sustainability*.
>
> (Blühdorn, 2011: 6–7, emphasis in original)

At the limits to growth then, democracy, far from enabling social transformation, is said to have become a tool for the defence of the status quo and the governance of unsustainability.

Approaching the issues from the optic of political philosophy rather than cultural theory, Susan Baker has recently argued in a comparable fashion that liberal democracy can be seen as inherently unsupportive of the norm of sustainable development since it takes human interests as the measure of all values. She therefore casts doubt on the capacities of representative democracy to advance sustainable ways of living, and argues 'that in promoting the common good as a base for sustainable futures we will preclude certain values and human behaviours that are currently cherished in our liberal political order' – and, in effect, she implies, so much the better for the planet! (Baker, 2012: 266–268).

One has to feel some sympathy for such forms of scepticism about liberal democracy, given that those defending its 'freedoms' are frequently so indifferent both to the real world of need formation and satisfaction, with its huge inequalities of income and opportunity, and to its ever more intractable environmental constraints on indefinite consumption. What one currently misses from the libertarian attacks on all forms of state governance over needs or policing of consumption is any recognition of the 'dictatorship over needs', as it were, that is now exercised by consumer society itself, a society in which corporate power, its lackey politicians, the media and advertising all combine to exercise a monopoly over ideas and visions of the 'good life' and to promote ever more intensive 'grooming' of each upcoming generation for a life devoted to working and spending (Haug, 1986, 2006; Schor, 2010). One would also like more recognition of the forces arraigned today against democratic discussion of political ends. Mainstream parties in most affluent Western societies contend with each other only about the best way of attaining a commonly agreed set of 'progressive' ends, defined in terms of economic growth and expanding material consumption. They do not invite their electorates to debate the fundamental purpose or value of economic activity.

Yet it has to be said, too, that all of these grounds for scepticism are, at a more fundamental level, targeting not so much democracy itself, but its partial and inadequate realization in affluent consumer societies. Moreover, insofar as such societies are indeed less than fully democratic, it is in large part due to the subordination of national governments to the power of transnational corporations – who will always wield what influence they can to keep us in the shopping malls. What Blühdorn and other commentators also fail sufficiently to acknowledge is that enhanced material consumption can be as restrictive on 'rights' to, for example, more free time, unpolluted environments, less noise, as it is 'permissive' in advancing the majority's 'rights' to go shopping. Nor do these commentators adequately recognize the conflictual nature of such 'rights' in contemporary affluent cultures – where the 'rights' of car users so often clash with those of cyclists and pedestrians; of those who want piped music in their shops and cafés with those who do not; of those who want airport expansion with those who do not, and so on. But it is democracy, too, that seeks to offer some representation of these different needs and aspirations, and deliberative procedures for resolving conflicts between them. It may in practice do so very inadequately, but even that is a considerable advance on any more elitist system. Importantly too, in the current context, there is evidence that people are 'conditional cooperators' who are much more likely to take action to combat climate change impacts and conserve resources if they are assured, by democratic voting, that their fellow citizens will do the same. Democracy, it seems, very considerably enhances the chances of reciprocal cooperation (Hauser *et al.*, 2014; World Bank, 2015: 167). Moreover, and on a more philosophical note, even if it were to be possible to impose sustainability through a top-down dictatorship of needs, this would, paradoxically, have to count as a failure. For it is surely part of the moral logic of sustainability that it is not achievable if it is only achievable by highly coercive means. As Peter Victor has insisted, policy changes cannot be driven solely from the top: 'they must be wanted and demanded by the public because they see a better future for themselves, their children, and the children of others, if we turn away from the pursuit of unconstrained economic growth'. In fact, Victor suggests, the only option is bottom-up – 'a groundswell of aversion to further growth in consumption' (Victor, 2008: 221–222).

But the key point here, in any case, is what the sceptics would put in place of democratic transition: how do they envisage the institution of the more autocratic form of governance that they recommend as necessary to the promotion of sustainability? Who is the 'we' that Baker tells us will preclude certain liberal values in the interest of environmental well-being, and how does she envisage them attaining a position in which to do so? Even if one concedes the possibility of a more benevolent, sustainable-friendly elite emerging (a kind of Platonic philosopher-king rule …?), how could this gain the necessary power in modern democratic societies other than through an electoral mandate? (And in this connection we might ask, too, of those who 'call' for global regulatory authorities to replace democratic process: to whom are they addressing the call?). In other words, whatever the power of the critiques of democracy (or its deficit) in affluent consumer societies – and there is no doubt that they can prove, at least on first reading, depressingly persuasive – these critiques are seriously flawed by reason of their failure to provide any compelling account of the alternative means of transition to their recommended forms of governance. And in the absence of that, it would seem that we must *either* accept that the radical changes required to promote sustainable welfare will never come about, *or* we must retain some faith in the power of democratic process in the more affluent parts of the globe to precipitate the forms of resource redistribution and economic and social restructuring essential to secure a viable global order in the future.

Alternative hedonism: an overly individualist approach?

It is true, however, that even if the 'alternative hedonist' approach can be defended in these ways against the blanket dismissals of its anti-democratic critics, it remains vulnerable to the charge that it may rely too heavily on individual consumer responses to 'change the world' instead of targeting the structural and institutional obstacles standing in the way of personal self-change in the first place. It has also been construed as neglecting the formative impact of production and marketing strategies on consumer attitudes and their objective constraints on personal consumption habits even in those cases where there was some interest in changing the latter. My engagement with consumer disaffection with the affluent lifestyle has furthermore been criticized for abstracting from the development needs of the more impoverished global communities.[5] Though understandable, these more specific charges stem from a misconception of the political rationale for attending to the constituency of the 'affluent disaffected' in the argument for 'alternative hedonism': a misconception that I would hope to have gone some way to correct in the discussion above. But I shall here, in conclusion, seek to add to that clarification by expanding both on the ways in which new forms of 'alternative hedonist' experience emerge out of and contribute to changed social policy and on the relay of pressures that it could come to exert – hence on the potential 'global' reach of an alternative politics of prosperity.

On the first point: we must indeed acknowledge the key role of production in eliciting and creating new needs and wants (or new ways of meeting existing needs and wants) through its provision of goods and services on the market. In this sense, as Marx pointed out some time ago, (Marx, 1973: 99–108; cf. Soper, 1981: 40–72), it is not so much needs that lead to products, but products that lead to needs. In the spirit of this argument, we should also accept the analysis of those who point to the revised paradigms of consumption accompanying new regimes of capitalist accumulation and reorganization of the labour process. Fordist production pressures did indeed bring with them very significant changes in consumption norms, like, for example: the commercialization of goods previously supplied at home, the individualization of lifestyles, suburbanization and the shift from public transport to private car use, and so forth (Koch, 2012: 68–75). These trends have continued in the era of the so-called IT revolution, but have been augmented by the internet's transformation of work and consumption, the pervasive acquisition of personalized electronic equipment of all kinds and the immense acceleration of the fast-fashion dynamic and brand marketing across a whole range of goods (Schor, 2013).

As already indicated, it would be a mistake to invoke the extensive correlation between economic regimes and consumption in order to justify a wholly deterministic account of consumer responses, since that will not reflect the options for more ethical and sustainable ways of living. What it does capture, however, are the systemic curbs on the exercise of these forms of alternative choice. And it is here that policy interventions that tap into subjective shifts of feeling, using them as legitimating springboards for introducing social policies that adjust or remove those restraints, can prove of critical importance in advancing more sustainable welfare.

One frequently cited example of this is the way in which expanded provision of safe routes and other facilities for cyclists not only leads to more cycling, with all the benefits to health and well-being that follow from that, but also initiates everyone into the pleasures of reduced motor traffic, thereby reinforcing support for the transition to a less car-centred way of living. A related example that I have noted elsewhere (Soper, 2007: 220–222) is that of congestion charging in Greater London, introduced in February 2003. Prior to its introduction, this was a policy that could claim some measure of public concern about the gridlock and pollution caused by city driving and in this sense could appeal beforehand to a predisposition in its favour. It could not, in other words, have been imposed had it not been for an already existing degree of disaffection among London car owners and users with the 'car culture' and its impact on city life. Yet the level of explicit support for the policy was fairly low, and much of the response to the idea of its introduction remained ambivalent. Had it been put to the vote, it would probably not have received majority support.[6] On being implemented, however, it offered forms of experience (quicker and more reliable buses, emptier and less noxious streets) that enhanced public appreciation of the charging policy and later allowed for its further extension.[7] The policy thus instantiates an 'alternative hedonist' dialectic whereby an initial and still rather equivocal 'structure of feeling', which serves to legitimate the experimental introduction of certain forms of 'policing' of consumption, is extended and consolidated by reason of the pleasurable consequences of that 'policing'. One might also note here the expanding culture of what has been termed 'collaborative' or 'connected' consumption: networks of sharing, recycling, exchange of goods and service provision (including of banking and other financial services) that bypass the mainstream market provision (Schor, 2010, 2013). Prompted in part by the financial crisis of 2008, these have helped to reduce carbon emissions and waste, while at the same time creating more eco-sensitive communities and cooperative ways of living. Such networks have come to be valued in themselves by participants for the novel forms of social interaction that they provide – and are illustrative of the potential role of 'social capital' in advancing welfare discussed in Chapter 1. If encouraged by policy moves designed to protect and consolidate their presence, they could well shift current thinking about material culture in quite significant ways (acting as a check, for example, on the individualization of consumption or challenging the dominant consumerist aesthetics of 'newness' or shunning high street-led fashions and mass production in favour of clothes-swopping and craft and homemade goods). They might also over time prove the hubs for exerting pressure for the stricter regulation of corporations in order to end their reliance on sweatshop labour and ever faster turnover times, and to render them much more accountable than they currently are for the pollution incurred in production. One might also note the potential for influencing policy on 'disinvestment'. As Klein has argued, the withdrawal of investment in fossil fuel companies does not immediately harm Shell or Chevron, but it does put pressure on politicians to introduce across-the-board emission reductions and acts as a first stage in the delegitimization of further fossil fuel extraction (Klein, 2014).

Since developments of that kind hamper profits, they will be intensely resisted by corporate power and by career politicians committed to the existing economic status quo. The anti-consumerist pressures noted here also remain relatively insignificant compared to the mandates for policing consumption that would be needed to advance a sustainable welfare programme on a global scale. But the model of democratic procedure that they instantiate, whereby greener proactive policy initiatives allow emergent structures of feeling to be actualized through the provision of alternative forms of experience is of some pertinence, I believe, in conceptualizing the larger scale shifts in experience and policymaking that will be essential for managing any transition to a sustainable economic order. What is key here, is that policymakers should emphasize the benefits that will follow from new forms of regulation and more sustainable modes of provision (improved health; richer sensual and aesthetic experience; enhanced well-being) and that they themselves can appeal to some form of pre-existing disposition in favour of the new regulation. Policy moves that are introduced on the basis of fairly minimal or low-profile manifestations of public support can, through the positive effects of their implementation, prove educative in ways that overcome subjective prejudice against objectively good practice. But it is also a 'dialectic' that endorses a more complex sense of needs than government policy on 'empowerment' has ever wanted to acknowledge. For, where the notion of 'empowerment' has been invoked ideologically (as it has in Britain in recent decades) in order to reposition claimants as 'consumers' exercising individualized choices, it has also sometimes served as the rationale for a new form of statist condescension rooted in the reduction of the self to a 'merely' consuming self that is incapable of looking beyond immediate personal need or of coming to decisions on the basis of 'objective' science. This can then result in a paradoxical disregard for the more citizenly dimension of public concern over environmental issues (Clarke, 2004a, 2004b, 2005) and allow 'experts' to profess their scepticism about the wisdom of any form of consultation exercise over such controversial issues as fracking or genetically modified (GM) crops (Soper, 2007: 219).

Hence the importance for the project of sustainable welfare for rendering explicit the desires and concerns implicit in current expressions of consumer anxiety and highlighting the alternative structure of pleasures and satisfactions to which they gesture. Hence, too, the importance of exposing the more puritanical and hedonistically repressive aspects of the affluent 'good life': a time-scarce and technology-driven mode of existence generating forms of alienating tolerance that ought more readily to be recognized as sources of deprivation (cf. Scitovsky, 1976; Soper, 2007: 221–222). But all this also means challenging the Janus-face responses from governments that, on the one hand, call on their publics to apply energy-saving measures and issue repeated warnings on the health risks of the 'fast food', low-exercise lifestyle, while giving every encouragement in their economic policies to the further expansion of consumerism. In furthering this, new forms of individual experience (involving revised ideas about the aesthetics of material culture and the satisfactions that it provides, and a heightened sense of the potential political power of consumption – or non-consumption) might not only force the hand of policymakers but also pressurize national governments into more open confrontation with their contradictory stance on the growth economy. And, since this confrontation is surely essential if the needs of the more impoverished communities are to be properly addressed, anything that helps to promote these new forms of experience within affluent societies can also be said to have its wider global relevance and to act as leverage for the macroeconomic changes needed at global level.

Conclusion

Without denying the importance of 'top-down' initiatives in promoting sustainable welfare, I have sought to show here how reliant they are in modern democracies upon electoral support and their necessary interaction with the experiences of individuals. I have also sought to illustrate the ways in which subjective support for new forms of 'policing' of consumption is reinforced and extended through provision for an 'alternative hedonist' experience of it. The avant-garde of consumers who will opt to 'self-police' their consumption in the interests of sustainable welfare is likely to remain an ineffective minority unless it is swelled by proactive public policy that allows new structures of feeling to be actualized through the provision of alternative forms of experience. In its application to public policy, 'alternative hedonism' is not a theory that ascribes needs in the absence of *any* subjective cognition of needs but a theory of the actualization of those needs through the provision that builds on their embryonic presence and potential for development. This is a 'dialectical' procedure that allows for some alleviation of the tensions between 'objective' and 'subjective' or 'empowering' approaches to welfare.

And, although the focus of this approach is on individual disaffection with affluent consumption, and thus with an elitist Global North response to consumerism, this is because of its possible leverage in bringing about a more egalitarian world order. The international agencies and institutions committed to a sustainable welfare agenda are likely to remain relatively powerless, and very little pressure will be applied on national governments to cooperate in promoting this agenda, unless and until their electorates come to perceive that as being in their own interests. 'Alternative hedonist' frameworks of thinking about the good life can alter conceptions of self-interest among affluent consumers and thus help to set off this relay of political pressures for a fairer global distribution of resources and more sustainable economic order. The development and communication of an 'alternative hedonist' political imaginary is, in this sense, of critical importance at the international level in helping to set off the relay of political pressures for a fairer global distribution of resources.[8] An alternative and ecologically sustainable conception of the good life can also hopefully not only win the support of consumers within the richer nations, but also come to figure as an ideal through which less affluent countries can critically consider the conventions and goals of 'development' itself – and thereby better understand the worst consequences of Global North 'overdevelopment' and how to avoid them.

Notes

1 It is true that the simple lack of a correlation between higher income and increased reported life satisfaction does not in itself entail that more consumption has not improved well-being. Feelings of satisfaction are not always the best guide to how well people may be faring, and the standards used by people in assessing their level of satisfaction may themselves become more stringent as their life experience changes with increased income (cf. O'Neill, 2006, 2007; Soper, 2014; Brandstedt, 2013 and Chapter 1 in this volume).
2 Although this relates to an emergent mood among consumers, especially in the UK, and draws on some media reflections of this, it is not offering an empirical survey or analysis of actual consumer behaviour. Its primary interest is in the conditions and forms of agency that might help over time to bring about a fairer allocation and more responsible and life-enhancing use of global resources.
3 By 'affluence' I refer to a lifestyle that is very prosperous relative to that of the majority of the world's population (but to which there is also very differing access within 'affluent' societies themselves). I associate 'consumerism' not only with an unprecedented expansion of market provision, but also with a resistance to non-commodified conceptions of the means of advancing the 'good life' and personal development. As both product and condition of existence of a fully fledged capitalist economy, it cannot be adequately analysed without reference to its role in realizing profit through the extension of material consumption and fostering of new consumer desires at every level.
4 However, I reject the neoclassical conception of the consumer as exclusively driven by self-interest and have discussed at some length the 'altruism' within the 'egoism' of alternative hedonist responses and the reasons why it is difficult in any theory of consumption to draw too sharp a distinction between self- and other regarding behaviours (Soper, 2008a, see also Chapter 1 in this volume).
5 Primarily in discussions following seminar and conference papers, but also, as indicated above, implicitly by all those who question the power of democracy to deliver the needed forms of action on climate change.
6 When a similar policy was put to the vote in Edinburgh, prior to any implementation, it failed to gain majority support.
7 For some reports on this, see Juliette Jowit, *The Observer*, February 15 2004; Andrew Clark, *The Guardian*, February 16 and 18 2004; Jackie Ashley, *The Guardian*, February 19 2004.
8 Academic thinking on sustainable welfare could have an important role in this by countering the supposed fixity and 'naturalization' of current attitudes to consumption. Certainly, it needs to move from how things are at present and to avoid overly utopian conceptions on social action and political change (for further discussion, see Chapter 4 in this volume). But it may also be mistaken to suppose that the only solutions on issues of sustainable welfare are those that conform to attitudes and interests as currently constituted.

References

Baker, S. (2012). Climate Change, the Common Good and the Promotion of Sustainable Development. In J. Meadowcroft, O. Langhelle, and A. Ruud (eds) *Governance, Democracy and Sustainable Development, Moving Beyond the Impasse* (249–271). Cheltenham: Edward Elgar.

Bauman, Z. (1993). *Postmodern Ethics*. Oxford: Blackwell.

Bauman, Z. (1998). *The Consumer Society: Myths and Structures*. London: Sage.

Bauman, Z. (2000). *Liquid Modernity*. Cambridge: Polity.

Bauman, Z. (2008). Exit Homo Politicus, Enter Homo Consumens. In K. Soper and F. Frank Trentmann (eds), *Citizenship and Consumption* (139–153). Basingstoke: Palgrave Macmillan.

Blühdorn, I. (2011). The sustainability of democracy: On limits to growth, the post-democratic turn and reactionary democrats. *Eurozine*, 11 July.

Blühdorn, I. (2013). The governance of unsustainability: Ecology and democracy after the post-democratic turn. *Environmental Politics*, 22(1), 16–36.

Brandstedt, E. (2013). *The Construction of a Sustainable Development in Times of Climate Change*. Lund: MediaTryck.

Brown, K. W. and Kasser, T. (2005). Are psychological and ecological well-being compatible? The role of values, mindfulness and lifestyle. *Social Indicators Research*, 74, 349–368.

Bunting, M. (2004). *Willing Slaves: How the Overwork Culture is Ruling Our Lives*. London: Harper Collins.

Campbell, C. (1995). The Sociology of Consumption. In D. Miller (ed.), *Acknowledging Consumption* (96–126). London and New York: Routledge.

Campbell, C. (2004). I Shop therefore I Know that I am: The Metaphysical Basis of Modern Consumerism. In K. M. Ekstrom and H. Brembeck (eds), *Elusive Consumption*. London and New York: Berg.

Clarke, J. (2004a). Unstable connections: Citizen-consumers and public services. Paper presented at the Consumers as Citizens seminar. 22 April 2004, HM Treasury, London.

Clarke, J. (2004b). A consuming public?, lecture in the ESRC/AHRB Cultures of Consumption Series, Royal Society, London, included in Research Papers (phase 1 projects), 21 June 2004.

Clarke, J. (2005). New Labour's citizens: Activated, empowered, responsibilised or abandoned? *Critical Social Policy*, 25(4), 447–463.

Easterlin, R. A. (2001). Income and happiness: towards a unified theory. *Economic Journal*, 111, 465–494.

Featherstone, M. (1991). *Consumer Culture and Postmodernism*. London: Sage.

Fevre, R. (2003). *The New Sociology of Economic Behaviour*. London: Sage.

Fiske, J. (1989). *Reading the Popular*. Boston, MA: Unwin Hyman. Giddens, A. (2009). *The Politics of Climate Change*. Cambridge: Polity.

Goodland, R. and Daly, H. (1992). *Ten Reasons Why Northern Income Is Not the Solution to Southern Poverty*. Washington, DC: Environment Department, World Bank.

Gorz, A. (1989). *Critique of Economic Reason*. London: Verso.

Gorz, A. (1999). *Reclaiming Work: Beyond the Wage-based Society*, trans. C. Turner. Cambridge: Polity.

Hardt, M. and Negri, A. (2002). *Empire*. Harvard, MA: Harvard University Press.

Haug, W. F. (1986). *Critique of Commodity Aesthetics*. Cambridge: Polity.

Haug, W. (2006). Commodity Aesthetics Revisited, *Radical Philosophy*, (135), Jan–Feb., 18–24.

Hauser, O. P., Rand, D. G., Peysakhovivh, A. and Nowak, M. A. (2014). Cooperating with the future. *Nature*, 511(7508), 220–223.

Heilbroner, R. (1974). *An Inquiry into the Human Prospect*. New York: W. W. Norton.

Honoré, C. (2005). *In Praise of Slowness: Challenging the Cult of Speed*. New York: Harper One.

Inglehart, R. and Klingemann, H. D. (2000). Genes, Culture, Democracy and Happiness. In E. Diener and E. Suh (eds), *Culture and Subjective Well-Being*. Cambridge, MA: MIT Press.

Intergovernmental Panel on Climate Change (IPCC) (2014). *Climate Change 2014: Synthesis Report. Summary for Policymakers*. New York and Cambridge: Cambridge University Press.

Jackson, T. (2004). *Chasing Progress: Beyond Measuring Economic Growth*, London: New Economics Foundation.

Jackson, T. (2009). *Prosperity without Growth: Economics for a Finite Planet*, London: Earthscan.

Kasser, T. (2002). *The High Price of Materialism*. Cambridge, MA: MIT Press.

Kasser, T. (2008). Values and prosperity, paper to the SDC seminar on Visions of Prosperity, 26 November 2008.

Kallis, G. (2011). In defence of degrowth. *Ecological Economics*, 70, 873–880.

Klein, N. (2000). *No Logo*. London: Harper Collins.

Klein, N. (2014). *This Changes Everything: Capitalism vs the Climate*. New York: Simon and Schuster.

Koch, M. (2012). *Capitalism and Climate Change: Theoretical Discussion, Historical Development and Policy Responses*. Basingstoke: Palgrave Macmillan.

Latouche, S. (2009). *Farewell to Growth*, trans. D. Macey. Cambridge: Polity.

Layard, R. (2005). *Happiness: Lessons from a New Science*. London: Allen Lane.

Levett, R. (2003). *A Better Choice of Choice: Quality of Life, Consumption and Economic Growth*. London: Fabian Society.

Lodziak, C. (1995). *Manipulating Needs, Capitalism and Culture*. London: Pluto.

Marx, K. (1973), *Grundrisse*. Harmondsworth: Penguin.

O'Neill, J. (2006). Citizenship, well-being as sustainability: Epicurus or Aristotle? *Analyse & Kritik*, 28(2), 158–172.

O'Neill, J. (2007). Sustainability, Well-being and Consumption: The Limits of Hedonic Approaches. In K. Soper, and F. Trentmann (eds), *Citizenship and Consumption* (172–190), Basingstoke: Palgrave.

Ophuls, W. (1977). *Ecology and the Politics of Scarcity*. San Francisco, CA: W. H. Freeman.

Osbaldiston, N. (ed.) (2013). *Culture of the Slow: Social Deceleration in an Accelerated World*. London: Palgrave.

Schor, J. (2010). *Plenitude: The New Economics of True Wealth*. New York: Penguin.

Schor, J. (2013). From Fast Fashion to Connected Consumption: Slowing Down the Spending Treadmill. In N. Osbaldiston (ed.), *Culture of the Slow: Social Deceleration in an Accelerated World* (34–51). Basingstoke: Palgrave.

Scitovsky, T. (1976). *The Joyless Economy*. London, New York, Toronto: Oxford University Press.

Shearman, D. and Smith, J. W. (2007). *The Climate Change Challenge and the Failure of Democracy*. Westport, CT: Praeger.

Soper, K. (1981). *On Human Needs: Open and Closed Theories in a Marxist Perspective*. Brighton: Harvester Press.

Soper, K. (2007). Re-thinking the 'good life': The citizenship dimension of consumer disaffection with consumerism. *Journal of Consumer Culture*, 7(2), 205–229.

Soper, K. (2008a). 'Alternative Hedonism' and the Citizen-Consumer. In K. Soper and F. Trentmann, (eds), *Citizenship and Consumption* (191–205). Basingstoke: Palgrave Macmillan.

Soper, K. (2008b). Alternative hedonism, cultural theory and the role of aesthetic revisioning. In S. Binkley and J. Littler (eds), Special Issue: Cultural studies and anti-consumerism: A critical encounter, *Cultural Studies*, 22(5), 552–567.

Soper, K. (2009). Introduction. In K. Soper, M. Ryle and L. Thomas (eds), *The Politics and Pleasures of Consuming Differently* (1–21). London: Palgrave.

Soper, K. (2014). Towards a Sustainable Flourishing: Democracy, Hedonism and the Politics of Prosperity. In M. L. Mueller and K. L. Lykke Syse (eds), *Sustainability, Consumption and the Good Life*, London: Routledge.

Thomas, L. (2008). Alternative realities: Downshifting narratives in contemporary lifestyle television. *Cultural Studies*, 22(5), 680–699.

Thomas, L. (2009). Ecochic: Green Echoes and Rural Retreats in Contemporary Lifestyle Magazines. In K. Soper, M. Ryle and L. Thomas (eds), *The Politics and Pleasures of Consuming Differently*. Basingstoke: Palgrave.

Victor, P. A. (2008). *Managing without Growth: Slower by Design, not Disaster.* Cheltenham: Edward Elgar.

Westra, L. (1998). *Living in Integrity: A Global Ethic to Restore a Fragmented Earth.* Lanham, MA: Rowman and Littlefield.

Wilkinson, R. and Pickett, K. (2009). *The Spirit Level: Why Equality is Better for Everyone*. London: Penguin.

World Bank (2015). *World Development Report 2015: Mind, Society, Behaviour.* Washington, DC: World Bank.

Conclusion

Looking back, looking forward: results and future research directions

Oksana Mont and Max Koch

Western welfare capitalism is in crisis. The dimensions of this crisis include unprecedented levels of inequality, unemployment and exclusion. Adverse demographic trends such as ageing populations and falling fertility rates call for more sophisticated and diverse services, especially in the health sector. 'Globalization', more specifically, the increased transnational mobility of capital, undermines the tax base of the original national welfare state and brings issues of fairness and equity into the spotlight, particularly the distribution of wealth and benefits, as well as access to resources. Quality of life indicators have not displayed the same growth rates as gross domestic product (GDP) during the post-war era (Max-Neef, 1995). Last but not least, as we have argued in the Introduction, Western welfare standards are being challenged by environmental issues such as climate change and biodiversity loss that have a global and intergenerational character. Taking environmental limits in welfare reasoning seriously means going beyond the national basis of the Western class compromise, exploring the potentials for new institutional agreements at global *and* local level, and systematically considering environmental and intergenerational concerns.

This volume set out to scrutinize the current direction of welfare development and to explore alternative pathways to a more sustainable society where well-being, justice and socio-economic stability can be secured for all, now and in future, and within the ecological limits of a finite planet. What we came to label 'sustainable welfare' calls for systematic explorations of potential solutions at the crossroads of sustainability science, welfare research and economic and policy strategies. The contribution of this book is threefold. First, as an 'academic' contribution in the narrow sense, it offers a kaleidoscope of views and proposals for how welfare and sustainability concepts, policies and practices could be integrated to advance the new research field of 'sustainable welfare'. Second, it contributes towards the sketching of the outlines of potential solutions to the real-life challenges represented by the multiple crises that real-world societies are facing. Third, this volume illustrates the importance of interdisciplinary approaches for addressing complex eco-social problems. Accordingly, the chapters of this volume have diagnosed and detailed the numerous challenges that contemporary welfare systems are facing and studied the kind of changes in mindsets, institutional settings, theoretical underpinnings and practices, and processes and actor compositions that could facilitate a transition towards sustainable welfare.

Avenues for integration of sustainability and welfare research

In revisiting our initial *concept* of sustainable welfare – directed towards the satisfaction of human needs within ecological limits within an intergenerational and global perspective (Introduction) – we begin with three of the relevant subconcepts: well-being, welfare and sustainability. Well-being is about our ability to prosper as human beings (Jackson, 2009: 136). Hence, it transcends material pleasures and is present in individual health, in close relations with family and friends and in our trust in the community. It manifests itself in our satisfaction at work and our sense of shared purpose and belonging. Welfare is often defined in similar terms, as a subjective condition of what is perceived as good for a person (Sumner, 1996). The most prominent subjective conceptions of welfare are hedonism, which understands it in terms of pleasurable experiences, and desire theories, which understand it in terms of desire satisfaction, that is, people getting what they want. Yet subjective accounts of well-being may be at odds with moral and political objectives, as Brandstedt and Emmelin (Chapter 1) have demonstrated, since maximizing one's utility may take place at the expense of others.

Objective accounts of welfare include the basic needs approach and are usually motivated by normative or moral reasoning. The two best-known human needs approaches were developed by Max-Neef (1991) and Doyal and Gough (1991). As demonstrated by Koch and Buch-Hansen (Chapter 2), both approaches recognize the difference between needs and wants and identify universal needs. However, the two approaches differ in terms of the nature of need-satisfiers. While according to Max-Neef satisfiers are culturally determined, Doyal and Gough highlight the universal character of satisfiers such as water and food, housing and a clean environment in order to satisfy the basic need of health. A critical issue is the level on which basic human needs can and should be satisfied. Here the concrete characterization of 'thresholds', especially for the throughput of matter and energy in production and consumption processes, becomes central since their structure and size have direct implications for the economy, society and the environment. This is a rather complex issue, since scientific knowledge about the availability of resources and environmental sinks, among many other factors, keeps advancing. It is however beyond academic dispute that, because of environmental limits, the needs and wants of the world population cannot be satisfied at the same level as currently is the case in the countries of the Global North. Doing so would indeed require four or five Earths.

The question of whether and to what extent welfare can be provided beyond 'mere' basic needs in a global and intertemporal dimension is also addressed in sustainability discourse. Here, the concept of needs is central, in particular the 'essential needs of the world's poor, to which overriding priority should be given' (WCED, 1987: 43). At the same time, the 'idea of limitations imposed by the state of technology and social organization on the environment's ability to meet present and future needs' is put forward (WCED, 1987: 43). In addition to the aforementioned discussion on thresholds, prominent in objective accounts of welfare, sustainability debates also consider issues of intra- and intergenerational fairness and equity as well as the recognition of ecological limits, and integrate these into definitions of well-being and welfare. Objective accounts of welfare that have basic needs as their starting point seem hence to be better positioned to meet societal sustainability targets than subjective accounts, but less so for the consideration of subjective well-being. Yet subjective accounts of welfare, which are often applied in research circles in the Global North, tend to neglect the welfare of geographically and temporally distant people. Brandstedt and Emmelin (Chapter 1) point to the difficulties in integrating the two concepts and suggest that, if the maximization of welfare is the primary goal, then focusing on the subjective understanding of welfare is more conducive for achieving this. If, on the other hand, the welfare provision is conditioned on a sustainability proviso, then some needs and wants will have to be restrained to leave space for welfare provision for others at present and in the future.

The sustainability discourse is also concerned with the question of how – more or less – sustainable societies can evolve over the long term. Will they always grow and expand in size? How will 'progress' and 'prosperity' be defined? Since the origins of the capitalist world system (Wallerstein, 1974), states and the global economy have mostly been expanding. However, classical economists such as John Stuart Mill, and subsequently John Maynard Keynes, recognized that a developmental stage might be reached where economic growth will actually stop. Herman Daly (1994) built on these authors and advanced the notion of a steady-state economy, which has more recently been taken up by the degrowth movement of researchers and activists who advocate a planned transition to a non-growing economy (see Chapter 2). The common point of departure is the critique of the broadly accepted view that economic growth is always linked to improvements in prosperity, usually defined in terms of material wealth. In 1987, Daly was already distinguishing between growth in terms of 'quantitative increase in the scale of the physical dimensions of the economy' and 'the qualitative improvement in the structure, design and composition of physical stocks and flows, that result from greater knowledge, both of technique and of purpose' (Daly, 1987: 323). Similarly, degrowth researchers have started to review our notions of economic growth and development (Latouche, 2009; Kallis, 2011). And even within policy circles, voices have been raised that economic growth and current development policies have failed miserably to alleviate poverty in many parts of the world or provide a fairer distribution of wealth (UNDP, 2013). In addition, research continues to demonstrate that Western countries, stylized as being 'progressive' and 'economically advanced', are in fact those with the highest ecological footprint and with the highest per capita levels of consumption and the associated environmental, social and health impacts (Wackernagel *et al.*, 1997: 33). Indeed, with increases in material standards of living come the ill-effects of modernization such as stress and mental health problems, obesity, smoking and addiction. Even the progress in 'empowerment of women' is double-edged if 'emancipation' is largely manifested through material consumption and by conforming to the social norms of commodified lifestyles (Chapters 3 and 12).

The imposition of Western lifestyles around the world is often insensitive to the traditions and cultures of local communities and their ways of providing welfare. In fact, less 'economically advanced' nations are in many respects more sustainable, especially in terms of social networks and the strength of their communities. Accordingly, the lesser economically developed nations may in fact inspire alternative modes of welfare provision at local and community level, as argued by Soper and Emmelin (Chapter 3). The precondition for this to happen is the overcoming of the notion that these nations are 'backward', 'marginal' or 'premodern' in any sense. Instead, the overdeveloped nations may need to be relabelled as materialistic, highly individualistic and environmentally and socially unsustainable. The degrowth community offers a more complex narrative where the link between progress and economic expansion is severed and local cultural and social values are celebrated, while individualistic materialism and consumerism are portrayed as being problematic and old-fashioned.

Yet for the time being it is not primarily the degrowth community that legitimately devises and shares visions, scenarios and models of the future, but rather government authorities, mainstream researchers and think-tanks. The corresponding assumptions and visions about the future as well as the type and extent of anticipated change are vital, since legitimate visions of the future also shape present-day actions or justify inaction. If the future is seen as bright, then there is no need to change the 'business as usual' of today. Indeed, Brandstedt and Mont (Chapter 4) demonstrate that mainstream policy visions rarely present alternatives to the Western way of life and its associated ideas of prosperity, welfare and progress based on economic growth. Instead, these are rather variations of 'modern life' that can be discussed without raising any inconvenient questions or scrutinizing the main principles and building blocks of Western society, economy and culture. In fact, all the mainstream Swedish visions of the future discussed here are optimistic and, should any problems arise, it is presumed that these will comfortably be solved by the magic of technological progress. Economic growth is here seen as the main prerequisite for societal development and is encouraged and safeguarded by various political, economic and social measures. Consumption, celebrated as an activity that will almost automatically propel us into a better future, is rarely acknowledged as a contributing cause to the environmental crisis. As a rule, mainstream visions of the future do not mention the downsides, and especially not the rebound effects, of the pursuit of economic growth.

So what if we reject such optimistic assumptions about the future? What if we assume that we are the last generation that is able to make the changes necessary to prevent the future from becoming a 'broken world' due to the environmental, economic and social crises caused by us? Tim Mulgan's (2011) book is used in Chapter 4 to explore these questions using a thought experiment. It shows that the differences between an affluent and a broken world lie in the background assumptions about the abundance of natural resources, optimism about the future and the role of technology, the acceptance of inequality, the advancement of the consumer society and economic growth. Many of the assumptions in the thought experiment that have led to the broken future are precisely those assumptions that are explicitly or implicitly used in visions of the future developed by mainstream public agencies that shape our minds and actions for the coming decades. The dire prospect of the broken world should further motivate actors beyond the degrowth community to look for alternative visions, actions and policies that could help avoid ecological disaster.

Policies

Unfortunately the mere academic production of concepts and alternative visions will not by itself bring about a steady-state economy and a sustainable welfare system. Understanding the numerous institutional obstacles, the structural forces and the ways in which these operate as barriers to the establishment of sustainable welfare at global, national and local levels is therefore vital – and the precondition for the identification of policies, factors and actors that may initiate such a transition. Part II has explored these obstacles and proposes alternative avenues and actors for advancing sustainable welfare. The no-growth community of academics and activists represents such a group of actors who aim to prevent the broken world from materializing. Khan and Clark (Chapter 5) contrast this perspective with that of proponents of pro-growth. The two authors demonstrate that the latter call for a reconfiguration of the current structures of the global economy, while the former mobilizes for a total trans-formation thereof. In some areas the two perspectives are not so far apart, for example, in relation to climate change mitigation and technology development. In contrast, with respect to the regulation of the financial and business sector, consumption and the distribution of income and wealth and labour, both perspectives suggest fundamentally different policies and practices. In the area of finance, the pro-growth perspective ascribes the leading role to private capital, leaving direct control over and regulation of financial resources to private financial organizations. In contrast, the no-growth perspective views the present financial system as one of the main causes of the economic and environmental crisis. Consequently the proposed policies include a range of measures to first regulate the financial system and then to redesign it in the long run to make it conducive to a steady-state economy. Major differences also exist in the area of labour market policies where pro-growth is primarily concerned with pre-paring markets for changes induced by the transition to a green economy, while the no-growth community of scholars acknowledges the challenge of main-taining full employment in a steady-state economy and discusses work time reduction and sharing as viable measures for the avoidance of unemployment and social exclusion. In terms of consumption, pro-growth supporters encourage shifting consumer behaviour towards green and more efficient consumption, while the no-growth community suggests reducing the levels of consumption in combination with the greening of consumption patterns. While pro-growth narratives advocate policies that are politically feasible to implement but insufficient or counterproductive to achieving sustainable welfare, no-growth suggestions may be politically more challenging to implement as they question the core premises of the global capitalist economy. To increase the feasibility of no-growth policies, Khan and Clark opt for the development of more credible visions of sustainable welfare in a steady-state economy, for an integration of the diverse no-growth perspectives into a positive transformation programme and for forming alliances to support the various policy elements of that programme.

Existing welfare states were created with the goal of reducing social risks associated with the work–welfare nexus (Esping-Andersen, 1990). The present-day risks highlighted in the welfare literature refer to globalization and growing international competition, the de-industrialization of the advanced economies and the associated changes in labour markets. However, Johansson, Khan and Hildingsson (Chapter 6) argue that a new kind of social risk related to environmental degradation and climate change is emerging. This, however, tends to be ignored by the established welfare scholarship, despite the fact that it is acknowledged in numerous environmental documents, including Intergovernmental Panel on Climate Change (IPCC) reports. The IPCC highlights that climate change to date has 'merely' aggravated existing social risks, but could well become the main driver of new risks in the long run. These new risks will have profound adverse effects on health, poverty and livelihoods, and corresponding implications for welfare systems for accommodating these effects. As demonstrated in numerous reports, climate change directly affects the less advanced economies as well as poor and vulnerable communities in both rich and poor countries. And it is the poor nations with non-existent or low-capacity welfare systems that have the greatest need to adapt to or mitigate the effects of climate change. To address this misbalance, Johansson, Khan and Hildingsson suggest developing an eco-social insurance capable of transcending both the work–welfare nexus and the nation state.

Developing sustainable welfare is a complex task that will require not only new welfare systems and regulatory measures but also various types of policy instruments that frame the behaviours of actors. In recent years, one type of eco-social policy instrument that has gained in popularity is emission trading schemes for companies and individuals such as pollution allowances and tradable rights, especially for carbon emissions (Chapter 7). However the effectiveness of these instruments is questionable, since the reduction of carbon emissions is intended to be the by-product of the search for new investment opportunities that such schemes offer for finance capital in particular. Another issue is fairness and, above all, the distributive implications of such schemes, since the groups that are likely to bear the financial brunt have the least resources to cope. Hildingsson and Koch argue that the carbon emission reduction potential and distributional impacts of personal carbon trading (PCT) schemes are uncertain. Alternatively, the two authors investigate the potential of voluntary grass-roots initiatives for reducing carbon emissions using the example of CRAGs (Carbon Rationing Action Groups). Unlike personal carbon trading schemes and the associated rationality of carbon commodification, CRAGs are based on a collective logic where mutual learning, trust and reciprocity are central. A study of ten CRAGs in the UK reports that, on average, their members managed to reduce their carbon emissions by 30 per cent (Howell, 2012). Similar to many other voluntary organizations, the main challenge for CRAGs is long-term maintenance. Municipalities and local governments could do a great deal more in assisting the sustainability of grass-roots movements and organizations.

It is impossible to discuss sustainable welfare without addressing the issue of the organization of work and leisure time and without analysing the effects of various policies on labour time reduction. Such policies were frequent and successful in the early and mid-twentieth century but have been discontinued since. A number of factors have contributed to a reorganization of work and employment – including flexible production, the robotization of work processes and the application of information and communication technologies, leading to a decrease in the demand for unskilled labour and an increase in the demand for non-standard employment (Koch and Fritz, 2013), including precarious work (Standing, 2011). Together, these factors have affected the shape and effectiveness of work time reduction policies. Using examples of France, the Netherlands and Belgium, Mont (Chapter 8) demonstrates that these policies have been relatively weak as employment-generating measures, but significantly more successful in improving the work/life balance. In terms of absolute reductions of work time, recent policy attempts have mostly failed. However, none of the work time reduction policies were devised to meet the triple goal of increased employment and well-being and a simultaneous reduction in environmental impacts. In this situation, it is encouraging that models are being developed that demonstrate that – under certain conditions and adequate policy interventions – economic stability can be maintained, while GDP growth can be slowed down or stopped, unemployment reduced and environmental impacts limited (Viktor, 2008; Jackson and Victor, 2011; Malmaeus, 2011). These models also show that achieving this triple goal requires a combination of measures, which include an environmental tax reform to limit the environmental impacts of production and consumption, basic income as a measure to counter the adverse effects of growing productivity and labour replacement, a shift to the service economy as a measure for reducing overall labour productivity and environmental impacts and an investigation of possibilities for encouraging leisure activities that increase individual well-being but have low environmental impacts.

Emerging practices

Though the above policy strategies and instruments can undoubtedly play important roles in establishing and shaping sustainable welfare, their socio-ecological effectiveness remains limited if the diversity of transition pathways and institutional conditions of different countries are not considered. In his account of the steady-state economy, Daly (1994) has advocated three institutional pillars: a physical depletion quota institution, a population stabilization institution and a distributist institution. Since none of these institutions is specifically designed to provide welfare, Koch and Buch-Hansen (Chapter 2) argue that the notion of a distributist institution should be complemented by an institutional perspective. The present diversity of welfare states and their institutions is likely to affect degrowth trajectories and the concrete forms of the resulting sustainable welfare systems. These will most likely not follow one unified ideal type, but rather a range of different models, comprising a great diversity of institutional arrangements, actors and practices, affected by different economic, cultural and socio-technical contextual factors. Chapter 9 explores this as yet under-researched field using the examples of France, the US and China. Buch-Hansen, Pissin and Kennedy demonstrate that, although these countries have specific political and economic challenges, each also has a unique set of opportunities to be capitalized on during the transition towards degrowth and sustainable welfare states. These correspond to particular divisions of labour between the state, market and commons including social enterprises (Chapter 10).

Any transition to sustainable welfare is facilitated by the formation of socio-political alliances with different actors in society and by engaging a broad range of such actors. One often neglected but nonetheless essential actor – especially in relation to future decisions – is present-day youth. Their dreams and aspirations, their energy and transformative force will greatly affect the future shape of society. China is a country with one of the largest youth populations who, at the same time, are one of the most vulnerable groups affected by climate change and environmental pollution. Kennedy and Pissin (Chapter 11) study how Chinese young people understand, imagine and practice low carbon life. Images of low carbon life emerge when rich and middle-class Chinese emulate wasteful Western urban lifestyles, but also when the 'Chinese Dream' – a low carbon motto – aims to redefine prosperity and put consumerism under scrutiny. As in many other countries, Chinese youth can be divided into four groups, where the first group associates low carbon life with a 'high-quality lifestyle' and the second group with a 'fashionable lifestyle'. The third group consists of young Chinese who resist or reject the idea of changes that need to take place in their daily lives in order to embrace a low carbon life, while the fourth group is a minority that comprises young individuals who lack awareness of environmental issues or perceive them as a temporarily necessary condition in the course of economic development. The diversity of perceptions about low carbon life suggest that different messages, imageries and even policy tools may be needed in order to engage and incentivize different groups of the population in the transition to sustainable welfare.

Soper (Chapter 12) addresses the relationship between individuals and governments in initiating transformative processes and legitimizing sustainable lifestyles. For governments to take the lead, they need to be supported by their electorates. Yet, given the extent to which sustainable welfare has been associated with perceived sacrifice, it is difficult to gain the necessary public support. Powerful business and financial actors usually object to any policy aiming for income and wealth redistribution, let alone a limitation of profits. Soper argues that the growing dissatisfaction of the public with the consumerist lifestyle may become the driving force for sustainable welfare. People are increasingly disenchanted with the consumer culture because of its growing negative side effects such as time scarcity, high levels of stress, traffic congestion and because of the increasing displacement of other pleasures of life and well-being through the shopping mall culture. To facilitate a democratic process of transition in Western countries, she calls for a changed perception of the 'good life' – an 'alternative hedonism' – that could provide a common platform and a vision of a societal order where individual lifestyles of personal fulfilment and enjoyment would be complemented by environmentally sound and socially just production and consumption methods, and corresponding modes of governance. According to Soper, the seeds of alternative visions and practices are to be found in craft movements, the service economy, socio-ecological enterprises and forms of collaborative consumption. A 'slower' life and more free time should therefore not be seen as a threat to 'culture' but as sources of individual and communitarian well-being, genuine individual fulfilment and opportunities for greater involvement with various social networks that have the potential of enhancing social capital and creating trust among individuals (Putnam, 2000). This could indeed be a way to sever the link between resource-intensive economic growth and societal progress – and to break the monopoly of the prevalent consumer culture over alternative and sustainable definitions of well-being and quality of life.

Future research pathways

The integration of social welfare and environmental sustainability has been the core purpose of this volume. Chapters have addressed conceptual issues, provided examples of policy strategies and instruments that could facilitate the transition towards sustainable welfare, and studied emerging practices, but also highlighted conceptual, political and structural challenges to this transition. We conclude by highlighting those theoretical, political and practical issues that should be further explored and tested in future research.

At the *conceptual level* we have identified difficulties in integrating subjective and objective accounts of well-being. Future research should therefore address the issue of whether and under what circumstances synergies between the two understandings of well-being and sustainability can be found and achieved. In this context, the role of extrinsic and intrinsic values can be highlighted. A related issue is the demarcation of thresholds for needs-satisfiers that would secure welfare for all within the limits of the finite planet – and potentially beyond mere 'survival'. This would indeed require a much improved division of labour between diverse scientists and policymakers. Finally, in order to contest the mainstream optimistic visions of the future that lull us into inaction and 'business as usual', more complex and concrete narratives and alternative visions as well as scenarios and models for a steady-state economy will need to be developed so that political alliances for avoidance of the 'broken world' can be formed. Despite considerable efforts in several of the chapters in this volume, this includes yet more precise definitions of 'prosperity', 'progress' and 'development' beyond material abundance.

In the *policy-oriented* Part II of this volume, several authors call for the development of various no-growth and degrowth visions into practical transformation strategies that could frame more specific policy packages. Here, research has a potentially vital role to play but can only do so in close dialogue with diverse societal actors. The identification of common interests and political alliances is an important further research step in itself. The case of policy instruments in climate change mitigation exemplifies this (see Chapter 7 by Hildingsson and Koch). While market-oriented policy tools such as carbon-trading schemes have turned out to be largely useless in relation to their original environmental goals, some of the voluntary grassroots initiatives have proven to be quite efficient in environmental terms but face difficulties in sustaining themselves over time. Here research into potential mechanisms, groupings of actors and their institutional embedding, especially at local levels, could support and facilitate the long-term achievement of environmental goals, particularly where local governments and governance networks support voluntary and civic bottom-up initiatives.

The potential roles of different actors in the transition towards sustainable welfare has been taken up in several chapters of this volume but should nevertheless be explored further. In fact, the concept of governance itself is in urgent need of renewal in a situation where governmental influence tends to be reduced to supporting the economic interests of powerful private actors. The role of businesses and civil society in the transition to sustainable welfare also deserves closer attention as different actors could take the lead in this transition in different national and local contexts (see Chapter 9). Hence the issue of what circumstances will enable particular actors to attain leadership roles is worth investigating closer. The same applies to the financing of welfare systems (see Chapters 5 and 8), since the current deceleration of economic growth in many Organisation for Economic Co-operation and Development (OECD) countries is putting existing welfare systems under financial pressure, while the demands on these systems are growing and diversifying. Since growth-critical scholars have dedicated little attention to welfare institutions within planned degrowth trajectories to date (Chapter 2), a critical question for future research is how the financial base of welfare systems can be sustained without economic growth, as well as which kinds of alternative welfare arrangements – and the division of labour across public, private and communal actors – this may presuppose.

If 'sustainable welfare' is going to be *practised* at all, then it will be most likely be in different ways in different countries. This is because sustainable welfare systems will differ substantially from country to country as a result of their diverse points of departure in terms of the institutional particulars of market coordination and welfare systems (Buch-Hansen, Pissin and Kennedy in Chapter 9). While research on the potential diversity of future welfare systems is still in its infancy, it is important to explore the opportunities and potential that exist within current welfare systems, since these must be built upon in any move towards sustainable welfare. Another potential opportunity for the establishment of sustainable welfare lies in the diversity of perceptions about the 'good life' and the relevant practices among different segments of the population (Chapter 11 by Kennedy and Pissin). In order to capitalize on this diversity, research is needed in order to develop customized approaches for different target groups. For some segments of the population, moral and ethical arguments may work well in order to help change people's behaviour in their everyday lives, while for others approaches that enhance their extrinsic values may be the best way to introduce such change. A final proposition worth exploring in comparative empirical research is that disenchanted consumers may become the main force of change, capable of influencing and supporting governments in the transition towards sustainable welfare (Soper in Chapter 12).

References

Daly, H. E. (1987). The economic growth debate: What some economists have learned but many have not. *Journal of Environmental Economics and Management*, 14(4), 323–336.

Daly, H. E. (1994). Steady-State Economics. In C. Merchant (ed.), *Ecology Key Concepts in Critical Theory*. Atlantic Highlands, NJ: Humanities Press.

Doyal, L. and Gough, I. (1991). *A Theory of Human Need*. New York: Guilford.

Esping-Andersen, G. (1990). *The Three Worlds of Welfare Capitalism*. Cambridge: Polity Press.

Howell, R. A. (2012). Living with a carbon allowance: The experiences of Carbon Rationing Action Groups and implications for policy. *Energy Policy*, 41, 250–258.

Jackson, T. (2009). *Prosperity without Growth? The Transition to a Sustainable Economy*. London: Sustainable Development Commission.

Jackson, T. and Victor, P. (2011). Productivity and work in the 'green economy': Some theoretical reflections and empirical tests. *Environmental Innovation and Societal Transitions*, 1(1), 101–108.

Kallis, G. (2011). In defence of degrowth. *Ecological Economics: The Journal of the International Society for Ecological Economics*, 70(5), 873–880.

Koch, M. and Fritz, M. (2013). *Non-Standard Employment in Europe. Paradigms, Prevalence and Policy Responses.* Basingstoke: Palgrave Macmillan.

Latouche, S. (2009). *Farewell to Growth.* Cambridge: Polity.

Malmaeus, M. (2011). *Ekonomi utan tillväxt. Ett svenskt perspektiv.* Stockholm: Cogito.

Max-Neef, M. (1991). *Human Scale Development: Conception, Application and Further Reflections.* New York: The Apex Press.

Max-Neef, M. (1995). Economic growth and quality of life: A threshold hypothesis. *Ecological Economics*, 15, 115–118.

Mulgan, T. (2011). *Ethics for Broken World: Imagining Philosophy after Catastrophe.* Durham: Acumen Publishing.

Putnam, R. D. (2000). *Bowling Alone: The Collapse and Revival of American Community.* New York: Simon & Schuster.

Standing, G. (2011). *The Precariat; The Dangerous New Class.* London: Bloomsbury Academic.

Sumner, L. W. (1996). *Welfare, Happiness, and Ethics.* Oxford: Clarendon Press.

UNDP (2013). *Humanity Divided: Confronting inequality in Developing Countries.* New York: United Nations Development Programme.

Viktor, P. (2008). *Managing without Growth: Slower by Design, Not Disaster.* Cheltenham: Edward Elgar Publishing.

Wackernagel, M., Onisto, L., Linares, A. C., Falfán, I. S. L., García, J. M., Guerrero, A. I. S. and Guerrero, M. G. S. (1997). *Ecological Footprints of Nations. How Much Nature Do They Use? – How Much Nature Do They Have?* Xalapa: Centro de Estudios para la Sustentabilidad, Universidad Anáhuac de Xalapa.

Wallerstein, I. (1974). *The Modern World-System, Vol. I: Capitalist Agriculture and the Origins of the European World-Economy in the Sixteenth Century.* New York/ London: Academic Press.

WCED (World Commission on Environment and Development) (1987). *Our Common Future: The Report of the World Commission on Environment and Development.* New York: Oxford University Press.

Index

'N' indicates a note; 't' indicates a table.

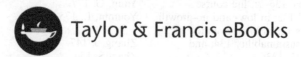
For Product Safety Concerns and Information please contact our EU representative GPSR@taylorandfrancis.com Taylor & Francis Verlag GmbH, Kaufingerstraße 24, 80331 München, Germany